What are people saying about this book?

Congratulations on putting together such an extensive and valuable book on Managing Agile Projects – this is the kind of contribution that will accelerate the adoption of Agile Development into large corporate Enterprises.

Managing Agile Projects is the kind of book that will make everyone realize that Agile Development is a true revolution in the way we manage software development — from its practices to its attitude.

This comprehensive book demystifies difficult issues such as facilitating social interactions, interacting with stakeholders, and producing just the right amount of artifacts such as documentation, while providing detailed explanations of practices to install day-to-day agile activities such as requirements gathering, testing, integration and release management.

This practical guide will help executives, managers, and developers to understand the true characteristics of agile development and agile project management, and how these characteristics are different than other types of development and management.

This book is an essential read for those who want to understand how to develop software with less risk, and less cost, while maintaining high quality and employee satisfaction.

Mike Beedle, CEO
New Governance Inc.

D0897219

Once again, Kevin Aguanno provides the Project Management Discipline with yet another tool to aid in the execution of projects. Not only does Managing Agile Projects *identify the areas of concern or potential issues associated with implementing new concepts, or even change, it also provides the mitigation tactics that a Project Manager can use in his Toolbox.* Managing Agile Projects *is easy to read and is written with practical examples to which we ALL can relate...a reference for ANYONE within the Project Management Discipline including educators, trainers, practitioners and those aspiring to be practitioners.*

Lisa Jacobsen
Project Management Institute (PMI)

Kevin Aguanno's Managing Agile Projects *is a welcome addition to the complex issues surrounding managing software development projects using agile methods. It is neither too extreme nor too general, it's "just right." The reader will find a broad set of experience based recommendations for managing projects that use agile methods as well as practical advice on how to introduce agile to an organization. Since agile is itself an emerging process, Kevin's is a critical step along the way to a mature process based on adapting the best practices from a variety disciplines ranging from XP to CMMI.*

Glen B. Alleman

Kevin Aguanno has brought together a book on project management that hits the target dead center. The target is, of course, that all projects are unique; therefore the approach should be unique, or "agile," as well. This book represents a consolidation of very powerful, practical, and applicable approaches to project management, a definite asset in my project management toolkit. Its relevance reaches beyond IT and into industries were constant changes and rapid responses are required to survive and deliver successful projects.
Stéphane Deschênes, PMP

Managing Agile Projects

Editor
Kevin Aguanno, PMP®, MAPM

First Edition

Multi-Media Publications Inc. ❖ Lakefield, Ontario

Managing Agile Projects

Edited by Kevin Aguanno

Published by:
Multi-Media Publications Inc.
R.R. #4B, Lakefield, Ontario, Canada, K0L 2H0

http://www.mmpubs.com/

ISBN (paperback edition):   1-895186-11-0
ISBN (PDF edition):   1-895186-12-9

First printing 2005.
Printed in USA. Published in Canada.

National Library of Canada Cataloguing in Publication

Managing agile projects / edited by Kevin Aguanno. -- 1st ed.

(The project management essentials library)
Issued also in electronic format.
Includes bibliographical references.
ISBN 1-895186-11-0 (pbk.)

1. Project management. I. Series.

HD69.P75A38 2004   658.4'04   C2004-902800-6

Table of Contents

Acknowledgments

This book is a testament to the innovative minds of its many contributors. Agile methods have evolved over the past two decades, yet they are only now entering the main stream. The people who have written chapters in this book have been some of the leading researchers and proponents behind the movement. Their drive to find ways to deliver business value in an efficient, customer-focused manner has led them to create new technical development methods, new techniques, and new project management paradigms. We must thank these visionaries for their dedication to the cause.

This book also could not have existed without the fine editorial team at Multi-Media Publications Inc. and the many reviewers of manuscript drafts. Thank you for the late nights and weekends wherein you helped make this book become a reality.

Thanks also go out to the many practitioners who have helped evolve the techniques discussed in this book, through heated email and newsgroup debates. The agile methodologies are a product of many minds. Thank you to all who believe.

Editor's Acknowledgments

In addition to those thanked above, I would like to thank Lisa Jacobsen of the Project Management Institute for her feedback, and Mike Beedle for catching a potentially embarassing error.

Finally, I would like to thank my beautiful wife, Alba, and my two children for allowing me to volunteer many of our evenings and weekends to this project. They have been a tremendous support to me in my own career development and in professional giveback activities such as this one. I am glad to have you in my corner.

Dedication

To all who strive to perform, despite bureaucratic processes and senseless constraints: let this book help you shed your fetters.

PART ONE

Introduction

CHAPTER ONE

Introduction

Kevin Aguanno

Extreme Programming,[1] Scrum,[2] Feature-Driven Development,[3] Lean Development,[4] Crystal Methods,[5] Agile Project Management:[15] these are just a few of the more common examples from a group of new product-development methods that have emerged over the past decade. While they were once relegated to back alley discussions between product development teams, they have emerged to become topics of mainstream discussion, appearing as topics in conferences and academic journals. Where did these "new" methods come from? What do they offer that is different from traditional methods? Is there anything really *new* in these methods? And do we need new project management techniques to manage these new methods?

Proponents have come together under the banner of Agile Methods in order to support the further development and promotion of these methods. The term *agile* was selected by these proponents at an initial meeting[6] in order to denote the ability of these methods to respond to changing requirements in a controlled but flexible manner. The runner-up moniker, Lightweight Methods, did not highlight the applicability of these methods to projects experiencing high levels of change, and also carried the negative connotations of the term *lightweight* – these are serious methods and deserve consideration.

The concepts of agile product development first emerged among Japanese automobile manufacturers in the 1980s.[7] These concepts quickly spread to North American car manufacturers and then their IT departments in the late 1980s. Once these ideas worked their way into the IT community, they quickly spread to other organizations and industries through exposure in software development conferences and journals. Naturally, several different approaches, or methods, evolved that incorporated these new product development ideas into a software engineering and development context.

While they first emerged as software development methods, these methods have been adopted more broadly. Scrum, for example, has been used as a general project management approach in non-software projects,[8] and agile techniques have been customized into methods for other industries, such as Lean Construction.[9] While the principles described in this book are generally applicable to most new product development scenarios, the discussions and examples are mostly from the software development world, where most of the research and work on agile methods is taking place.

Why do we Need New Methods?

In the face of changing requirements, traditional project management "best practices" suggest that we try to

1   Lock down requirements to form a baseline,

2   Implement change control, and

3   Fall back on the documented requirements or the contract as means to enforce the change control.

Lock down requirements. The purpose behind this technique is to document the requirements as of a single point in time and then get those requirements "approved" (signed off by the sponsor) to provide a baseline against which further changes can be measured. Having such a baseline allows the impact of new changes to be assessed and a set of metrics (usually budget and timeline) that are used as negotiating points for accepting the changes.

Implement change control. Once the baseline is in place, any scope discussions can refer back to the baseline to see if features are covered under the existing scope or form new requirements. New requirements will require an impact analysis that estimates the effect of the changed requirements to the budget, timeline, risk, etc. of the project. For changes to be accepted by the project team, and for the baseline to be updated to reflect the newly approved scope, the project sponsor signs a change authorization document that grants the formal approval to update the approved budget, timeline, and scope baselines. In many environments, this includes changing signed contracts.

Fall back on the documented baseline. As discussed above, whenever there is a question about whether a feature is to be implemented by the project team, the team can refer back to the documented baseline. Any difference will have to be handled through the change control process. Often disputes erupt about whether a feature is new, or just a "clarification" to an existing feature that is already part of the baseline. In most projects, the baseline is never 100% clear, and negotiations are needed to resolve different interpretations of the baseline.

While these methods may appear to work in theory, in practice they lead to chaos and dramatic project underperformance. "Junior" project managers – those without a lot of real-world experience – will usually err by being either too lenient, and allowing too much change to the baseline without triggering the change control processes (in the interest of customer satisfaction), or err by being too strict, and refusing to accept changes to the baseline. Sometimes the latter approach leads to irate customers as they are told that changes will be deferred until the next release of the product to avoid delays to the release of the initial project scope baseline. Either approach can lead to project underperformance. In the first case, projects may go way over budget and may be late due to additional features being added in a haphazard way by the project team in response to changing customer whims. In the second case, projects may go over budget and may be late due to the extra work and delays caused by assessing the changes to the baseline and the often contentious negotiations with the customers.

The Standish Group, in their ground-breaking Chaos Reports[10] first noted that approximately 16 percent of all IT projects are successful. The rest are either late, over budget, deliver only a fraction of their original scope baseline in order to meet their time or budget restrictions, or are cancelled altogether. Many in the IT industry were initially shocked by these results, but soon realized the truth behind them. IT projects, especially software development projects, are different from more traditional projects in that they are *new product development projects* with a number of unusual characteristics:

- At the early design stages, the intangible nature of most software leads to difficulties in communicating design and vision in an easily-understandable way.

- Progress is often hard to assess, given the intangible nature of the deliverables.

- They are usually trying to create unique products with few available analogs for comparison.

- The tools for building software (programming languages) are constantly changing, often mid-way through the project.

- The building blocks (computer hardware, operating systems) are constantly changing.

- The industry standards that the software must support are constantly changing.

When dealing with all of this uncertainty, of course there is going to be a high level of change during a project.

Now add to this a reality of today's business world: with a global economy and the faster pace of today's business (working in Internet time), no set of requirements will stay the same for very long. A competitor comes out with a new product. Government legislation changes. Your company is bought out by another one with a different strategy. An organizational restructuring results in you having a new boss who wants to make a mark and who wants to redirect your priorities. Many different forces of change are at work in our world, and we cannot control these sources of change. The concept of *change control* is a misnomer: we cannot "control" these factors, nor can we control the changes that they generate. What we can do, however, is manage how we adapt to these changes.

What is Different about Agile Methods?

Agile methods, at their core, are all about managing the impact of change on a project. When change occurs, these methods provide ways of allowing that change to be introduced to the project in an orderly way that attempts to maximize the benefits for the sponsor, while controlling the risks that the change introduces.

In traditional product development lifecycles, such as the Waterfall Method,[11,12] there is a design developed, then the product is developed according to that design, then the product is tested to determine how well it adhered to the design. Design changes introduced during the development or testing portions of the project cause chaos, in that they require the project to stop dead in its tracks and cycle back to the beginning design phase. If these changes occur late in the project, the resulting delays and increased costs can skyrocket. (See Figure 1-1.)

Agile methods share some common characteristics that allow them to respond better to change. These characteristics are discussed at greater length throughout this book.

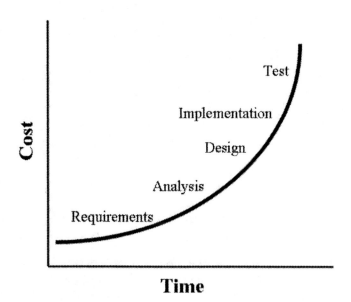

Figure 1-1: Boehm's cost of change curve[13] shows the exponentially higher cost of making changes late in a project.

Iterative and Incremental Development. Agile methods break down the development of their new products into a number of repeating cycles called *iterations*. Each iteration builds upon the last, adding additional layers of functionality. This allows the product to grow much in the same way that an onion or a pearl grows by adding layers. Starting from an initial kernel of functionality, over time (and several iterations) the product becomes more and more complete. This provides delivery of some functionality early in the project, and then regularly throughout the remainder of the project.

Short Iterations. By using short iterations, agile methods keep the feedback cycle short, allowing more responsiveness to change, and reducing the risk of building "the wrong thing" based on unclear or changing requirements.

Progress Measured via Completed Features. Rather than trying to track progress by measuring percent complete on intangible elements such as design, agile methods track progress by fully-completed and tested features. Progress is measured by the percent of features that are complete and ready for the sponsor to review or deploy. This avoids the Vaporware Syndrome, where functionality is "mocked up" (faked) or features are not properly developed in order to meet a timeline or budget constraint. Then, when a sponsor seeks to deploy the product, the truth is revealed – that a lot of additional work is still required to "finish the job."

Open, Flexible Design. Designs are flexible and extensible using open standards wherever possible. Since the full set of requirements may be unclear at the beginning of the project, and will likely change anyway, prepare a flexible, extensible design that will allow you to add on features to support new requirements as they emerge. There is always the risk of some rework to incorporate complex requirements, but often the impact is offset by the other benefits gained by using agile methods.

Empowered Teams. Teams of specialists who know their jobs well and have the experience (and maturity) to decide for themselves how best to approach the problems at hand. Instead of imposing a design on the team, let the people who know best how to implement the details decide how they are going to do the work. This often allows for more flexibility in a system than is usually found in a more traditional, centralized design.

Personal Communications. Rather than focus on producing written documents to communicate design decisions, technical approaches, and other normally-documented items, agile methods suggest that teams work in shared physical environments. Speaking face to face, perhaps with the support of a whiteboard for drawing diagrams, is a much more efficient way of working out design details. It is easier to update a design on a whiteboard, a design that is shared in the minds of a room full of people, than to update hundreds (or thousands) of pages of design documents. As we will see later in this chapter, many large projects have failed because of the reliance on written documentation to communicate design. While written documentation has its place on agile projects (as discussed in Chapter 9) teams need to seek opportunities to discuss approaches verbally to capture nuances not reflected always in documents, and to provide a fast way of asking (and answering) questions to ensure comprehension.

Using these common characteristics, the creators of the various agile methods have produced a variety of approaches, each emphasizing different aspects. No single agile method is "better" than the rest – they all have their strengths and weaknesses – yet employing them can often lead to some significant benefits for the sponsor and for the project team.

What are the Benefits of Being Agile?

While agile methods may not fit every project, they do provide valuable benefits when applied against specific business problems. Consider each of these benefits when evaluating whether a particular agile technique may be of use on your own project, as each technique puts a different emphasis on the different benefits.

There are three main types of benefits from agile techniques: reducing risk, improving control, and improving communications. Each of these benefits has a number of aspects that are detailed below.

Reducing Risk

Of all three benefit types, reducing risk is perhaps the most significant. The benefits from improved control and improved communications largely lead to reduced risks themselves, so we should put extra emphasis on discussing the use of agile techniques for the reduction of risk.

While risks may be categorized in many different ways, in this chapter we will look at three specific risks: the risk of building (or doing) the wrong "thing;" the risk of building the right thing, but poorly; and the risk of being stuck in an endless cycle of design updates and reviews due to changing requirements or high levels of complexity. There are other risk-reduction benefits, but these are the three that I have found to be easier to sell to your project sponsors and team members, as they help avoid concrete, measurable impacts when these risks are left uncontrolled.

25

Building the Wrong Thing

As one of my primary specialties, I spend a lot of time reviewing (and correcting) troubled software development and systems integration projects. When I first come onto these projects, I interview all the main project stakeholders. Of course, one of my first stops is the desk of the sponsor. Something that I have heard repeatedly from sponsors of troubled projects is a variation of the phrase "They gave me what I may have asked for, but that was not what I meant." This is an indication of a serious disconnect in expectations that can be improved with better communications.

There is nothing better on a project than having actively-involved stakeholders who work closely with the project team reviewing the work in progress, answering questions as they arise and providing immediate feedback. Imagine managing one of these projects – you would never be concerned about acceptance of the final deliverables, since the approvers were providing you their feedback throughout the project, ensuring that what you created was aligned with their expectations. Agile techniques realize that documentation is a poor means of communications. Writing down requirements may help some people better understand the "thing" they desire, but you need to supplement the written documents with many discussions and joint design reviews to ensure that you capture the nuances that sometimes cannot be put onto paper.

Some people are visual learners. No matter how detailed (and thick!) a requirements document becomes, these people will not be able to relate the document to their mental vision for the product. In fact, I have personally seen one project sponsor hold a two-inch-thick binder filled with detailed technical specifications, shake it up and down a couple of times in her hand, and comment that since the document is so obviously thick and heavy, that it *must* be correct. She signed off on the document without even opening up the binder! For people like this, creating more and more detailed specifications is not going to solve the problem. Even if they *do* attempt to read the document, their eyes are going to glaze over after the first few pages, and they will drift off to sleep. You need a different approach.

Agile methods adapt a technique borrowed from the movie industry called "storyboarding." In storyboarding, you create a visual representation of the "flow" of a movie, sketching out visually what each shot will look like. Then, those who are visual thinkers will have something other than the written script to which they can relate, and get a better sense of what you are proposing. In agile software development, we do this by creating "use cases" or "user stories" that give a simple, task-oriented view of what people will need to be able to do when using the system. The specifications are created from the user's perspective, focusing on the functionality that is demonstrable and that performs some business function. We don't "storyboard" database optimization algorithms – no user or sponsor will likely be able to understand the technical details of such a work component anyways, except at the most general levels – stakeholders do not even think of such features, or if they do, they just assume them to be in the project anyway. You can "storyboard" a transaction or use case by sketching out the user interface (the screen) and the changes that appear on that interface as the various steps of the use case are completed. This will help visual thinkers get a better feel for what you are proposing, they can better understand how it relates to how they perform their jobs today, and you can get some early usability feedback.

Gone are the days when the technical people get a written specification, create something, and then hand it back to the sponsoring group claiming that they are done. Now, sponsors are more astute, taking a more holistic view of project success: the real measure of success they use is not conformance to the written requirements, but rather the achievement of the business case benefits that prompted the funding of the project in the first place. Sponsors are demanding a seat at the table, and a chance to provide some feedback during the development of the project's "product."

The close involvement of sponsors and other stakeholders during iterative product development through the use of end of iteration reviews, allows stakeholders to provide guidance to the project team that will avoid the "you built what I asked for, not what I wanted" situation discussed earlier. It also has an added benefit of allowing a more adaptive approach to changing requirements.

On many projects, especially where the project is creating something that the sponsors have never had before, the true requirements are often not known or understood. Sometimes these projects are reactions to external forces beyond the sponsor's control, and about which little is currently known:

•   New government legislation that will change regulations affecting how the organization carries out its business,

•   Changing consumer preferences, and

•   Customers demanding new features to match a competitor's newly announced offering.

In these (and related) situations, the sponsor will not know all of the detailed requirements at the start of the project. Instead, enough will be known to get started, and the rest of the requirements will be discovered or fully explored during the course of the project. In these cases, it is sometimes better to "just get started" and then figure out the details later.

I once had the challenge of building a new software system for a government body to allow the automation of some processes to meet service availability and responsiveness targets proposed by upcoming legislation. The legislation, when passed, would require the immediate availability of the supporting information systems to support the new regulations.

Like most proposed government legislation, by the time it gets approved and turned into law, it goes through many changes as a result of negotiations with the various political parties and the influence of lobbyists. While the final requirements would not be known until the law was passed, we needed a system running days after the proposal became law. What were we to do?

The use of agile techniques made this process much simpler. We started by building the pieces that were not likely to change, and demonstrated increasingly more complete versions of the system through our end of iteration reviews. The specialists in the government department, who were closely monitoring the current state of the legislation and the direction of the political winds, gave us feedback at each stage that allowed us to adapt the system to the prevailing concept of what the final legislation would look like. In four months, we developed and tested the complete system, and it was ready the day the legislation was passed into law.

Traditional methods, where one waits for a signed-off requirements document before starting work, would have led to long delays before we could start, numerous change request forms that would have been caught up in the government bureaucracy awaiting approval, and a delivery date that would have been months behind the required (legislated) product availability date. If we had not accepted any change requests until we were done (one common response to this type of situation), we would have built what was originally asked for, but not what was required at the time of completion, due to the many requirements that had changed. The project output would have been useless. In this real-world example, agile techniques saved the day.

Building the right thing wrong

Assuming we managed to build the right thing for the customer (that is, we completely and accurately understood the customer's requirements and expectations, and managed to build a product that met those expectations) there is still a major product risk left to consider. We may have built the right thing, but we may have done a poor job building it. In other words, we may "have built the right thing wrong."

Quality should be a concern for every product development effort, whether that product is computer software, a bridge, or a consulting report. Dr. William Edwards Deming, the guru of the revolution in quality management that took over the business world in the 1980s and 1990s, tells us that quality needs to be designed into a product development process. More simply: we need to find ways of ensuring that barriers to quality are removed at every step in the process.

In the software development world, quality is usually addressed through various types of testing at the end of the software development process: unit testing, integration testing, usability testing, and others that all culminate in customer acceptance testing. One of the major reasons why most software development projects run over budget and behind schedule is that this testing happens only at the end of the project. Defects are found late in the project lifecycle, leaving little time to fix them. When a design defect is found, the implications are disastrous – the project team must revisit the initial designs, make updates, change the software that was developed based upon those updated designs (and the changes may ripple throughout all areas of the software application) and then start the testing process all over again. Just one of these defects can lead to a delay of many months and the associated increased costs. We need to find a way to design quality into the software development process to avoid these costly late-cycle quality issues.

One solution to this problem, and one easily addressed by the agile techniques of iterative and incremental development is the use of continuous testing. All agile methods are structured around iterative and incremental development. Using these methods, every iteration delivers fully-tested and functional deliverables. The completeness of those deliverables increases with each succeeding iteration, but the portions that are developed in each iteration need to be properly working for the iteration to be considered complete. This means that testing needs to happen in every iteration.

Testing during each iteration means that defects are found much earlier in the development cycle. This allows more time than the traditional "test at the end" methods for fixing these defects. More importantly, critical design-related defects may be uncovered much sooner. As Boehm points out in Figure 1-1, the later a change (or, by extension, design defect) occurs in a project, the greater the cost of incorporating the change. Identifying design defects early on is critical.

I once had a case where my team was one month into an agile development project. We had two-week iterations, and were at the end of our second end-of-iteration review. The project sponsor had pulled in an external reviewer to assess our progress and approach. With a concerned look on his face, the external reviewer announced that a new corporate standard for user interface design was just announced that we would have to live by on our project. Unfortunately, the new standard required us to significantly redesign how we were building the user interface for our application. Essentially, about half of our work over the prior four weeks had to be discarded and done over again. The sponsor was *not* happy about this. That is, until I explained the impact on the project (and his budget) if we had not been using an agile development method. If the first time that a reviewer had seen our work and noticed the non-compliance with the new standard was during the traditional "user acceptance testing" phase at the end of our eight month project, we would have needed to discard months of work completed to that point in time – a much greater impact than the couple of lost weeks that we were really facing. The sponsor immediately saw the value in iterative delivery and mandated the use of agile development methods (in this case, Scrum) on his future projects.

Another benefit to testing in each iteration is the greater amount of testing that generally takes place under these approaches. Additionally, through the regression tests required to ensure that the incremental development does not break portions that were developed earlier, the initially-developed portions are tested over and over again, increasing the chance that the initially-developed pieces work as they were intended. One way to ensure this is through the practice of test-driven development, where we design the tests first – tests designed to test that the application will meet the requirements – and then use the tests as design input into our development process. This way, we can use what will be the eventual "acceptance tests" as the unit and systems tests performed by the programmers. Running the relevant acceptance tests in each iteration means that the code is more likely to work as expected, since there are a greater number of opportunities to fix identified defects and then retest again during subsequent iterations.

Getting Stuck in "Design Churn"

Agile methods are not necessarily the best methods for every project; however, they do have a lot to offer certain types of project. Projects that benefit the most from the use of agile methods are those in which the requirements are either unclear or evolving. If you expect a high level of requirements change during a project, then traditional methods simply will not work.

Peter Coad and Jeff DeLuca were brought on to one of these projects in their notorious "Singapore" project.[3] This project, to develop a commercial leasing system, had such a complex design that no single team member could keep the entire design in his or her mind. To compensate for this complex design, the team had developed thousands of pages of documentation (over 3,500 pages of use cases, class diagrams, etc.) in which they captured the design and worked out the complex component interaction issues. The problem was that there were continual changes occurring that required them to review and update these 3,500 pages of documentation to incorporate the impact of each change. Obviously, this took a lot of time, and by the time the changes were incorporated into the designs, more change had occurred. The changes were sparking additional changes, and the team was stuck in the dreaded cycle of "design churn." The sponsor, frustrated with this lack of progress, fired the original development team and brought in Coad and DeLuca to try and find a way out of this problem and start developing usable software.

To break out of the vicious cycle, Coad and DeLuca decided to take the pieces that they could understand clearly, and that were reasonably well-defined and stable, and build them first. By completing these simpler pieces first, visible progress was demonstrated to the sponsor, usable software started evolving, and the project became "unstuck." While the initial pieces were being built, the design team picked up another discrete piece and designed that piece enough that development could start on it, and so on. This process works as long as the overall design uses open standards, and is flexible and extensible. (A similar process was used to break out of the design churn encountered by Kent Beck, Ron Jeffries, and the rest of the C3 Team on the Chrysler Comprehensive Compensation system,[16] discussed later in this book.)

33

Another side benefit of this overall approach is the ability to procrastinate – that's right, procrastinate. If you are facing a project scope element where the requirements are not stable, why not delay starting on the design and development of that piece as long as possible? Work on other pieces during the initial iterations, and push the scope elements full of uncertainty to future iterations. In this manner, you can deliberately delay working on components whose requirements are likely to change for as long as possible. The longer you wait, the greater the chance of the requirements becoming more stable as more is known about the emerging solution that you are enhancing through each iteration. Once a requirement is stable enough to start work, then *that* is the time to start working on it – to start earlier, you risk too much rework and wasted effort.

Now, I am not advocating that you push out *all* components with unclear requirements until late in the project. This would be foolish. You need to use this technique judiciously, balancing the benefits of delaying the start of a project component with unstable requirements with other techniques that reduce other risks. In fact, there are times when you may want to do the exact opposite.

Sometimes, the way of getting out of a design dilemma is through experimentation. If you are not sure how to overcome a design issue with certainty, or if you are faced with competing approaches and cannot make up your mind which is best, try conducting an experiment to see which approach is better. Take a page from the Rational Unified Process (RUP) playbook, and schedule the areas of greatest uncertainty (or risk) first, allowing you to perform experiments to validate assumptions, remove technical uncertainty, and establish an approach that can work. Sometimes this approach will allow you to "prove" a design through demonstration long before you could "prove" it on paper with supporting design details.

Use these techniques as different tools in your toolbox. Do not pick one tool and try to apply it to every situation, but rather learn all of the tools and learn when each one is best employed. In other words, use the right tool for the job at hand.

Improving Control

In addition to reducing risk, agile methods allow the project manager to improve his or her control over the project. This may sound counterintuitive, but in practice, it is true: using a less-rigid, structured approach allows the manager to better control the project in situations where there will be high levels of change on the project. In effect, the agile methods allow the manager to better respond and adapt to changing requirements in a way that does not lead to design churn, confrontational contract negotiations, and angry stakeholders.

Generally, control is improved through a number of mechanisms that are common results of all agile methods:

• Frequent delivery of working code means progress is objectively measurable,

• More chances for stakeholders to provide early feedback and redirect project priorities where necessary increases the chance of delivering real value,

• Misunderstanding are surfaced earlier, avoiding late-lifecycle design changes mentioned earlier in this chapter, and

• The sponsor has the ability to end a project early and still get measurable benefits.

Frequent Delivery means Measurable Progress

By breaking the project lifecycle down into a number of short, recurring design-develop-test iterations, the functionality being developed that meets the business requirements can be delivered in small increments, each providing business value. When facing highly-complex or risky projects, sponsors and managers have a much better read on the real progress of a project when actual progress is visible to everyone on a frequent basis. Without the visibility of real progress, there is little management control that can be meaningfully exerted to correct the course of the project or to deal with performance issues.

Consider a traditional waterfall-type development process. The team designs a solution, builds it, then tests and perfects it before handing it over to a project sponsor for review and acceptance. If this whole process was 18 months long, the sponsor will have no means by which to measure progress until he or she gets access to the completed product for the acceptance review. Until the product is ready for review, the sponsor has no concrete means by which to measure progress. If the team says they are 90% complete, who can argue? The next weeks, when they say they are 91%, 92%, and then 93% complete, there is still no evidence by which to question or argue this progress.

Instead, agile methods allow you to improve visibility into real progress by focusing on user-visible features or transactions. For example, let us look at an application with ten user-visible features (such as menu options in a software application). When you can demonstrate that the four of the ten are complete and working, you can claim you are 40% complete, and have a sound basis against which to measure that progress.

Visible progress reduces uncertainty. It also puts sponsors at ease – especially those who may have gambled their careers on the success of your project. Showing them real progress will ease their concerns, increase their satisfaction, and reduce their need for micromanaging you and your team.

Feedback and Redirection means Delivering More Value

End-of-iteration reviews allow sponsors and other stakeholders a chance to review the work performed to date. This introduces an opportunity for them to provide feedback. You may hear that what was developed was perfect. More likely, you will hear feedback such as one of the following:

- What you delivered may be what I asked for, but not what I meant (a misunderstood requirement).

- What you delivered does not work properly (a defect).

- Now that I see what you have built, I have thought of something that would make it even better (a new requirement).

- Now that I see what you have built, I realize we forgot something (a missed requirement).

- Something has come up – I need you to do that a different way (a change).

No matter which of the above types of feedback you receive, if you can incorporate the feedback into your next iteration, you will bring the project closer to delivering the business value that the sponsor needs. There is no point in sticking to the original scope baseline and deferring change until the end of the project (or for another product version/release) – doing so will mean that you deliver something to the sponsor that he or she cannot use. Since you have not adapted to his or her changing business requirements, your deliverable is now based on obsolete requirements and will exist solely as "shelfware" – a useless effort and expenditure of funds unless you can make the changes to the product to bring it back in line with the sponsor's *current* business needs.

Capturing and responding to feedback at the end of each iteration will help you be more responsive to your sponsor's changing business priorities, and will help you better deliver a product at the end of the project that will deliver *some* business value, rather than *no* business value (as would happen if you did not respond to the changes). The feedback will not be just changes to what you have already built, but it will also help you reprioritize what you are planning to build next, to ensure that you are focusing on the pieces that will deliver the greatest benefits. Both the sponsor and the project manager can better control the delivery of business value.

Early Feedback means Lower Cost of Change

Getting feedback earlier in the project will allow changes to be incorporated earlier. As pointed out in Figure 1-1, this means that design changes have a greater chance of being surfaced and acted upon earlier in the product development cycle, when the costs of those changes are the lowest.

End Early with Measurable Benefits

Another benefit of this approach allows the sponsor control over the level of quality (completeness) of the product at the end of the project. At the end of each iteration, the included features should be fully functional and tested. Theoretically, it would be possible for the sponsor to release (deploy) the product at the end of any iteration, allowing the sponsor to realize several benefits:

- If the product is the first to address a niche in the marketplace, early deployment may allow the sponsor to gain marketshare well ahead of any competition.

- If the contents of the early iterations are selected carefully, then the sponsor may choose to deploy a partially-completed product to gain immediate benefits of the completed portions, before the full product is completed. In some cases, the benefits from early deployment may help offset (or even pay for) the costs of completing the full product.

- If the contents of the iterations are continually reprioritized at the start of each iteration, focusing on the items that are most important first, then at some point later in the project, all of the high-priority items will have been developed, and the only remaining items to be developed will be of marginal value to the sponsor. The sponsor may decide to forego developing these low-priority features, deeming the product to be "good enough" for general rollout.

Improving Communications

Finally, agile methods foster better communications among team members than traditional product development methods. Communications is key to any project, and all good project managers know that 80% of the job of a good project manager is facilitating communications, whether it be communicating status, discussing solutions to problems, notifying others of dependencies, or ensuring that everyone shares the same project vision and strategy.

Once, on one of those "take a student to work days," I had a Grade 9 student assigned to me. His task was to shadow me for the day, and then write a report for his class on the role of a project manager.

For the entire day, the student followed me to meetings, watched me working at the computer, and listened to me calling project stakeholders to gain insight or to share information. Only at the end of the day, before leaving work, did I find out that the student was the son of an executive several layers above me in the organizational hierarchy. That made me wonder: did I do my job well, did I look professional, did I make a lasting impression? I hoped that when the boy's father asked who he shadowed at work that day, and how things went, that I would get a glowing report.

About a week later, I received a copy of his school report via internal company mail along with a short note. The report described the day-to-day job of a project manager as being

> the most fun job in the company – you get to talk to your friends all day on the phone, stop by their desks for a chat, and send them emails. You don't have to do any real work!

I was mortified. What would my executive think about my job performance? I opened the note with shaking hands and read

> Sounds like my son doesn't get it yet. Maybe he's too young to understand, but it seems to me like you are focusing on exactly the right thing – communications. That's the key to running a successful business, and a successful project. Good work.

I learned a lesson that day, about the importance of communications. I was never conscious of what I was doing, but that day opened my eyes. Since then, I have deliberately crafted communications plans for my projects, and have designed project teams to maximize the flow of information and knowledge.

Co-located teams

There is tremendous value to be gained from using collocated teams on a project. These are teams where most (if not all) team members work in the same location, preferably with adjacent desks. Later in this book we will delve into this topic in more detail, but in my experience, the direct benefits of collocated teams are experienced through several means.

Whiteboarding. Instead of crafting long-winded, complicated emails or documents describing issues and suggesting design approaches, when the team members are all in one location, someone can simply tap others on the shoulder and ask them to step over to a whiteboard. By drawing diagrams, making quick changes, erasing and redrawing, and through immediate feedback from others, solutions to problems can be quickly and effectively described, modified, and agreed upon or rejected. This is what Cockburn describes[14] as high-bandwidth communications. This beats the long delays in trying to do the same problem solving via long strings of emails back and forth between team members, or via slowly-evolving documents.

Looking over the shoulders of others. I once worked in an environment where we needed to boost the productivity of a team building a Web application. We moved the graphic designer into the same office as the two developers. There was an immediate improvement in the performance of the team, all attributable to better communications. When the designer created the mockup for a new Web page, he could simply ask one of the developers to turn around in his chair and take a look at the design while it was on the screen. The developers could immediately say whether the design was "build-able" or not, and could ask the designer to make immediate corrections that would prevent much later problem solving and rework. Similarly, the designer could review the Web pages as the developers built them to give feedback on whether they were turning out as intended. Finally, the two developers were able to help each other out with technical problems, reducing the time spent on problem-solving and fixing defects. Over all, it was the most effective management change that we implemented on the project. The improved communications gave us greater control over the project's outcome.

Non-verbal communications. The majority of the information we convey (approximately 70%, by some estimates) is through non-verbal means. This includes body language (nervousness, hesitation), tone of voice (sarcasm, uncertainty), and eye contact (or the lack thereof). Sometimes, more is revealed by the topics that are avoided than by the topics that are discussed. By working in a collocated environment, we avoid the use of impersonal communications vehicles such as email and documents that convey only 30% of the meaning; instead, we get to use face-to-face conversations that allow us to take advantage of the full 100% of what information is being transmitted. This allows faster and more thorough communications. It allows us to "read" the other person in a conversation to try and determine whether they really do understand what we just said. Sometimes we have to work remotely, but even then, if a team has worked together before, and knows each others' working styles and personalities, then teleconferences are an acceptable alternative that still allow a lot of non-verbal transfer of information. Greater understanding and faster transfer of knowledge and information: why would you ever want to work apart again?

Short daily meetings

By holding regular (but short) daily team meetings, team members can share their successes and problems with each other. Following the lead of Scrum, agile meetings are best when team members briefly share three pieces of information:

1   **What they have just completed** – so that others who may be dependent upon the completion of that work may get immediate notice of its readiness, and to give a measure of visible progress to the team's efforts.

2   **What they are about to work on next** – so that team members will be aware of what others are doing and can able to help out or provide advice based upon past experiences. This also may bring other dependencies to light that the team may not have been aware of at first.

3   **Any issues that are slowing down or halting progress** – if facing technical issues, other team members may be able to help, or the project manager may be able to find assistance from outside of the team. If the issues are organizational or administrative, the project manager can take immediate actions to remove the barriers. If the issues are personal, the project manager can seek out assistance, training, or whatever other help is required for the team members to maximize their performance.

Employing short daily meetings allows the project manager to get earlier notice of problems (and thus more time to act upon them before they balloon into big issues). Additionally, project managers can better ensure steady progress with these meetings by highlighting cross-dependencies and offering a chance for team members to share their tacit knowledge to solve issues. Of course, the lengthy dialogues that might be required to impart knowledge or solve problems do not happen in the meeting – they are handled through follow-up conversations between the team members affected – rather, the meetings are used to highlight the need for these follow-up conversations.

Close customer (sponsor) involvement

Another way of improving control over the project through improved communications is by having the project sponsor, or a customer representative involved daily in project meetings. The immediate and regular access to someone who understands the business situation that gave rise to the project, who understands the requirements, and who is authorized to make decisions regarding the project can greatly improve control over the project schedule, budget, and scope. In Extreme Programming, we call this the On-Site Customer, while in Scrum, this is referred to as the Product Owner. There are three main ways in which this improved level of communications with the sponsor can be used to help control the project.

Quick and easy escalation. By having ready access to a decision-maker who understands the business requirements and the project's business case, the project manager can quickly escalate any issues requiring a decision or action within the sponsor's organization. Usually, this role is held by someone with authority who can move roadblocks that the project manager cannot resolve without assistance. The quick communication of these issues helps speed up the project, avoiding costly delays.

Snap decision-making. In addition to the ability to quickly escalate issues to the sponsor or other key decision-makers, close customer involvement in the daily happenings within the project allows you to contact a decision-maker immediately when a snap decision is required. No more struggling to find a decision maker and get a decision made. By having someone involved who is authorized (and willing) to make decisions, you can communicate your decision point requests quickly,

Instant feedback. As discussed earlier in this chapter, one of the big benefits of agile development methods is that you have regular opportunities for stakeholder feedback at the end of

44

each iteration. Having close customer involvement in the project, however, leverages this benefit to even higher levels. Instead of waiting for end of iteration reviews for feedback, team members can bounce ideas or approaches off of the customer representative at any point during the project to get immediate, valuable feedback. This increased communications helps control quality by even further reducing the likelihood of "building the wrong thing."

As I have described above, there are three main categories of benefits from deploying agile development methods on projects, and each plays an important role in improving project control. While agile methods are not the right solution for *every* project situation, they *do* provide a means by which to increase control over projects where the requirements are constantly changing – projects that are notoriously hard to control using traditional methods.

Why do we Need This Book?

There are many publications in the marketplace that describe the various agile methods and techniques. Yet, most of these discuss these techniques from the perspective of a team member who will be employing these methods in the performance of their technical development activities. Very few publications present the agile methods from the perspective of a project manager.

Additionally, most of the existing publications focus on a single method or agile technique; there are few that discuss all of the most common techniques. This book presents techniques from many different agile methods, and compares the various methods in the context of these techniques. (I should note here that many of the discussions deal primarily with Extreme Programming – not because the techniques are not applicable to other agile methods, but rather because

Extreme Programming is the agile method that has been most written about and most studied to date. When reading this book, when you read "Extreme Programming" consider that in most instances the statement will apply to most other agile methods as well.)

This book combines the work of many experts into one volume. These are the luminaries of the field – the people who invented some of these agile methods and techniques. The chapters in this book have been prepared by these experts both from previously published (and now updated) articles, and from new original works, appearing in this book for the first time.

Part One: Introduction

The first section of this book, its introduction, presents an overview of what agile methods are about, and a brief history of how they came to be.

Chapter 1 – This chapter provides a brief overview of reason why agile methods were developed in the first place, and the major benefits to be gained from employing them. The author, Kevin Aguanno, is a consultant, teacher, and keynote speaker on agile development methods. He focuses on bringing agile methods out from under the software development umbrella and into the world of project managers. He has introduced hundreds of companies (and thousands of project managers) to agile development principles and techniques.

Chapter 2 – For those who want to understand more about how these methods have evolved, this chapter provides a brief history of the major agile methods and describes how they interrelate with the Software Engineering Institute's Capability Maturity Model (SEI CMM). The authors of this chapter, David Cohen, Mikael Lindvall, and Patricia Costa performed an extensive study of agile software development methods for the U.S. Air Force through the Fraunhofer Center for

Experimental Software Engineering at the University of Maryland. This chapter is a brief extract from their full report.

Part Two: Managing Agile Projects is Different

The second section of this book explores how managing agile projects is different from managing projects following more traditional methods. This section takes a more holistic view from the project management perspective, rather than the specific agile techniques that are deployed on projects.

Chapter 3 – Written by Kevin Aguanno, this chapter presents a brief overview of how agile project management is different from the project management approaches presented by bodies such as the Project Management Institute (PMI).

Chapter 4 – There is a lot of confusion between the terms *iterative* and *incremental*. Each means a very different thing, yet agile methods bring both together for the first time in a unique way. Pascal Van Cauwenberghe is a noted author, teacher, and speaker on Extreme Programming and other agile methods and techniques, and has prepared an excellent tutorial on the differences between iterative and incremental development approaches and the advantages from each.

Chapter 5 – As one of the leading luminaries in the agile development movement, Alistair Cockburn has written numerous books, published scores of articles, and speaks regularly at software development conferences on agile principles and techniques. He is the developer of a group of related agile methods called, collectively, the Crystal Methods, and is one of the early proponents of using "use cases." Mr. Cockburn is one of the founders of the Agile Alliance, and a co-author of the *Agile Manifesto*. In this chapter, adapted from a series of articles he published in *Crosstalk: The Journal of Defense Software Engineering*, he takes his experiences from agile software development and applies them to the topic of project management in general.

Chapter 6 – Agile project managers must walk a fine line between too much control, which destroys the benefits from flexibility that agile methods provide, and too little control, which will allow a project to degrade into chaos. Learning from the science of Complex Adaptive Systems, Sanjiv Augustine and Susan Woodcock propose a number of practices that will allow project leaders to keep the project balanced between too much order and too much chaos, the so-called *chaordic edge.*

Chapter 7 – When requirements are constantly changing, documenting and rationalizing requirements – the practice of requirements engineering – becomes very challenging. Jim Tomayko, a professor of computer science at Carnegie Mellon University and a scientist of the Software Engineering Institute (SEI), presents a brief comparison between requirements elicitation in traditional and agile projects, highlights the related difficulties when working with requirements in agile projects, and highlights one of the advantages.

Chapter 8 – One way in which agile projects are quite different from traditional projects, is in the level of involvement required from project stakeholders, and in particular, the project sponsor. Scott Ambler, a noted expert on object-oriented software development techniques, the developer of the Agile Modeling technique, and a widely-published author presents in this chapter the reason behind the need for active stakeholder participation on agile projects. In addition, he presents some tips for ensuring that you get the most benefit out of your stakeholder involvement, and avoid some of the pitfalls.

Chapter 9 – Scott Ambler contributes again to this book by providing a chapter on the reliance of agile methods on higher-bandwidth communications; for example, focusing on face-to-face communications over written documentation. With a different focus on communications than traditional project methods, agile methods require some extra attention from project managers in this key area. Ambler's contribution in this chapter is an update from material presented in his book *Agile Modeling: Effective Practices for Extreme Programming and The Unified Process.*

Part Three: Agile Management Techniques

Now that we have discussed how agile projects are different from traditional projects, this section addresses a number of individual agile management techniques that are common to most agile methods.

Chapter 10 – Kevin Aguanno provides an overview of the agile management techniques presented in this section.

Chapter 11 – While in Chapter 7 we discussed the need for a different approach to requirements engineering, this chapter provides the details on how to conduct such a different approach. Kirstin Kohler and Barbara Paech are active researchers in requirements engineering, having published many journal articles in the field. Kohler is a researcher and consultant with the Fraunhofer Institute for Experimental Software Engineering in Germany, and Paech is the Chair of Software Engineering at the University of Heidelberg. Both share their extensive experience in this area to provide practical approaches to overcoming the challenges surrounding changing requirements on agile projects.

Chapter 12 – As a frequent speaker and teacher on agile development methods, perhaps the most frequently-asked question I receive is "How do you estimate and deliver agile projects under fixed-price contracts?" While recognizing that time and materials contracts are the easiest under which to deliver agile projects, the reality in the business world is that these types of contracts require a large amount of trust between the sponsor and the delivery team – trust that is often not present. In this chapter, Pascal Van Cauwenberghe provides us with some good options for preparing fixed price contracts for agile projects.

Chapter 13 – The focus that agile methods place on feature-based prioritization, design, and progress reporting changes the paradigm under which a project operates. To focus so much on user-facing features, requires that the project adopt a user-centric view of requirements and design. Larry Constantine, one of the founders (and leading proponents) of usage-centered design, first presented the contents of this chapter as an article in *Information Age*. This chapter presents the pros and cons of taking such as user-focused design approach, and shares a step-by-step process that managers can understand for performing user-focused design.

Chapter 14 – Documentation: how much is enough? In Chapter 9, we talked about the preference for other means of communication. Yet in Chapter 11, we explored the need for requirements documentation. Where is the balance? In this chapter, Scott Ambler answers that question, providing an approach and some tips to help you prepare "just enough" documentation.

Chapter 15 – One of the key benefits from (and requirements of) iterative development is the need for continuous testing. In this chapter, Ron Jeffries explores the different types of testing you will need to perform in an agile environment, and tips for performing each. He also includes some tips on how to get your project teams to adopt the agile testing techniques such as automated regression testing. Jeffries is one of the co-founders of the Extreme Programming method, and is a well-known author and speaker in this field.

Chapter 16 – While we discussed how to do create agile documentation in Chapter 14, we still need to focus on face-to-face communications as our primary means of sharing information. In this chapter, Linda Rising, one of the leading experts in object-oriented design and the use of "patterns," shares techniques for holding agile meetings that first appeared in *STQE: Software Testing and Quality Engineering*.

Part Four: There is No Silver Bullet

To prepare a balanced view of agile project management, one must look at the criticisms of the agile methods as well. This section presents some of the shortcomings and possible misrepresentations of the agile methods.

Chapter 17 – No single method can address all situations. In this chapter, Kevin Aguanno describes the types of projects wherein agile methods can play a valuable role, and those that might best be served through more traditional methods. There is no one-size-fits-all method: project managers should understand a number of different methods and be prepared to select the appropriate one for the project at hand.

Chapter 18 – Perhaps the most damning of all the critics of any agile method, Gerold Keefer is known for his in-depth analysis of the research supporting Extreme Programming and for his sharp (and well-supported) criticism of some of the claims made by XP proponents. Keefer is president of a quality management consultancy that specializes in helping organizations take a common-sense approach to implementing best practices like CMMI.

Chapter 19 – Sometimes, the rapid pace of agile projects can cause problems. In this chapter, David Hussman, a noted speaker and author on agile development practices, discusses the problems caused by agile projects locally-optimizing for their own projects, and the management problems that result from having multiple agile projects with interface interdependencies. He doesn't leave us high and dry, however: he does provide us with a suggested risk reduction strategy for use when managing this type of situation.

Chapter 20 – So, you have decided to adopt a whole agile method, or just some of these agile techniques, into your own organization. How do you combat the resistance of those who are comfortable with the traditional techniques? How can you convince others that their methods are not the best ones for high-change projects? How do you get the organization to change its official project management (and product development) methods? Kevin Aguanno addresses these – and other – questions in this chapter on "stealth" methodology adoption.

All of us who have contributed to this book hope that you enjoy it and welcome any questions that you may have about the contents herein. At the end of the book you will find biographical information on each author along with an email address and (in most cases) a Web site address. Feel free to visit the Web sites for more information and email the authors with your questions or feedback.

For those wanting more details on these topics, most of the chapters have included extensive end notes including supporting references. Browse through these end notes for additional sources of information.

CHAPTER TWO

The Roots of Agililty

David Cohen
Mikael Lindvall
Patricia Costa

A gile Methods are a reaction to traditional ways of developing software and acknowledge the need for an alternative to documentation driven, heavyweight software development processes[1]. In the implementation of traditional methods, work begins with the elicitation and documentation of a complete set of requirements, followed by architectural and high-level design, development, and inspection. Beginning in the mid-1990s, some practitioners found these initial development steps frustrating and, perhaps, impossible[2]. The industry and technology move too fast, requirements change at rates that swamp traditional methods[3], and customers have become increasingly unable to definitively state their needs up front while, at the same time, expecting

This chapter is extracted from *Agile Software Development: A DACS State-of-the-Art Report* (New York: Data and Analysis Center for Software, 2003). Some of the material also appeared in "An Introduction to Agile Methods," *Advances in Computers*, Elsevier Science (USA), Volume 62, 2004. Used with permission of the authors.

more from their software. As a result, several consultants have independently developed methods and practices to respond to the inevitable change they were experiencing. These Agile Methods are actually a collection of different techniques (or practices) that share the same values and basic principles. Many are, for example, based on iterative enhancement, a technique that was introduced in 1975[4].

In fact, most of the Agile practices are nothing new[5]. Instead, the focus and values behind Agile Methods differentiate them from more traditional methods. Software process improvement is an evolution in which newer processes build on the failures and successes of the ones before them, so to truly understand the Agile movement, we need to examine the methods that came before it.

According to Beck, the Waterfall Model[6] came first, as a way in which to assess and build for the users needs. It began with a complete analysis of user requirements. Through months of intense interaction with users and customers, engineers would establish a definitive and exhaustive set of features, functional requirements, and non-functional requirements. This information is well-documented for the next stage, design, where engineers collaborate with others, such as database and data structure experts, to create the optimal architecture for the system. Next, programmers implement the well-documented design, and finally, the complete, perfectly designed system is tested and shipped[7].

This process sounds good in theory, but in practice it did not always work as well as advertised. First, users changed their minds. After months, or even years, of collecting requirements and building mockups and diagrams, users still were not sure of what they wanted — all they knew was that what they saw in production was not quite it. Second, requirements tend to change mid-development, when it is difficult to stop the momentum of the project to accommodate the change. The traditional methods may well start to pose difficulties when change rates are still relatively low[8] because programmers, architects, and managers need to meet, and copious amounts of documentation need to be kept up to date to accommodate even small changes[9]. The Waterfall model was supposed to fix the problem of changing requirements once and for all by freezing requirements and not allowing any change, but practitioners found that requirements just could not be pinned down in one fell swoop as they had anticipated[7].

Incremental and iterative techniques focusing on breaking the development cycle into pieces evolved from the Waterfall model[7], taking the process behind Waterfall and repeating it throughout the development lifecycle. Incremental development aimed to reduce development time by breaking the project into overlapping increments. As with the Waterfall model, all requirements are analyzed before development begins; however, the requirements are then broken into increments of stand alone functionality. Development of each increment may be overlapped, thus saving time through concurrent multitasking across the project.

While incremental development looked to offer time savings, evolutionary methods like iterative development and the Spiral Model[9] aimed to better handle changing requirements and manage risk. These models assess critical factors in a structured and planned way at multiple points in the process rather than trying to mitigate them as they appear in the project.

Iterative development breaks the project into iterations of variable length, each producing a complete deliverable and building on the code and documentation produced before it. The first iteration starts with the most basic deliverable, and each subsequent iteration adds the next logical set of features. Each piece is its own waterfall process beginning with analysis, followed by design, implementation, and finally testing.

Iterative development deals well with change, as the only complete requirements necessary are for the current iteration. Although tentative requirements need to exist for the next iteration, they do not need to be set in stone until the next analysis phase. This approach allows for changing technology or the customer to change their mind with minimal impact on the project s momentum.

Similarly, the Spiral Model avoids detailing and defining the entire system upfront. Unlike iterative development, however, where the system is built piece by piece prioritized by functionality, Spiral prioritizes requirements by risk. Spiral and iterative development offered a great leap in agility over the Waterfall process, but some practitioners believed that they still did not respond to change as nimbly as necessary in the evolving business world. Lengthy planning and analysis phases, as well as a sustained emphasis on extensive documentation, kept projects using iterative techniques from being truly Agile, in comparison with today s methods.

Another important model to take into account in these discussions is the Capability Maturity Model (CMM[10, 11]), a five-level model that describes good engineering and management practices and prescribes improvement priorities for software organizations[12]. The model defines 18 key process areas and goals for an organization to become a level 5 organization. Most software organizations maturity level is Chaotic (CMM level one) and only a few are Optimized (CMM level five). CMM focuses mainly on large projects and large organizations, but can be tailored to fit small as well as large projects due to the fact that it is formulated in a very general way that fits diverse organizations needs. The goals of CMM are to achieve process consistency, predictability, and reliability[12].

Ken Schwaber was one practitioner looking to better understand the CMM-based traditional development methods.

He approached the scientists at the DuPont Chemical's Advanced Research Facility posing the question: Why do the defined processes advocated by CMM not measurably deliver?[13]. After analyzing the development processes, they returned to Schwaber with some surprising conclusions. Although CMM focuses on turning software development into repeatable, defined, and predictable processes, the scientists found that many of them were, in fact, largely unpredictable and unrepeatable because[13]:

- Applicable first principles are not present

- The process is only beginning to be understood

- The process is complex

- The process is changing and unpredictable

Schwaber, one of the lead proponents of Scrum, realized that to be truly Agile, a process needs to accept change rather than stress predictability[13]. Practitioners came to realize that methods that would respond to change as quickly as it arose were necessary[14], and that in a dynamic environment, creativity, not voluminous written rules, is the only way to manage complex software development problems[5].

Practitioners like Mary Poppendieck and Bob Charette also began to look to other engineering disciplines for process inspiration, turning to one of the more innovate industry trends at the time, Lean Manufacturing. Started after World War II by Toyoda Sakichi, its counter-intuitive practices did not gain popularity in the United States until the early 1980s. While manufacturing plants in the United States ran production machines at 100% and kept giant inventories of both products and supplies, Toyoda kept only enough supplies on hand to run the plant for one day, and only produced enough products to fill current orders. Toyoda also tightly integrated Dr. W. Edwards Deming's Total Quality Management philosophy with his process. Deming believed that people inherently want to do a good job, and that managers needed to allow workers on the floor to make decisions and solve problems, build trust with suppliers, and support a culture of continuous improvement of both process and products[15]. Deming taught that quality was a management issue and while Japanese manufacturers were creating better and cheaper products, United States manufacturers were blaming quality issues on their workforce[15].

Poppendieck lists the 10 basic practices which make Lean Manufacturing so successful, and their application to software development[15]:

1   Eliminate waste — eliminate or optimize consumables such as diagrams and models that do not add value to the final deliverable

2   Minimize inventory — minimize intermediate artifacts such as requirements and design documents

3   Maximize flow — use iterative development to reduce development time

4   Pull from demand — support flexible requirements

5   Empower workers — generalize intermediate documents, tell developers what needs to be done, not how to do it

6   Meet customer requirements — work closely with the customer, allowing them to change their minds

7   Do it right the first time — test early and refactor when necessary

8   Abolish local optimization — flexibly manage scope

9 Partner with suppliers — avoid adversarial relationships, work towards developing the best software

10 Create a culture of continuous improvement — allow the process to improve, learn from mistakes and successes

Independently, Kent Beck rediscovered many of these values in the late 1990s when he was hired by Chrysler to save their failing payroll project, Chrysler Comprehensive Compensation (C3). The project was started in the early 1990s as an attempt to unify three existing payroll systems[16] and had been declared a failure when Beck arrived. Beck, working with Ron Jeffries[3], decided to scrap all the existing code and start the project over from scratch. A little over a year later, a version of C3 was in use and paying employees. Beck and Jeffries were able to take a project that had been failing for years and turn it around 180 degrees. The C3 project became the first project to use Extreme Programming[3], relying on the same values for success as Poppendiek's Lean Programming.

Similar stories echo throughout the development world. In the early 1990s, the IBM Consulting Group hired Alistair Cockburn to develop an object-oriented development method[3]. Cockburn decided to interview IBM development teams and build a process out of best practices and lessons learned. He found that team after successful team apologized for not following a formal process, for not using hightech tools, for merely sitting close to each other and discussing while they went, while teams that had failed followed formal processes and were confused why it hadn't worked, stating maybe they hadn't followed it well enough[3]. Cockburn used what he learned at IBM to develop the Crystal Methods.

The development world was changing and, while traditional methods were hardly falling out of fashion, it was obvious that they did not always work as intended in all situations. Practitioners recognized that new practices were necessary to better cope with changing requirements. And these new practices must be people-oriented and flexible, offering generative rules over inclusive rules which break down quickly in a dynamic environment[5]. Cockburn and Highsmith summarize the new challenges facing the traditional methods:

- Satisfying the customer has taken precedence over conforming to original plans

- Change will happen — the focus is not how to prevent it but how to better cope with it and reduce the cost of change throughout the development process

- Eliminating change early means being unresponsive to business conditions — in other words, business failure

- The market demands and expects innovative, high quality software that meets its needs — and soon

The Agile Manifesto

A bigger gathering of organizational anarchists would be hard to find Beck stated[1], when seventeen of the Agile proponents came together in early 2001 to discuss the new software developments methods. What emerged was the Agile Software Development Manifesto. Representatives from Extreme Programming (XP), Scrum, DSDM, Adaptive Software Development, Crystal, Feature-Driven Development, Pragmatic Programming, and others sympathetic to the need for an alternative to documentation driven, heavyweight software development processes convened[1]. They summarized their viewpoint, saying that the Agile movement is not anti-methodology, in fact, many of us want to restore credibility to the word methodology. We want to restore a balance. We embrace modeling, but not in order to file some diagram in a dusty corporate repository. We embrace documentation, but not hundreds of pages of never-maintained and rarely used tomes. We plan, but recognize the limits of planning in a turbulent environment[1]. The Manifesto itself reads as follows:

> We are uncovering better ways of developing software by doing it and helping others do it. Through this work we have come to value:
>
> • Individuals and interaction over process and tools
> • Working software over comprehensive documentation
> • Customer collaboration over contract negotiation
> • Responding to change over following a plan
>
> That is, while there is a value in the items on the right, we value the items on the left more[1].

The Manifesto has become an important piece of the Agile Movement, in that it characterizes the values of Agile methods and how Agile distinguishes itself from traditional methods. Glass amalgamates the best of the Agile and traditional approaches by analyzing the Agile manifesto and comparing it with traditional values[17].

Individuals and interaction over process and tools: Glass believes that the Agile community is right on this point: "Traditional software engineering has gotten too caught up in its emphasis on process[17]. At the same time most practitioners already know that people matter more than process" [17].

Working software over comprehensive documentation: Glass agrees with the Agile community on this point too, although with some caveat: "It is important to remember that the ultimate result of building software is product. Documentation matters but over the years, the traditionalists made a fetish of documentation. It became the prime goal of the document-driven lifecycle" [17].

Customer collaboration over contract negotiation: Glass sympathizes with both sides regarding this statement: "I deeply believe in customer collaboration, and without it nothing is going to go well. I also believe in contracts, and I would not undertake any significant collaborative effort without it." [17]

Responding to change over following a plan: Both sides are right regarding this statement, according to Glass: "Over the years, we have learned two contradictory lessons: (1) Customers and users do not always know what they want at the outset of a software project, and we must be open to change during project execution, and (2) Requirement change was one of the most common causes of software project failure." [17]

This view, that both camps can learn from each other, is commonly held, as we will see in the next section.

Agile and CMM(I)

As mentioned above, Agile is a reaction against traditional methodologies, also known as rigorous or plan-driven methodologies[8]. One of the models often used to represent traditional methodologies is the Capability Maturity Model (CMM)[10, 11] and its replacement[18] CMMI, an extension of CMM based on the same values[19]. Not much has been written about CMMI yet, but we believe that for this discussion, what is valid for CMM is also valid for CMMI.[20]

As mentioned above, the goals of CMM are to achieve process consistency, predictability, and reliability. Its proponents claim that it can be tailored to also fit the needs of small projects even though it was designed for large projects and large organizations.[12]

Most Agile proponents do not, however, believe CMM fits their needs at all. If one were to ask a typical software engineer whether the Capability Maturity Model for Software and process improvement were applicable to Agile Methods, the response would most likely range from a blank stare to a hysterical laughter.[21] One reason is that CMM is a belief in software development as a defined process that can be defined in detail, that algorithms can be defined, that results can be accurately measured, and that measured variations can be used to refine the processes until they are repeatable within very close tolerances.[22] For projects with any degree of exploration at all, Agile developers just do not believe these assumptions are valid. This is a deep fundamental divide — and not one that can be reconciled to some comforting middle ground.[22]

Many Agile proponents also dislike CMM because of its focus on documentation instead of code. A typical example is the company that spent two years working (not using CMM though) on a project until they finally declared it a failure. Two years of working resulted in 3,500 pages of use cases, an object model with hundreds of classes, thousands of attributes (but no methods), and, of course, no code.[22] The same document-centric approach resulting in documentary bloat that is now endemic in our field[23] is also reported by many others.

While Agile proponents see a deep divide between Agile and traditional methods, this is not the case for proponents of traditional methods. Mark Paulk, the man behind CMM, is surprisingly positive about Agile Methods and claims that Agile Methods address many CMM level 2 and 3 practices.[24] XP,[28] for example, addresses most level 2[28] and 3[29] practices, but not levels 4 and 5.[12] As a matter of fact, most XP projects that truly follow the XP rules and practices could easily be assessed at CMM level 2 if they could demonstrate having processes for the following:[25]

- Ensuring that the XP Rules and Practices are taught to new developers on the project

- Ensuring that the XP Rules and Practices are followed by everyone

- Escalating to decision makers when the XP Rules and Practices are not followed and not resolved within the project

- Measuring the effectiveness of the XP Rules and Practices

- Providing visibility to management via appropriate metrics from prior project QA experience

- Knowing when the XP Rules and Practices need to be adjusted

- Having an independent person doing the above

Glazer adds, with a little work on the organizational level, CMM level 3 is not far off.[25]

So according to some, XP and CMM *can* live together,[25] at least in theory. One reason is that we can view XP as a software development methodology and CMM as a software management methodology. CMM tells us *what* to do, while XP tells us *how* to do it.

Others agree that there is no conflict. Siemens, for example, does not see CMM and Agility as a contradiction. Agility has become a necessity with increasing market pressure, but should be built on top of an appropriately mature process foundation, not instead of it.[26] Many make a distinction between turbulent environments and placid environments, and conclude that CMM is not applicable to the turbulent environments. These claims are based on misconceptions. In fact, working under time pressure in the age of agility requires even better organization of the work than before![26]

Regarding the criticism about heavy documentation in CMM projects, Paulk replies: over-documentation is a pernicious problem in the software industry, especially in the

Department of Defense (DoD) projects.[24] Plan-driven methodologists must acknowledge that keeping documentation to a minimum useful set is necessary. At the same time, practices that rely on tacit knowledge[30] may break down in larger teams.[24] Others claim that CMM does not require piles of process or project documentation and there are various organizations that successfully can manage and maintain their process with a very limited amount of paper.[26]

CMMI is the latest effort to build maturity models and consists of Process Areas (PA) and Generic Practices (GP). CMMI is similar to CMM, but more extensive in that it covers the discipline of system engineering. In an attempt to compare Agile and CMMI, Turner analyzed their values and concluded that their incompatibilities are overstated and that their strengths and weaknesses complement each other.[21]

While many tired of traditional development techniques are quick to show support for the Agile movement, often as a reaction against CMM, others are more skeptical. A common criticism, voiced by Steven Rakitin, views Agile as a step backwards from traditional engineering practices, a disorderly attempt to legitimize the hacker process.[31] Where processes such as Waterfall and Spiral stress lengthy upfront planning phases and extensive documentation, Agile Methods tend to shift these priorities elsewhere. XP, for example, holds brief iteration planning meetings in the Planning Game to prioritize and select requirements, but generally leaves the system design to evolve over iterations through refactoring, resulting in hacking.[31] This accusation of Agile of being no more than hacking is frenetically fought[32] and in response to this criticism, Beck states: Refactoring, design patterns, comprehensive unit testing, pair programming — these are not the tools of hackers. These are the tools of developers who are exploring new ways to meet the difficult goals of rapid product delivery, low defect levels, and flexibility.[3] Beck says, the only possible values are excellent and insanely excellent depending on whether lives are at stake or not You might accuse XP practitioners of being delusional, but not of being poor-quality-oriented hackers.[3] Those who would brand proponents of XP or Scrum or any of the other Agile Methodologies as hackers are ignorant of both the methodologies and the original definition of the term hacker.[1] In response to the speculation that applying XP would result in a Chaotic development process (CMM level 1), one of the Agile proponents even concluded that XP is in some ways a vertical slice through the levels 2 through 5.[33]

The question of whether Agile is hacking is probably less important than whether Agile and CMM(I) can co-exist. This is due to the fact that many organizations need both to be Agile and show that they are mature enough to take on certain contracts. A model that fills that need and truly combines the Agile practices and the CMM key processes has not, that we are aware of, been developed yet.

PART TWO

Managing
Agile Projects
is Different

CHAPTER THREE

Managing Agile Projects is Different

Kevin Aguanno

As discussed in Chapter 1, agile methods share a number of common characteristics that arise from their approach to dealing with change:

- Iterative and Incremental Development

- Short Iterations

- Progress Measured via Completed Features

- Open, Flexible Design

- Empowered Teams

- Personal Communications

While each of these characteristics can be found in more traditionally-managed projects, agile methods combine all of these together and define how they interact to lower risk and increase control in response to project change. What is more important than these characteristics, however, is the common underlying philosophy of agile projects. Jim Highsmith notes:

> Lightweight [processes] is only one aspect of agile, the other two are collaborative values and principles and a fundamental understanding of the unpredictability of project activities.[1]

It is in this fundamental belief that project outcomes cannot be predicted where agile methods differ from traditional project management philosophies, such as the one commonly attributed to the Project Management Institute (PMI). Agile project management is based upon the belief that every project is unique (else it would not be a "project" but rather normal business operations) and as such the processes used by the project team should be adapted to the specific needs of the individual project. With processes and people changing from project to project, traditional management methods that were derived from the statistical science of manufacturing process management fail to deliver the ongoing performance improvements they promise from their practice of continual improvement.

Agile project managers understand that since we cannot predict with any certainty or specificity all changing requirements, technical issues, and the like, then we cannot manage projects using predictive techniques based upon defined processes and known past performance against those processes. Agile managers understand that many projects require the use of empirical management methods that are different from our traditional methods and are much more adaptive to project changes while still giving the manager control.

Ken Schwaber, the founder of the agile Scrum methodology, relates a story of a time when he took a number of "traditional" software development processes to a group of leading process control theory experts at Dupont. They immediately noted the mismatch between the reality of software development projects and traditional (defined) management methods. Schwaber describes the difference between defined and empirical management methods as explained to him by the scientists:

> The "defined" process control model requires that every piece of work be completely understood. Given a well-defined set of inputs, the same outputs are generated every time [. . .] The methodologies that I showed him attempted to use the defined model, but none of the processes or tasks were defined in enough detail to provide repeatability and predictability. [The chief scientist] said my business was an intellectually intensive business that required too much thinking and creativity to be a good candidate for the defined approach [. . .] The empirical model of process control, on the other hand, expects the unexpected. It provides and exercises control through frequent inspection and adaptation for processes that are imperfectly defined and generate unpredictable and unrepeatable outputs.[2]

This concept of varying levels of uncertainty requiring different types of management processes is generally recognized within the agile world. Highsmith makes the same distinction, noting that

> projects also run the gamut from production-style ones in which uncertainty is low, to exploration-style ones in which uncertainty is high. Exploration-style projects are characterized by a process that emphasizes envisioning and then exploring into that vision rather than detailed planning and relatively strict execution of tasks. It is not that one is right and the other wrong, but that each style is more or less applicable to a particular project type.[3]

It is generally agreed that production-style projects (low uncertainty, more akin to manufacturing processes) can be managed well with traditional (or "classic") project management methods. Agile proponents also believe that exploration-style development projects (high uncertainty, unique) can be managed best with agile project management methods. Where there is some confusion, however, is in categorizing a large number of real-world projects that fall somewhere between these two extremes. One approach to clarifying this boundary is shown in Table 3-1 from a recent book[4] by Gary Chin. In this table, "Operational Projects" is the same as the "production-style" projects we have been discussing. What is interesting in this approach is the recognition that even exploration-style development projects may be better served by traditional methods when facing complex situations involving numerous external stakeholders. In these circumstances, the formality introduced by traditional methods will help eliminate the risks of dealing with so many stakeholders, each with their own unique needs and perspective

Table 3-1: The applicability of traditional and agile project managers changes based upon project type and organizational stakeholders.

	Multiple, External Stakeholders	Multiple, Internal Stakeholders	Single Organization
Operational Projects	Classic	Classic	Classic
Product / Process Development Projects	Classic/Agile	Classic/Agile	Agile
Technology / Platform Development Projects	Classic/Agile	Agile	Agile

on the project. Alistair Cockburn also recognizes this need to "shift" the project management techniques from more agile techniques to less agile techniques as the complexity of project communications increases. Cockburn addresses this need by providing different "flavours" of his Crystal Methods, each becoming more formal as project team sizes grow, with each heavier method having a darker and darker colour, as shown in Table 3-2.

Table 3-2: The Crystal Methods grow in formality as the team size or project complexity grows.

Method Name	Team Size
Crystal Clear [8]	3 to 6
Crystal Yellow	Less than 20
Crystal Orange [9]	Less than 40
Crystal Red	Less than 80

While the two project approaches (agile and traditional) appear to be at odds with each other, once you understand their underpinnings, you will soon see that, at least at a philosophical level, agile methods address specific project niches that are not well served by traditional management methods.

CHAPTER FOUR

An Introduction to Iterative and Incremental Delivery

Pascal Van Cauwenberghe

S urprisingly, many people *still* wonder what is wrong with the safe and predictable, sequential-phased approach, also known as "waterfall." This is despite the fact that a lot has been written about iterative and incremental development over many years. Still, most people involved in software development cannot give you a clear definition of what those two words mean to them. When they are able to give definitions, they often contradict each other.

Into this confused world, the proponents of Agile Development and especially Extreme Programming proclaim that they go beyond "traditional" iterative and incremental development methods. What are we to do? How do we approach software projects? How do we reach our targets reliably, quickly, and efficiently?

Defining our terms

"When I use a word," Humpty Dumpty said in a rather scornful tone, "it means just what I choose it to mean – neither more nor less."
Lewis Carrol, *Through The Looking Glass*.

We must first choose what we want our terms to mean.

A Phase: A period in which some clearly defined task is performed. Just imagine that we require the following phases: Analysis, Design, Coding, Testing, Integration, and Deployment. Each phase has some inputs and some outputs.

To Iterate: To perform some task in multiple passes. Each pass improves the result, until the result is "finished." Also called *rework*.

An Iteration: A period in which a number of predefined tasks are performed. The results are evaluated to feed back to the next iteration.

An Increment: A period in which some functionality is completed to a production-quality level.

A Release: Some coherent set of completed functionalities that is useful and useable to the intended users of the system.

To illustrate the difference between iterative and incremental, imagine a project where we need to develop a system that has three functions: A, B and C. Each of the functions requires the same amount of work: one month. Thus, we have a three month project.

With these definitions we can have a look at different ways to organize a software project.

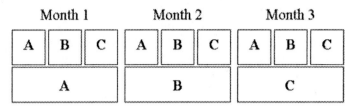

Iterative (top) vs Incremental (bottom)

Figure 4-1: A comparison of iterative and incremental development models.

Different ways to plan a project

The waterfall – straight to the target

The **sequential, phased** approach, better known as "Waterfall" is the simplest and potentially fastest approach: we analyze the problem, design the solution, implement the code, test the code (are we allowed to fix the coding bugs?), integrate if necessary, and then deploy. Done.

The attraction of this process model is its simplicity: you do each of the steps and then you are done. If you want to know how long the project takes, just add up the time required for each phase. These times are just estimates, so your total is also an estimate. But it makes following up on the project's schedule easier. For example, once analysis and design are complete, they will not be worked on again.

The simplicity of this model attracts two kinds of people:

• Remote stakeholders like upper level managers or end-users who have no need to know the exact process. They really just want to know when the outputs will be delivered.

- Teachers and educators who need to present a simplified model of a process as a first, simplified introduction to the subject. Unfortunately, it is this first approximation that sticks in the minds. Or do students skip all the following lectures?

The spiral – iterate to incorporate feedback

Of course, it is never as simple as the waterfall process suggests: we do make errors during analysis and design. When Walker Royce[1] originally described his process, there were feedback loops back to analysis and design. They were quickly "simplified" away. So, this was the original **phased, iterative** approach:

- Perform analysis, until you think you are ready

- Design, until you think you are ready. Should you find any problems in the analysis, feed them back to the analysis. Perform another iteration of the analysis, to improve it.

- Code the design, until ready. Should you find any problems in the design, feed them back. Perform another iteration of the design, to improve it.

- Test the code. Should you find any problems, start another iteration of the coding.

- Integrate and deploy. Feed back any problems you encounter.

In short, you go sequentially through the phases. Some phases have more than one iteration if we see that the output of that phase is not perfect. In more than one sense, the waterfall is the optimist's interpretation of the spiral model.

As Boehm[2] noted, the later a defect is caught, the higher the cost to fix it. We are therefore encouraged to only proceed cautiously to the next phase if the previous phase is relatively complete. As software engineers have noted, the likelihood of finding defects becomes higher as we come to the later phases. This is because each phase delivers a more precise, more "testable" output than the previous phases.

There is one management problem with the spiral model: how do you schedule the iterations? How many iterations will be needed? This makes estimating and tracking the project's progress more difficult and unpredictable.

Iterative development – getting better all the time

Where the spiral process views feedback and iteration as exceptional events, iterative development assumes we will make mistakes, we will need feedback, and we will need several iterations before we get it right.

In **iterative, phased** development we design our project plan around the idea of iterations and fit the phases in them. For example, we can plan to have five iterations:

- In the first iteration we will do 90% analysis, 10% design

- In the second iteration we will do 30% analysis, 50% design, 20% coding

- In the third iteration we will do 10% analysis, 30% design, 70% coding

- In the fourth iteration we will do 10% design, 50% coding, 40% testing and bug fixing

- In the fifth iteration we will do 50% testing and bug fixing, 30% integration, 20% deployment.

This process takes into account the reality that we almost never get anything completely right the first time. At first, we will get a lot of feedback. Gradually, with each iteration, the output from each phase stabilizes and we need to do less rework.

Iterative development with incremental delivery – growing software

One complaint we could have with the previous process is that it takes too long to see the results of the work. Indeed, the software is not ready until the absolute end of the project. What if we need the results faster? We could use **iterative development with incremental delivery**, a variation on the previous process.

The basic idea is to release the software several times to its users, each time with more functionality. Each release is complete, useable and useful to its users. Each release adds more functionality, preferably the most important functionality first. How do we schedule our project?

*   First, we go through several iterations of analysis and design, until we are pretty sure these phases are mostly complete. We can then select the content and schedule of the increments to be developed. Let's say we have identified three increments A, B and C, to be delivered in this order to the users.

*   For increment A, we iterate through all required phases, until the software can be released. We expect to rework the analysis and design very little.

*   For increment B, we iterate through all required phases, until the software can be released. We expect almost no analysis or design work.

- For increment C, we iterate through all required phases, until the software can be released. We expect almost no analysis or design work.

We can picture this process as four applications of the above process. The amount of analysis and (architectural) design decreases in each step. The process delivers functionality after the second, third and fourth steps.

How do we select the contents of the increments? Architecture-driven processes would select the elements that have the most impact on the architecture (and thus the design). Risk-driven processes would select the most risky elements. Users would prefer the most useful or urgent functionalities.

Agile software development – extremely incremental

Agile software methods like Extreme Programming[3] take another approach, based on the following assumptions:

- You should welcome feedback and rework, instead of trying to avoid it

- You should deliver software to your users in small increments and deliver functionality in the order that the users want.

The development process is then scheduled as follows:

- Decide on the length of incremental releases. All increments are the same length. Decide which ones will be internal releases (used internally for evaluation and feedback) and external releases (released to the end-users).

- Gather an initial list of requirements. New requirements can be added at any time.

- Before the start of each increment: users (or their representative) prioritize the requirements and assign the requirements to releases. As many releases as required can be planned, but typically the contents of all releases, except the one being implemented, are subject to change.

- During the increment, the requirements are analyzed and broken down into small micro-increments. These increments are small enough to be fully implemented in a day or less.

- To implement a micro-increment, the developers analyze, design code, test, integrate and deploy iteratively. They iterate very quickly, so as to get a lot of feedback to guide their work.

- Each increment has a fixed length. If needed, scope is reduced/increased by the user to meet the target date.

What's so extreme in Extreme Programming?

What is the difference between Extreme Programming-style planning and iterative development with incremental delivery, such as is possible with the well-known and accepted Unified Process framework?

Incremental Architecture and Design

One difference is the assumption that **you can do architecture and design incrementally**. Indeed, XP spends very little time up front to define an architecture and overall design. Instead, we immediately start with the first increment to deliver functionality. All architecture and design work is done to satisfy the requirements of the current increment. XP does design in the following ways:

- A *System Metaphor* describes an overall architecture and vocabulary that all participants understand and agree with. The Metaphor is refined iteratively over the whole project.

- *Test-First* programming designs the code incrementally by defining executable tests with which the program unit must comply.

- *Refactoring* reworks the design to iteratively adapt the design to changing knowledge, environment, or requirements.

- Whiteboard design sessions, CRC card sessions, and other group design techniques.

Incremental Analysis

An even more controversial assumption is that **you can do analysis incrementally.** At the start of each increment, we only examine the requirements that have been scheduled for this increment. XP does analysis in the following ways:

- Brief requirements, called *Stories*, are elaborated interactively between the development team and the story author just before and during implementation.

- Requirements are formalized into executable "*Acceptance*" tests, which specify and verify the compliance of the software with the requirement.

- Requirements are allocated to releases using the *Planning Game*, where developers and customers optimize delivered value versus development cost.

Incremental Development in a Customer-Selected Order

A final difference is the assumption that **you can deliver software features incrementally, in whatever order yields most benefit for the customer.** If the software can be delivered incrementally, the users will get the benefit of the functionality sooner and thus get a faster return on their investment. As the customers can choose the delivery order, they receive the most important and valuable features first. The use of these increments generates lots of valuable feedback to drive the following increments.

What's the best way to plan a project?

The short answer is that it depends. It depends on your project, your team, and your environment. If the assumptions of XP hold, we can gain a lot of **benefits** from working incrementally:

- Early delivery of useful software.

- Delivery of functionality based on the value users give to that functionality (business value-driven instead of architecture- or risk-driven).

- Clear, tangible feedback on progress: each increment delivers *finished, production-quality* functionality.

- Clear and regular feedback on the quality and fit of the software from the users to the development team.

- The ability to adapt the project plan.

- Clear scheduling and predictable delivery.

- The development of the simplest possible system that satisfies the requirements, without any unnecessary adornments and complexity.

What are the **dangers** of this approach?

*   By only looking at small pieces (increments) of the software, we may have to do massive rework, which *might* have been avoided if we analyzed or designed the whole system correctly.

*   We might "paint ourselves into a corner;" that is, we can get a system that is incapable of supporting some new requirement.

*   We may be unable to add global requirements, such as alternate language support, performance, and security. A typical example is trying to retrofit "security" to an application that was not designed with this requirement in mind.

*   We might go slower because we have to restart analysis and design sessions for each increment, instead of doing it once at the start of the project.

A few heuristics

If your requirements are volatile or incomplete, if the environment changes, or if you wish to be able to anticipate to future events, work incrementally. If the requirements and environment are stable, you can optimize your process by looking at all the requirements upfront.

If you are not familiar with the domain, or have not built a similar architecture, work incrementally. Use the feedback to design your system and to avoid unnecessary complexity. If you have created many similar systems, you can do more design work up front. Still, you can always use the feedback to keep your system simple.

If you cannot deliver incrementally, then don't deliver incrementally. But, even if you cannot deliver incrementally to your final user, you might deliver incrementally to internal users, such as the quality assurance team, or product managers. Even if you cannot do that, deliver incrementally within your team. That way you still get the benefit of early feedback.

If you know a requirement is going to be more difficult to work on if you only tackle it later, work on it now. This might happen with global properties of software systems like localization, scalability, and security. You can still get the benefit of business value-driven scheduling for most requirements if you take those few exceptions into account: "Did you want security with that, Sir? With security, this feature will cost you X. Without security, it will cost you Y. If you wish to add security later, it will cost you Z." Iterative (re) design techniques like refactoring and the emphasis on simplicity does help to keep your software "soft"—more malleable—more accepting of changes.

If your team is big, do enough work upfront with a small team so that you can decompose the work on the system on the basis of a reasonable (but not perfect or final) architecture.

Conclusion

Incremental software development, with short increments, reduces project and functional risk and allows us to deliver value faster to users. Each release provides opportunities for useful external (customer/user) feedback and replanning, so that we are more likely to deliver what the customer needs. Within those increments, one iterates based on internal feedback (tests, reviews), to reduce technical risk, so that we are more likely to deliver the quality the customer needs.

The project is at its most agile when we use fast iteration and short increments, as the regular feedback allows us to make continuous small course corrections to our project.

CHAPTER FIVE

Learning from Agile Software Development

Alistair Cockburn

Being *agile* is a declaration of prioritizing for project maneuverability with respect to shifting requirements, shifting technology, and a shifting understanding of the situation. Other priorities that might override agility include predictability, cost, schedule, process-accreditation, or use of specific tools.

Most managers run a portfolio of projects having a mix of those priorities. They need to prioritize agility, predictability, and cost sensitivity in varying amounts and therefore need to mix strategies. This chapter focuses on borrowing ideas from the agile suite to fit the needs of plan-driven and cost-sensitive programs.

This chapter originally appeared in two parts in the October and November 2002 issues of *CrossTalk: The Journal of Defense Software Engineering*. It has been reprinted with permission of the author, and is also available at http://Alistair.Cockburn.us.

Our industry now has enough information to sensibly discuss such blending. The agile voices have been heard,[1,2,3,4,5,6,7] the engineering voices have been heard,[8,9,10] articles have been published[11,12] illustrating the differences in world view, and some authors have discussed the question of their coexistence, and the principles underlying successful development strategies.[3,8,13]

Buy Information or Flexibility

Many project strategies revolve around spending money for either information or flexibility.[3,14]

In a *money-for-information* (MFI) proposition, the team can choose to expend resources now to gain information earlier. If the information is not considered valuable enough, the resources are applied to other work. The question is how much the team is willing to expend in exchange for that information.

In a *money-for-flexibility* (MFF) proposition, the team may opt to expend resources to preserve later flexibility. If the future is quite certain, the resources are better spent pursuing the most probable outcome, or on MFI issues.

Different project strategies are made by deciding which issues are predictable, unpredictable but resolvable, or unresolvable, deciding which of those are MFI or MFF propositions, and how best to allocate resources for each.

Predictable issues can be investigated using breakdown techniques. Such an issue might be creating a schedule for work similar to that successfully performed in the past.

Unpredictable but resolvable issues can be investigated through study techniques such as prototypes and simulators. Such issues include system performance limits, and are also MFI propositions. Agile and plan-driven teams are likely to use similar strategies for these issues as part of basic project risk management.

Unresolvable issues tend to be sociological, such as which upcoming standard will gain market acceptance, or how long key employees will stay around. These issues cannot be resolved in advance, and so are not MFI propositions, but are MFF propositions. Agile and plan-driven teams are intrinsically likely to use different strategies for these issues. Agile teams will set up to absorb these changes, while plan-driven project teams must, by definition, create plans for them.

Teams will differ on which issues are resolvable, and how much money should be spent in advance on predictable issues. A plan-driven team is more likely to decide that creating the project plan is basically a predictable issue, and that a good MFI strategy is to spend resources early to make those predictions.

In contrast, an agile team might decide that the project plan is fundamentally unresolvable past a very simple approximation. There being no effective MFI strategy, it adopts an MFF approach, making an approximate plan early and allocating resources for regular re-planning over the course of the project.

Both agile and plan-driven developers might agree that the question of system performance under load is an important MFI issue, and so both might agree to spend money early to build a simple system simulator and load generator to stress-test the design.

They are likely to spend money differently on design issues. The plan-driven team, viewing it as a sensible MFI proposition, will spend money early to reduce uncertainty about the future of the design. Agile teams are more likely to view design as either being inexpensive to change (a poor MFI candidate) or unresolvable (making it an MFF proposition).

They are therefore more likely to choose a design early and allocate money to adjust it over time. This difference on design issues is fundamental, since the two groups view the matter from different decision arenas.

Ten Principles

The following 10 principles have shown themselves to be useful in setting up and running projects. Most of these are known in the literature.[3,4,8,21] My phrasing of them may be slightly different.

1 Different projects need different methodology trade-offs.

2 A little methodology does a lot of good; after that, weight is costly.

3 Larger teams need more communication elements.

4 Projects dealing with greater potential damage need more validation elements.

5 Formality, process, and documentation are not substitutes for discipline, skill, and understanding.

6 Interactive, face-to-face communication is the cheapest and fastest channel for exchanging information.

7 Increased communication and feedback reduces the need for intermediate work products.

8 Concurrent and serial development exchange development costs for speed and flexibility.

9 Efficiency is expendable in non-bottleneck activities.

10 Sweet spots speed development.

Different Projects Need Different Methodology Trade-offs

This should be obvious, but it seems to need re-stating at frequent intervals.[15,16,17,18]

Figure 5-1, adapted from Boehm and Port,[8] shows one particular aspect of these differences. In this figure, the two diminishing curves show the potential damage to a project from not investing enough time and effort in planning. The two rising curves show the potential damage to the project from spending too much time and effort in planning.

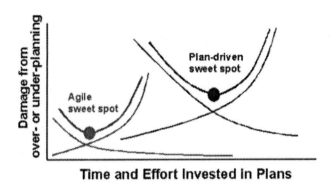

Figure 5-1: Balancing discipline and flexibility with agile and plan-driven models.

The lines crossing on the left indicate a project for which potential damage is relatively low with under-planning, and relatively high with over-planning. Much commercial software, including Web services fall into this category. The lines crossing on the right indicate a project for which potential damage is relatively high with under-planning, and for which much more planning would have to be done before damage would accrue from delays due to planning. Safety-critical software projects fall into this category.

91

The curves should make it clear that when there is risk associated with taking a slow, deliberate approach to planning, then agile techniques are more appropriate. When there is risk associated with skipping planning or making mistakes with the plan, then a plan-driven approach is more appropriate. The curves illustrate clearly the home territory of each.

Figure 5-2 shows a different characterization of project differences.[3] The horizontal axis captures the number of people needing to be coordinated, rising from one on the left to 1,000 on the right. The idea is that projects need more coordination elements to their methodology as the number of people increases.

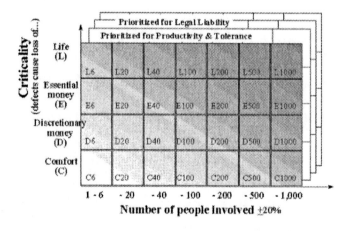

Figure 5-2: Projects by communication, criticality, and priorities.[3]

The vertical axis captures the potential damage caused by undetected defects in the system, from loss of comfort to loss of life. The idea is that projects need more validation elements as the potential damage increases.

Each box in the grid identifies a set of projects that might plausibly use the same combination of coordination and validation policies. The label in the box indicates the maximum damage and coordination load common to those projects (thus, D40 refers to projects with 20-40 people and potential loss of discretionary monies). Projects landing in different boxes should use different policies.

The different planes capture the idea that projects run to different priorities, some prioritizing for productivity, some for legal liability, and others for cost, predictability, agility, and so on.

Any one methodology is likely to be appropriate for only one of the boxes on one of the planes. Thus, at least 150 or so methodologies are needed (Capers Jones identifies 37,000 project categories[17]). That number is increased by the fact that technology shifts change the methodologies at the same time.

A Little Methodology Does a Lot of Good; After That, Weight is Costly

Figure 5-3 relates three quantities: the weight of the methodology being used, the size of the problem being attacked, and the size of the team. (*Problem size* is a relative term only. The problem size can drop as soon as someone has an insight about the problem. Even though problem size is highly subjective, some problems are clearly harder for a team to handle than others.) This figure illustrates that adding elements to a team's methodology first helps then hinders their progress.[3]

The dashed line shows that a small team, using a minimal methodology, can successfully attack a certain size of problem. Adding a few carefully chosen elements to the methodology allows them to work more effectively and attack a larger problem. As they continue to add to the methodology, they increase the bureaucratic load they put on themselves and, being only a small team, start expending more energy in

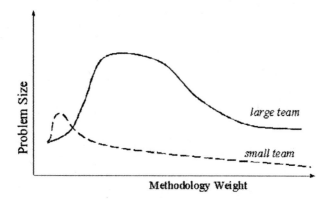

Figure 5-3: A little methodology goes a long way.

feeding the methodology than solving the problem. The size of the problem they can successfully attack diminishes.

The curve is similar for a large team (the solid line), but not as abrupt. The large team needs more coordination elements to work optimally, and has more people to feed the methodology as it expands. Eventually, even the larger team starts being less productive as the methodology size grows and solves the larger problems less successfully.

Larger Teams Need More Communication Elements

Six people in a room can simply talk amongst themselves and write on white boards. If 200 people were to try that, they would get in each other's way, miss tasks, and repeat each other's work. The larger team benefits from coordination. This is the slower rise in the large-team curve in Figure 5-3. The smaller team needs fewer coordination mechanisms and can treat them with less ceremony than can the larger team.

Although this principle should be obvious, many process designers try to find a single set of coordination elements to fit all projects.

Projects Dealing with Greater Potential Damage Need More Validation Elements

A team of developers charged with creating a proof-of-concept system does not have to worry about the damage caused by a system malfunction in the same way that a team charged with developing a final production system to be produced in vast quantities does. Atomic power plants, automated weapons systems, even cell phones or automobiles produced in the millions have such economic consequences that it is well worthwhile spending a great deal more time locating and eliminating each additional remaining defect. This is an MFI situation: It is worth spending a lot of money now to discover information about where those next defects are located.

For a system in which remaining defects have lower economic consequences (such as ordering food online from the company cafeteria), it is not worth spending as much money to discover that information. The team will consequently find it appropriate to use fewer and lighter validation techniques on the project.

Formality, Process, and Documentation Are Not Substitutes for Discipline, Skill, and Understanding

Highsmith[4] points to the difference between discipline and formality, skill and process, understanding and documentation.

Discipline is an internal quality of behavior; formality is an externally visible result. Many of the best developers are very disciplined in their actions without using formal methods or documents.

Skill is an internal quality of action, typically of a single person, while process is an externally declared agreement, usually between several people. Individuals operating at high levels of skill often cannot say what process they follow. Processes are most useful in coordinating the flow of work between people.

Understanding is an internal realization; documentation is external. Only a small part of what people know can be put into external documentation, and that small part takes a lot of time.

Process designers often forget these differences, thinking that enough formality will impart discipline, enough process will impart skill, and enough documentation will impart understanding. An agile project manager relies on

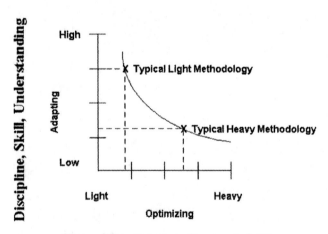

Formality, Process, Documentation

Figure 5-4: Differences between adapting and optimizing approaches.

96

discipline, skill, and understanding, while requiring less formality, process, and documentation (Figure 5-4). This allows the team to move and change directions faster.

Interactive, Face-to-Face Communication Is the Cheapest and Fastest Channel for Exchanging Information

Understanding passes from person to person more rapidly when two people are standing next to each other, as when they are discussing at a white board. At that white board, they can use gestures, facial expressions, proximity cues, vocal inflection and timing, cross-modality (aural-visual) timing, and real-time feedback along modalities to discover what each knows, needs to know, and how to convey it.[3,19] They use the white board as an external-marking device not just to draw, but also to hold some of their discussion points in place so they can refer back to them later.

As characteristics of that situation are removed, the communication effectiveness between the two people drops (Figure 5-5). On the phone, they lose the entire visual channel and cross-modality timing. With email or instant messaging, they lose vocal inflection, vocal timing, and real-time question and answer. On videotape, they have visuals, but lose the ability to get questions answered. On audiotape, they again lose visuals and cross-modality timing. Finally, communicating through documents, they attempt to communicate without the benefit of gestures, vocal inflection and timing, cross-modality timing, proximity cues, or question-and-answer.

This principle suggests that for cost and efficiency improvements, a project team employ personal, face-to-face communication wherever possible. A decade-long study at

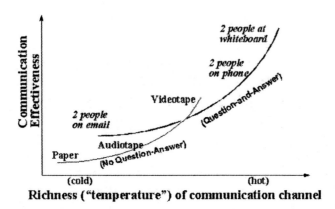

Figure 5-5: Increasing communication effectiveness through using richer communication channels.

MIT's Sloan School of Management in the 1970s and a recent research compilation both concluded that physical distance matters a great deal.[20,21]

The cost of imposing distances between people can be seen with a simple calculation. Suppose that a developer earns $2 per minute, and two people working side-by-side on the same problem exchange questions and answers at the rate of 100 questions each per week. Thus, for each minute on average that gets interposed between thinking the question and hearing the answer adds $200 of salary cost to the project per person per week, or about $10,000 per year. For a 10-person project, that one-minute average delay costs the organization $100,000 per year. Two offices being a few meters apart creates a one-minute delay. For offices around the corner or up a flight of stairs, the average delay is more on the order of five minutes ($500,000 per year).

The salary cost is actually the smaller cost. The larger cost is that when two people are more than about half a minute's travel apart, they simply do not ask each other many of those questions. Instead, they guess at the answers. Some percentage of those guesses are wrong, and those mistakes end up as defects in the system that must be found through debugging, external test, integration test, or even through system use.

Increased Communication and Feedback Reduces the Need for Intermediate Work Products

Intermediate work products - those not required by the final users of the system or the next team of developers - tend to have two forms:

* promises as to what will eventually be constructed, and

* intermediate snapshots of the developers' knowledge (design descriptions).

This understanding, as we have already seen, moves faster through interactive than paper-based communication. Increasing the use of interactive communications will never entirely eliminate the need for archivable design documentation, but it can reduce it, particularly during the design and development stages of the project. Eventually, external documentation will be needed when none of the original designers are around, but that does not count as *intermediate* documentation.

Users who regularly get to see the developing system stop needing elaborate promises of what they will be given. This is an MFI issue. If the users are not going to get to see the result for a year or two, then it is worth a lot to create the most accurate promise possible. If on the other hand, the users get to see results every few days or weeks, then a better use of the project's money is to simply build the system and show it to the users.

There is, however, a MFF issue at play here as well since there are diminishing returns on the MFI issue of creating that promise. No amount of care in crafting a detailed promise can capture the unpredictable reaction of the users on seeing the final product in their own environment as they perform their work assignments. The time and money spent on guessing at the users' response to the delivered system would be better allocated to deal with their response on seeing the real system.

Mock-ups, prototypes, and simulations deal with the MFI aspects of the situation. They are an expenditure of resources to discover information sooner. The MFF aspects of the situation are handled through incremental delivery with iterative re-work, allocating resources for the inevitable surprises resulting from real delivery.

Concurrent and Serial Development Exchange Development Cost for Speed and Flexibility

On a predictable project, the project coordinator can arrange for each work specialist to show up at just the right moment, perform the needed work, and leave. Such scheduling, common in the construction and book publishing industries, minimizes salary cost in exchange for extending elapsed time (see Figure 5-6). The hazard is that a surprise might show up in an already-completed task forcing the previous task item to restart, in which case neither time nor cost is minimized.

Concurrent development runs teams in parallel, even when they have dependencies between them.[3] The teams will make and change decisions as they gain information, causing the other teams some rework. With careful management of

Serial
Development

Requirements	▨▨▨▨▨
Design	▨▨▨▨▨
Program	▨▨▨▨▨
Test	▨▨▨▨▨

Concurrent
Development

Requirements	▨▨▨▨▨
Design	▨▨▨▨▨
Program	▨▨▨▨▨
Test	▨▨▨▨▨

Figure 5-6: Serial development vs. concurrent development.[3]
Serialized development takes longer but costs less than concurrent
development.

their dependencies, the teams can complete the final work
sooner even though their salary costs are higher (see Figure
5-1). Effective concurrent development demands that
communication between people is fast, rich, and inexpensive
(as discussed in principles 6 and 7). The hazard in concurrent
development is that if work is started too early, rework costs
dominate the project.

Serial and concurrent development have opposing
characteristics. Cost-sensitive projects should use serial
development where they can, while projects sensitive to shifting
requirements benefit more from concurrent development.

Agile project teams almost always use concurrent
development assuming a significant number of surprises will
arise during development. The close communication needed
for effective concurrent development also lets them respond to
latebreaking changes effectively.

Efficiency Is Expendable in Non-Bottleneck Activities

Effective concurrent development requires calculating the moment at which to start a downstream activity. Goldratt's process theory[22] and theory of constraints[23] provide advice here.

Suppose that one requirements gatherer feeds information to five designers, who in turn feed their results to a single database analyst (DBA, see Figure 5-7). It is clear that the DBA will not be able to keep up with the work (and rework). Prudence insists that the designers get their work to a complete and stable state before passing it to the DBA.

Figure 5-8 illustrates this idea. The vertical axis indicates how complete and stable each group's work is. Completeness refers to how much they have done, and stability refers to how unlikely they are to make changes. For simplicity, the figure illustrates them as joint: The work becomes more complete and more stable over time, shown in an S-type of curve. For each curve, the solid downward-arrow indicates at what point a dependent activity gets initiated.

If the designers take work from a single requirements gatherer as in Figure 5-7, they can start work on their assignments when the requirements are only slightly complete

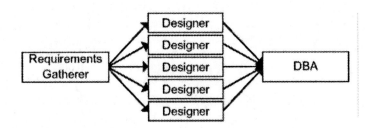

Figure 5-7: The Database Analyst (DBA) bottlenecking five Designers.[3]

102

and stable and still handle the consequential rework. Figure 5-8 shows the trigger event (the solid vertical arrow from requirements to design) occurring close to the left, while the requirements are not yet very complete or very stable. This figure also shows information continuing to pass from the requirements gatherer to the designers as the requirements work progresses. Once requirements become complete and stable, it will not take long to finalize work. The designers can complete the extra rework because there are five of them to one requirements gatherer.

The DBA, having no excess capacity, needs to be handed work that is more complete and more stable. The solid rightmost vertical arrow in Figure 8, which shows when the DBA's work gets initiated, starts higher on the designer's completeness and stability scale.

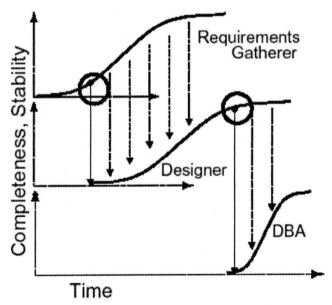

Figure 5-8: Completeness and stability over time. The designer-programmer benefits the schedule by starting earlier and accepting more rework.[3]

Note that in Figure 5-8 each designer uses much more time than the DBA. This is appropriate, since there is only one DBA for five designers.

The principle says that rework is an expendable commodity everywhere except at the bottleneck station (the DBA, in the above example). Rework can be expended to improve a design, to investigate multiple designs, or to get a head start on a downstream activity. Applying this principle to different circumstances produces different optimal project strategies.[2]

Although this is the most complicated principle presented so far, I find that most project leaders have, in fact, used this principle in responding to standard project pressures through common sense and intuition.

Sweet Spots Speed Development

The ideal project uses dedicated, experienced people who sit within earshot of each other; use automated regression tests; have easy access to the users; and deliver running, tested systems to those users every month or two. Such a project is clearly in a better position to complete successfully than one missing those characteristics. The surprise is that sponsoring executives do not pay more attention to these important success factors.

When the team cannot hit one of those sweet spots, then they need to invent a way to get closer to it. The farther away they are, the more difficult the project becomes. Below, we will discuss the six sweet spots.

Dedicated Developers

There is a large emotional and mental cost to a person having to switch between multiple assignments.[3,24] In my project reviews, I find that once people get interrupted at the rate of about three times per day, they stop even trying to focus on their main assignment and simply wait for the next interruption to happen. One senior project manager reported that he simply does not count as productive staff anyone assigned less than half-time to the project.

Experienced Developers

Experienced developers know the domain, they know the technologies or how to adopt them, and they know their computer science material. They move at multiple times the speed of their slower colleagues.

Small Collocated Team

Two to eight people sitting in the same room can ask each other questions without raising their voices. They are aware of when others are available to answer questions. They overhear relevant conversations without pausing in their work. They keep the design ideas and project plans on the board in ready sight and share information faster. The developers I have interviewed uniformly say that while the environment can get noisy, they have never been on a more effective project than when a small team sat in the same room.

Technology can mitigate the situation somewhat. One project team installed cameras on every workstation to display the image of the other people on the project in their various offices.[25] This gave them a sense of each other's presence, and indicated when people were not at their workstations or not to be disturbed with a question. They used online chat boxes to fire off and get answers to the many small questions that constantly arise. They were creative in mimicking the sweet spot in an otherwise unsweet situation.

Automated Regression Tests

With automated regression unit and acceptance tests, the developers can revise the code base and retest the entire system at the push of a button. Teams who have such tests report that they freely replace and improve awkward modules. They also report relaxing more on the weekends since they will run the tests on Monday morning and discover if someone has changed their system out from under them. These tests improve both the design quality and the programmers' quality of life. Experienced developers spend quite some effort to minimize the amount of the system not amenable to automated regression tests.

Easy Access to Users

Having a *customer* or usage expert available at all times means that the feedback cycle from nominated solution to evaluated idea is much shorter, often in the range of minutes to a few hours. The development team gains a deeper understanding of the users' needs and habits and makes fewer mistakes nominating ideas. It also means that more ideas can be tried, allowing for a better final product.

Missing this sweet spot lowers the likelihood of making a really useable product. Teams unable to have a usage expert available at all times have substituted weekly sessions with the users, studying the user community in depth before and during the project, using surveys, or using friendly alpha-test groups.

Short Increments and Frequent Delivery to Real Users.

There is no substitute for rapid feedback, both on the development process and the product itself. Some colleagues say that even one month is an intolerably long time. However, there is also a cost to deploying a product, which makes this a MFI proposition (discussed in the previous article).

With short increments, the process itself gets tested and can be repaired quickly, and the requirements for the product can be tested and varied quickly.

Projects that cannot deliver to an end user every few months should integrate a full build every few months and pretend as though it were delivered. This way, they exercise every part of the development process.

Differences Between Approaches

At this point, we have listed the issues that bear on how cost- and plan-driven projects can borrow from agile approaches. Some cause intrinsically different responses; other responses are more a matter of habit.

Intrinsic Differences

Statistics vs. heuristics. Some project leaders believe software development is a statistically controllable process; others do not. Their resulting strategies are incompatible. This is one of the places where friction arises between agile and plan-driven project leaders.

Individuals and interactions vs. processes and tools. Some leaders believe that with the right process, they can become immune to the turnover of key people. Others believe that no process can offer that immunity; the heart of good software development will always reside in the individual people on the project. As with the statistical approach, we are more likely to find process-centric leaders running plan-driven projects, and individualcentric leaders running agile projects.

Responding to change vs. following a plan. It is a fundamental difference between the two project types whether the team is encouraged to or penalized for responding to changes. Even though business needs, requirements, technologies, and people are constantly moving these days, some projects are still fixed in some combination of time, scope, and cost, and must operate in the plan-driven range.

Project plan as MFI or MFF. If the requirements or technologies are likely to change late in the game or without notice, or the team does not have experience with the technology, then it is a poor strategy to treat the project plan as a MFI issue. In those situations, the agile leader's mindset that the plan is a MFF proposition works better. The leader allocates energy to replanning coarsely but frequently.

Design as MFI or MFF. A plan-driven project team, believing that the design can be worked out in advance (MFI), expends resources early to gain that information and lock down the design. For those design elements that cannot be foreseen (MFF issues), plan-oriented design teams often design the system so that a range of future design constraints can be easily incorporated - expending extra design energy early in anticipation of having a more adaptable design.

Many agile designers find those resulting designs overly complicated. Agreeing that certain issues are MFF issues, they argue that a better MFF strategy is to make a simpler design in the first place, with less built-in flexibility. The saved money can then be allocated to change the design on an as-needed basis.

Some agile designers argue that the MFI component of the design activity is negligibly small, thus little or no effort should be expended on anticipated design changes.

Serial vs. concurrent development. There is a fundamental difference in the strategies applied when agility is a priority compared with when cost is the priority. As Principle No. 8 describes, cost-sensitive projects do better with serial development when that can be successfully executed. Unfortunately, there are so many surprises in projects that it is very difficult to execute successfully.

Surmountable Differences

Working software vs. comprehensive documentation. One tends to find more initiatives for comprehensive documentation on statistics-, process- and plan-driven projects, but this is not intrinsic. Many experienced managers use prototypes, simulators, and incremental development to reduce risk and gain early information on both agile and plan-driven projects, feeding that information into the plan as quickly as possible.

Customer collaboration vs. contract negotiation. Plan-driven project leaders clearly can improve their situation by increasing the collaboration in their customer relations, even if they must write and enforce contracts. This is a case in which plan-driven project leaders can employ some of the same work practices as agile project leaders.

Project plan and design on costsensitive projects. A detailed plan does not, by itself, confer cost savings or safety to a project. Detailed plans and detailed designs enable an estimable base-line cost. The manager can then tell if the cost is going up or down over time. It is not the detail of the plan, but successful application of MFF and MFI decisions that makes the difference in the result.

109

Borrowing From Agile

Drawing from the above, we see that the plan-driven project can streamline its development operations, improve predictability, and hedge its bets by borrowing in various ways from the agile approach. Following are examples of these.

Streamlining

A plan-driven project leader should still try to hit the six sweet spots: dedicated, experienced and collocated staff; using automated regression test suites; having easy access to knowledgeable users; and showing and delivering incrementally growing, running, tested systems to them regularly.

In addition to these, the project members can question to what extent they can lower the documentation burden through a more informal information exchange.

Improving Predictability

Good project leaders already use prototypes, simulators, and incremental development to get early information on their project. However, in my experience, many leaders of plan-driven projects do not avail themselves of these techniques, which are standard business among agile developers.

Of the above techniques, the most important for the plan-driven team to adopt is incremental development. By delivering a few increments, the leader gains invaluable information about *this* team, *this* problem, and *this* technology. That data are more appropriate to the project plan than estimates from other people working on other problems in other technology.

110

Hedging Bets

Surprises can show up even on a plandriven project. Based on where they estimate those surprises are, the plan-driven project leaders can incorporate some of the agile mindset into their strategy. Once again, the use of incremental development is key. The delivery, or even just integration, of each increment offers the team a chance to deal with whatever surprise showed up, whether in the requirements, the technology, or the process. The other technique to borrow is concurrent development, which offers a way to speed development and respond to late-breaking changes.

Lowering Costs

Customer collaboration over contract negotiation. The most important agile value for the cost-sensitive project leader to adopt is customer collaboration. When told that varying a requirement converts an expensive design into a simple, inexpensive one, a customer often is willing to change the requirements to allow the less expensive design. To the extent that the customer and the development team are on good terms, this happens more often.

Working software over comprehensive documentation. Tacit knowledge and informal communication are much less expensive than complete documentation. The cost-sensitive project will play a game of documentation brinkmanship, creating only minimal documents needed to keep the project from falling apart.

Responding to change vs. following a plan. Optimizing from an accurate plan is clearly a winning strategy. The only time that responding to change is advantageous to a cost-sensitive project team is when they discover a shortcut later in the project. At that point, they obviously benefit from changing the plan.

111

Summing Up

The natural tension between agility-focused, plan-driven, and cost-sensitive project teams is explained in part by their interpretations of what counts as a *money-for-information* proposition, what counts as a *money-for-flexibility* proposition, and how much money to spend on each. We have seen how people with various priorities use those economic strategies differently.

It is particularly important, in working with these principles, that each be used to tune a project's running rules, of particular importance is that each project team declares its priorities as well as its communication and validation requirements. With those in place, the team can orient itself to the amount of face-to-face communication it can manage, and the extra methodology weight it should appropriately set in place.

The principles are intended to be used as slider scales. Too much toward each end of the sliding scale brings its own sort of damage.

Agile teams put more emphasis on the ideas presented in this chapter than do plan-driven teams. Most of the ideas are not particularly new. What is surprising is the extent to which these known, old practices are ignored. It is sobering to re-read the paper, "Disciplines Delivering Success," presented at the 1997 Software Technology Conference in Salt Lake City[26] in which Brown points out the following: *"project-saving disciplines ignored by management*: good personnel practices, planning and tracking using activity networks and earned value, incremental release build plan, formal configuration management, test planning and project stability, and metrics." Of all the practices, the agile strategy of using concurrent development is intrinsically in opposition to cost-minimization under predictable circumstances. However, cost-sensitive project teams can benefit from all four of the agile values and all six of the project sweet spots. Customer collaboration and making good use of close, informal communications are key among those.

Of the differences between development styles, agile developers typically believe that software development is not amenable to statistical process control, and so heuristic project controls must be used.

CHAPTER SIX

Emergent Order Through Visionary Leadership

Sanjiv Augustine
Susan Woodcock

Today's Information Technology (IT) manager is under ever-increasing pressure to deliver results – applications that drive improvements to the bottom line – even while IT budgets are being significantly slashed. Meanwhile, despite the fall of the Internet economy, business environments continue to change at a rapid pace leaving many IT shops struggling to keep up. These changes have led to an increased interest in agile software development methodologies, with their promise of rapid delivery and flexibility while maintaining quality.

Agile methodologies such as Extreme Programming (XP), Scrum, and Feature-Driven Development strive to reduce the cost of change throughout the software development process. For example, XP uses rapid iterative planning and development cycles in order to force trade-offs and deliver the highest value features as early as possible. In addition, the constant, systemic testing that is part of XP ensures high quality through early defect detection and resolution.

In spite of some early success with agile methodologies, a number of factors are preventing their widespread adoption. Agile methodology advocates often find it difficult to obtain management support for implementing what seem like dramatic changes in application development. These methodologies require developers, managers, and users alike to change the way they work and think. For example, the XP practices of pair programming, test-first design, continuous integration, and an on-site customer can seem like daunting changes to implement. Furthermore, these methodologies tend to be developer-centric and seem to dismiss the role of management in ensuring success.

As managers of several successful XP projects, we have found that strong management is absolutely critical to the successful adoption and application of agile methodologies. But we have also discovered a lack of alignment between the methodologies and tools of traditional project management, and those of newer agile methodologies. Furthermore, we believe this misalignment is symptomatic of a deeper problem – differences in fundamental assumptions about change, control, order, organizations, people, and overall problem solving approaches. Traditional management theory assumes that

- Rigid procedures are needed to regulate change

- Hierarchical organizational structures are a means of establishing order

- Increased control results in increased order

- Organizations must be rigid, static hierarchies

- Employees are interchangeable "parts" in the organizational "machine"

- Problems are solved primarily through reductionist task breakdown and allocation
- Projects and risks are adequately predictable to be managed through complex up-front planning

Within this context, it is small wonder that the new methodologies appear informal to the point of being chaotic, egalitarian to the point of actively fostering insubordination, and directionless in their approach to problem solving. We believe that the slow adoption of agile methodologies stems mainly from this misalignment between the fundamental assumptions of traditional management and those of the new agile development methodologies. As such, we believe there is a significant need for a change in assumptions and a new management framework when working with agile methodologies.

In the search for a new framework, we have come to believe strongly in emerging management principles based on the "new science" of complexity that exploit an understanding of autonomous human behavior gained from the study of living systems in nature. Specifically, we have begun to build the notion of complex adaptive systems (CAS) into our management assumptions and practices. Complexity scientists have studied the collective behavior of living systems in nature such as the flocking of birds, the schooling of fish, the marching of ants and the swarming of bees. They have discovered that, while the individual "agents" in these complex adaptive systems possess only local strategic rules and capacity, their collective behavior is characterized by an overlaying order, self-organization, and a collective intelligence that is greater than the sum of the parts. The theory of CAS has been applied successfully in several areas – economics, life sciences and more recently, to management.

The concepts of CAS led us to the inspiration that like the XP team, project managers also need a set of simple guiding practices that provide a framework within which to manage, rather than a set of rigid instructions. Following these practices, the manager becomes an adaptive leader – setting the direction, establishing the simple, generative rules of the system, and encouraging constant feedback, adaptation, and collaboration. This management framework, covered in detail later in this chapter, provides teams implementing agile methodologies with

- An intrinsic ability to deal with change.

- A view of organizations as fluid, adaptive systems composed of intelligent living beings.

- A recognition of the limits of external control in establishing order, and of the role of intelligent control that employs self-organization as a means of establishing order.

- An overall problem solving approach that is humanistic in that

  - It regards employees as skilled and valuable stakeholders in the management of a team.

  - It relies on the collective ability of autonomous teams as the basic problem solving mechanism.

  - It limits up-front planning to a minimum based on an assumption of unpredictability, and instead, lays stress on adaptability to changing conditions.

The Problem: Project Manager as Uninspired Taskmaster

Traditional software lifecycle development methodologies grew out of a need to control ever-larger development projects, and the difficulties of estimating and managing these efforts to reliably deliver results. These methodologies drew heavily on the principles from engineering such as construction management. As a result, they stressed predictability (one has to plan every last detail of a bridge or building before it is built), and linear development cycles (requirements led to analysis which led to design which in turn led to development). Along with predictability, they inherited a deterministic, reductionist approach that relied on task breakdown, and was predicated on stability: stable requirements, analysis and stable design. This rigidity was also marked by a tendency towards slavish process "compliance" as a means of project control.

While these methodologies may have worked for some organizations in the past and may still work in some circumstances, for many companies, these methodologies only added cost and complexity while providing a false sense of security that management was "doing something" by exhaustively planning, measuring, and controlling. Huge costs were sunk in premature planning, without the rapid iterative development and continuous feedback from customers that we have come to realize are prerequisites for success today.

The results are stark – repeated, public failures such as the London Ambulance System and the Denver Airport Baggage system earned the software industry a reputation for being "troublesome" with huge cost overruns and schedule slippages. Consider the results of the Standish Group's CHAOS surveys. In the first survey, it was estimated that only 16 percent of all software projects were considered successful, 31 percent were failures and 53 percent were challenged. Comparatively, the 1998 figures showed a marked improvement in which 26 percent were successful, 46 percent were challenged and 28 percent were failures. The study attributed the increase in success to scaling the size of projects back to manageable levels, and using smaller teams. This result is clearly in line with the principles of agile methodologies. Furthermore, we have found that many established project management practices still apply to agile development projects – with some adaptation and a strong dose of leadership.

While managers designed traditional methodologies in an effort to control projects, the technical community gave birth to agile methodologies in response to their frustrations with traditional management (or lack thereof) and the resulting impact on their products and morale. For example, the principles of XP are focused almost entirely on the development process. While the technical community has championed these principles, very little has been written about the management side of agile development projects. The implication is that there is little need for a project manager since XP teams develop and monitor their own tasks. No wonder that corporate management has been skeptical of agile methodologies and slow to embrace them. Managers conjure up an image of a room full of developers doing their own thing… and the name "eXtreme" doesn't help matters either!

Regardless of the particular methodology, the traditional project manager is often seen as a "taskmaster" who develops and controls the master plan that documents (often in excruciating detail) the tasks, dependencies, and resources required to deliver the end product. The project manager then monitors the status of tasks and adjusts the plan as necessary. Underpinning this mechanistic approach is the assumption that equates individuals to interchangeable, controllable commodities.

So for many managers comfortable with traditional methodologies, the prospect of implementing agile methodologies on their development projects can be daunting. But it does not need to be. In fact, independent of agile methodologies, other trends in project management indicate a point to a convergence between the management community and the technical community.

The Solution: Project Manager as Visionary Leader

The best project managers are not just organizers: they combine business vision, communication skills, soft management skills, and technical savvy with the ability to plan, coordinate, and execute. In essence, they are not just managers, they are leaders. While this has always been the case, agile project management places a higher premium on the leadership skills than ever before.

For example, XP teams create and monitor their own iteration plans in collaboration with customers. Customers create stories (features) and prioritize them based on business value. The developers divide up the tasks themselves as they work and measures progress for each iteration (time-boxed development cycle), adjusting plans with the customers as necessary. So, if the project no longer needs a detailed master project plan, why does it need a project manager?

Every project needs a leader. Agile methodologies free the project manager from the drudgery of being a taskmaster thereby enabling the project manager to focus on being a leader – someone who keeps the spotlight on the vision, who inspires the team, who promotes teamwork and collaboration, who champions the project, and who removes obstacles. Rather than being an operational controller, the project manager can become an adaptive leader if he or she can relinquish reliance on old-style management.

The basic phases of an agile development project are really no different from those of any other project. You still must define and initiate the project, plan for the project, execute the plan, and monitor and control the results. The manner in which these steps are accomplished, however, are different, and requires the project manager to retrofit what he or she knows about traditional management to a new way of thinking – the thinking of complex adaptive systems. The practices outlined below provide a framework for project managers working in this new world.

The Means: An Agile Project Management Framework

The authors have applied XP successfully on several projects over the past years, and have evolved the use of XP practices as an integral part of a CAS inspired framework for agile project management. Below, we provide a guiding philosophy of the team as a complex adaptive system.

A Guiding Philosophy: Projects as a Chaordic Complex Adaptive Systems

As the literature will attest, traditional command-and-control management is largely derived from the principles of Frederick Taylor's *scientific management*. Taylor's scientific management approach was based, in turn, on the seventeenth century science of Newton that saw the world as a vast and magnificently ordered "clockwork universe" governed by the classical laws of nature. Scientific management is recognized as the prime mover in lifting the "working masses" in developed countries to new levels of affluence in the 20th century.

In today's world, however, we have trouble imposing command-and-control management on teams because knowledge workers have replaced the "working masses." In the computer software industry, for example, we have situations where skilled software developers are often worth as much or more to their employers than their managers. In Taylor's world, it was the manager who had the specialized problem-solving knowledge. In ours, this key problem-solving knowledge resides with the knowledge workers, and not the manager. So, how do we adapt project management techniques to deal with this reality?

The scientific world has changed. For nearly two centuries after Newton, his ideas held sway, and found widespread adoption in many other disciplines. Subsequent advances in the sciences – from Einstein's relativity thinking to quantum physics – have since replaced the Newtonian worldview in many disciplines. A more recent revolution in the scientific community looks set to finally change the traditional views of management – the new science of *complexity.*

Over the past two or three decades, scientists have explored living systems in many fields – as diverse and biology and economics – to search for common properties that explain complex phenomena such as Darwinian natural selection and increasing returns on the stock market. They have uncovered that many natural systems (such as brains, immune systems, ecologies, and societies) and many artificial systems (parallel and distributed computing systems, artificial intelligence systems, artificial neural networks, and evolutionary programs) are characterized by complex behaviors that emerge as a result of interactions among their component systems at different levels of organization.

These results have been used to unravel the mysteries of the collective behavior of living systems in nature such as the flocking of birds, the schooling of fish, the marching of ants, and the swarming of bees for strategic purposes. While the individual "agents" in these groups possess only local strategic rules and capacity, their collective behavior is characterized by an overlaying order, self-organization, and a collective intelligence that is greater than the sum of the parts. In addition, these living systems regularly display a remarkable ability to adapt to a complex and dynamic environment. Recognizing projects as CAS allows us to manage them as *chaordic* organizations. A chaordic project harmoniously blends characteristics of both chaos and order – freedom and control, optimization and exploration, competition and cooperation. Chaordic characteristics of interest to agile managers are:

- *Alignment and Cooperation*: When agents are aligned, they eschew competition and cooperate to work with each other for mutual gain. Shared vision keeps agents in alignment and acting toward common purpose.

- *Emergence and Self-Organization*: In a CAS, semi-autonomous *agents* follow *simple, local rules* that guide their behavior. Complex behavior *emerges* from the interaction between many agents following these simple rules. Self-organization is the spontaneous emergence of new patterns, behavior or structure from agent interactions.

- *Learning and Adaptation*: Continuous learning and adaptation are crucial to keeping projects on their *chaordic edge* – the edge between chaos and order – where there is "just enough" interaction, structure, exploration and cooperation. Too little structure and a chaordic project swings toward chaos, too much and it gets mired down. Too little exploration and the project has to rely on unreliable predictive methods, too much and it veers off-course.

If we view our projects as chaordic CAS, the rules of traditional project management can be retrofitted to a new CAS model. The authors have applied XP successfully on several projects over the past years, and evolved the use of XP practices as an integral part of a CAS inspired framework for agile project management.

A CAS-Based Project Management Framework: Six Practices for Managing Agile Development Projects

We have established a CAS-based project management framework with six Agile Project Management (APM) practices for managing agile development projects – *Guiding Vision, Organic Teams, Light Touch, Simple Rules, Open Information,* and *Adaptive Leadership.*

Together, these practices help us to steer our projects as chaordic complex adaptive systems while allowing us the freedom to overlay our own personal leadership styles. The six practices build on the fundamentals of CAS, as shown in Table 6-1. These practices are explained in further detail later in this chapter.

Table 6-1: Chaordic characteristics, CAS principles, and corresponding APM practices.

CAS Principle	Corresponding Agile Project Management Practice
Non-material fields exert force on material objects.	*Guiding Vision.* Recognizing vision as a non-material field rather than an elusive destination results in vision continuously guiding and influencing behavior in positive ways.
Autonomous, intelligent agents form the basis of CAS. *Interactions* between these agents result in *self-organization* and other *emergent* phenomena.	*Organic Teams.* Recognizing individual team members as intelligent, skilled professional agents and placing a value on their autonomy is fundamental to all other practices.

125

CAS Principle	Corresponding Agile Project Management Practice
	Teamwork and collaboration form the basis for rich interactions and cooperation between team members.
Local, strategic rules support complex, overlaying behavior in a team environment.	*Simple Rules.* Rules such as XP practices support complex, overlaying team behavior.
Information is energy that serves as an agent of change and adaptation.	*Open Information.* Open information is an organizing force that allows teams to adapt and react to changing conditions in the environment.
Emergent order is a bottom-up manifestation of order, while imposed order is a top-down manifestation.	*Light Touch.* Intelligent control of teams requires a delicate mix of imposed and emergent order.
Non-linear dynamic systems are continuously adapting when they reach a state of *dynamic equilibrium,* termed the *edge of chaos.*	*Adaptive Leadership* Visionary leadership implies continuously monitoring, learning, and adapting to the environment.

Practice #1: Guiding Vision – Keep the team aligned and directed with a shared mental model.

CAS agents' mental models are mechanisms for anticipation and adaptation. As articulated by Margaret Wheatley,[1] when a project vision is translated into a statement of the greater purpose and dreams of the organization, and communicated to all members of the team, it serves as a field that has a powerful effect on their behavior. It can permeate the project environment and influence team behavior in extremely positive ways, much more so than a simple task can. The vision needs to become a guiding force that helps the team make consistent choices, rather than embody an elusive end state on a piece of paper.

A real example of this principle is the use of the *commander's intent* in the U.S. Army. The Army knows that its leaders cannot be everywhere in the field of combat controlling all the decisions. Therefore, Army leaders clearly establish the "commander's intent" to serve as a guide on which soldiers can base their own initiatives, actions and decisions. Thus, even if the mission falls on the shoulders of the lowest ranking person, he or she must be able to understand and carry out the mission.

Likewise, you, the agile manager, can guide the team and continuously influence team behavior by defining, disseminating and sustaining a guiding vision. At the outset of the project, work closely with the customer to understand the vision for the project, how it is expected to support business goals, and how it will be used. To promote team ownership of the vision, facilitate a group discussion with the team to build a joint project vision. A strong grasp of the vision will help the team through difficult decisions about business value and priority and keep them focused on and inspired by the ultimate goal.

The traditional process of reducing project tasks into ever-smaller components for assignment and tracking often causes degeneration into "fractal" tasks, tasks at ever repeated smaller scales. The traditional tool for guidance – a project plan with fractal tasks – often has tasks at too small a level to be really meaningful. Instead, maintain a focus on the forest over the trees and promote a planning process that keeps tasks at a level that sets intent and desired outcome, while preserving flexibility for team innovation and autonomy.

Throughout the project, gently guide the team to maintain focus on the vision. Everyday decisions and interactions are opportunities to reinforce the vision and create positive energy. Beware of actions that are not consistent with the vision and your message, this kind of dissonance creates the negative energy that deflates teams and inspires many Dilbert comic strips. For example, in planning sessions, ask questions to provoke thinking about whether stated requirements and the assigned business value are in line with the vision.

Practice #2: Organic Teams – Enable collaboration and adaptation through close relationships on small, organic teams.

Self-organization and emergent order are due in part to rich interactions between agents in a CAS. These phenomena are explained by expressing the sum of the interactions of a CAS as a gestalt *connectivity* with each agent working in alignment with other agents. It is this connectivity that we believe can be manifested through organic teams.

Organic teams are clusters of specialized groups coordinated by communications and relationships. They reduce centrally coordinated bureaucracy in favor of more autonomous units with close *connections*. Flexibility and adaptability are provided by close connections of people, problems and resources. By increasing communication across group boundaries, increasing relationships among people and building trust, organic organizations spark innovation and adaptation.

We have all seen that when people work together leveraging complementary individual strengths the results can be exceptional. But getting people to work this way can be a challenge and it cannot happen by mandate. The project manager's role is to actively facilitate collaboration and adaptation by establishing the conditions for good relationships.

Good relationships among team members starts with the project manager's relationship with the team members. You set the standard and are the role model for the others. You need to take steps to get to know each team member as a person – know what makes each of them tick outside of work and what motivates each of them at work. In addition, by treating each person with respect you establish the model for working relationships on the team.

In addition to getting to know the team members yourself, you should help team members get to know each other also by creating opportunities and the right conditions. Opportunities can be created from planning games, everyday interaction, and special events. To set the right conditions, you must establish an environment in which team members treat each other with respect. You may even need to intervene to stop disrespectful behavior.

We recognize many managers may not be able to pick and choose their team but, if at all possible, the first practical step in building a collaborative team is selecting team members with the right attitude and complementary skills. Particularly, if the organization has not worked with XP before, the team members should be people who are adaptable and willing to try new ways of working, although having a few non-believers can have its advantages. In theory, XP teams have no experts – all developers work on all aspects. In reality, sometimes experts are needed when the team is learning some new tools or a specific component requires technology with which the organization has no experience. You must ensure that the role of experts and learning goals are clearly defined in order to achieve positive collaboration.

This initial stage of the project also provides the project manager with opportunities to get to know the team and help them get to know each other. The time-honored kick-off group lunch can be combined with techniques often used in training sessions such as sharing personal and professional information with a colleague who then makes the group introduction. In addition, the project manager should ensure that the physical workspace is arranged in a way that facilitates collaborative activities such as pair programming and team problem solving. Ideally, the team should be located in an open space with both individual and common areas.

Keep in mind that such open but close quarters have the potential to both encourage and inhibit collaboration. Some people may not be comfortable bringing their technical problems to the group. You should be finding ways to gradually get developers used to this mode of working such as beginning with pair programming, smaller groups, and demonstrating that bringing a problem to the group is not a sign of weakness. Some developers want to ask for help but aren't good at coming out with it. Start to learn individual team members' signals. For example, on one project a developer would signal interest in starting a dialogue by taking his earphones of and "coughing."

Planning sessions are fertile ground for developing a common understanding and respect between the developers and the Customer – something that is often sadly lacking in many application development projects. With the right kind of leadership, as the project progresses these sessions can become highly collaborative and creative resulting in improved morale and a better product. Basic facilitation techniques such as making sure all parties have an opportunity to speak, summarizing and confirming, and drawing out concerns can help to build the team.

There are many situations that can impede collaboration such as disrespectful treatment, egotism, and non-performing team members. The project manager must monitor the team dynamics and decide when to intervene.

As the project progresses, continue to look for special opportunities to get to know people better and to help the team know each other. For example,

• Establish a regular day for group order-in or potluck lunches,

• Give team members fun (positive!) nicknames, and

• Celebrate successes and milestones with nominal gifts that reflect knowledge of staff interests (e.g., music, gift certificates, special foods).

The team that laughs and plays together works better together.

Practice #3: Simple Rules – Establish and continuously refine a set of simple process rules for the team.

In a CAS, agents follow simple rules, but their interactions result in complex behavior emerging from the bottom-up over time. For example, birds in a flock follow simple rules such as avoiding objects, keeping pace, and staying close to other birds. By following these simple rules, flocks of birds exhibit complex, collective behavior by flying in formation for long distances and adapting to changing conditions along the way. The gestalt order that emerges is a result of following these simple rules.

We have used the twelve standard practices of XP as a set of simple rules for our software development projects. The XP practices provide the team with a flexible structure within which to work. To use the XP practices as simple rules, they must be explicitly stated and agreed to by all members of the team at the outset, although the team should have the ability to modify practices that are not working or add new practices. If the developers and the customer have not used XP before, provide the team with training on the full set of XP practices. Often, a one-day seminar on the practices including some XP exercises to simulate the planning game and short development iterations is sufficient. Based on this knowledge the team can discuss how best to apply the practices on the particular project at hand.

Take a leading role in encouraging the team to try certain practices about which team members may be doubtful. For example, on one of our XP projects a developer doubted the effectiveness of the *test-first design* practice but was able to quickly see the value after being encouraged to try it.

In applying the XP practices, you set up simple generative rules that are just enough to provide clear boundaries, but no so much as to restrict the autonomy and creativity of the team. Throughout the project, appropriately point out when practices are not being followed and seek to understand why, looking for opportunities to adjust and improve on the practices or their practical use.

Practice #4: Open Information – Provide free and open access to information.

In a CAS, information is the lifeblood of change and adaptation. Interactions between agents involve the exchange of information. The richness of the interactions between agents therefore, depends in a large part on the openness of the information.

For an agile team to be able to adapt, information must be open and free flowing. Traditional managers have long prevented this openness and freedom because of a fear that it will result in chaos. Because of this fear, traditional managers have controlled information and meted it out on a "need to know" basis. On traditionally managed projects, teams often feel like they don't know what is going on – only the project manager has the "master plan" and only the project manager interacts with project sponsor.

In the agile world, information is freed to leverage its power. XP practices, for example, promote open access to information– story cards are public property, as is visible documentation of all status information such as the tracking data. *Collective code ownership* encourages everyone to contribute to the project. Customers and developers are placed in close proximity via *on-site customer* to promote an open exchange of information.

To promote open information, try a variety of techniques:

- Place team members within close proximity of each other whenever possible.

- Make use of information radiators[2] such as whiteboards and charts to disseminate information.

- Rather than have status meetings with the project sponsor in an office or conference room, bring him or her to the project room for public status reports and hands-on demos.

- Use a team wiki[3] (free form web site written by users) to share information.

- Establish daily status meetings to promote the flow and exchange of information.

- Sustain open information exchange between business domain experts and the development team.

Practice #5: Light Touch – Apply intelligent control to foster emergent order.

In traditional management, everything is seen through the prism of control: change control, risk control, and most importantly – people control. Elaborate methodologies, tools and practices have been evolved to try and "manage" an out-of-control world. But tools fail when neat linear task breakdowns cannot easily accommodate cyclical processes, and neat schedules require frequent updating to reflect the reality of changing dates and circumstances. Complex start-to-finish plans laid out in advance of a project carry a certain naïve optimism that the future will not stray too far from what has been laid out.

In the zeal of imposing more and more control, managers seem to have forgotten the original purpose of control – to create order and to deliver value. As traditional managers, we had come to believe that more control would give us more order. Unfortunately, this conventional view does not really help us in the uncertain real world because life is characterized by probabilities, not certainties. As experience teaches, unforeseen events can lay the best of plans to naught in an instant. Skilled professionals do not take well to micromanagement. Tools and techniques reach their limitations quickly when used inappropriately.

Instead, if we realize that increased control does not cause increased order, we can approach management with courage, we can recognize – that we do not know *everything* in advance, so we cannot really plan it *all* out on a project plan in minute detail. We do not *really* know when things are going to get done in advance, so we cannot really pinpoint when they will be done in *minute* detail in a project schedule. So, we will need to relinquish some control in the interests of achieving greater order. Therefore, we have established the final principle – apply "just enough" control.

We believe that control and order are related, as illustrated in Figure 6-1. Without any control at all, there exists a certain level of order due to self-organization, depending on the team skills and dynamics. Initially, as control increases, order increases somewhat linearly, and reaches a narrow plateau quickly, decreasing very rapidly afterwards. Of course, the conventional view holds that the initial condition of no control starts off without any order at all, with an increasing linear relationship.

Visionary control is a delicate mix of emergent and imposed order. To impose order, you must impose some control but do it with a "light touch." With a progressive "light-touch" mindset, lay out project plans at a high-enough level to give the team room for innovation, creativity and rapid response to dynamic environments. Ensure that the project plans are synchronized with your guiding vision, and that they are based on functionality to be delivered and not tasks. Give your teams a level of autonomy to quickly adapt solutions to changing situations on their own. Dismantle rigid command-and-control structures to allow teams to follow a more adaptive, organic model. Step back from your project just a bit and give the team a chance to self-organize; you will be thrilled at the result!

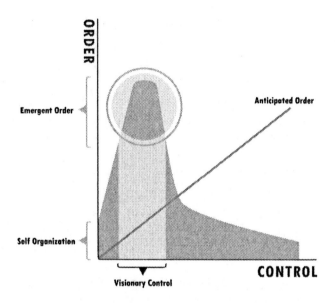

Figure 6-1: The relationship between control and order.

Complexity science brings us the concept of *strange attractors* – graphs of a system's behavior that reveal in visual form its unpredictable nature when it does not behave the same way twice, yet demonstrates inherent orderliness by being "attracted" to a particular, beautiful pattern. For example, vortexes such as dust storms or whirlpools exhibit a familiar spiral strange attractor. With visionary leadership and a light touch, your project teams will be drawn to a unique pattern of orderly behavior, representing their own particular "strange attractor."

Of course, viewed too closely, this emergent order may seem like disorder or chaos to the conventional eye. But to the courageous manager, who is willing to relinquish some control, the rewards of this practice are manifold – a dynamic and fulfilled team, innovative solutions and continuous adaptation.

Practice #6: Adaptive Leadership – Steer the project by continuously monitoring, learning and adapting your approach.

The common thread throughout all six practices is this final practice – Adaptive Leadership. In computer simulations, artificial systems that operate within a framework of simple rules can sometimes display amazingly lifelike behavior such as reproduction. Their most interesting behavior occurs at the border between order and chaos – unpredictable enough to be interesting and ordered enough to avoid falling into chaos. It is our contention that the most creative and agile work of a team occurs at this hypothetical edge of chaos. However, just as in dynamical non-linear systems, we believe that operating on this edge requires continuous learning and adaptation to changing environmental conditions.

Of course, all good things come with a price. To paraphrase Thomas Jefferson, the price of agility on the edge of chaos is eternal vigilance. In leading a team by establishing a guiding vision, fostering teamwork and cooperation, setting simple rules, championing open information, and managing with a light touch, the job of the agile manager has been likened to herding cats – each person has his or her own ideas, and is likely to behave in accordance with those ideas.

You, the agile manager, therefore must be continually vigilant to merit the mantle of leadership: monitoring progress, and keeping a finger on the pulse of the development team. This does not mean hovering and controlling everything – remember, you have established simple rules and must trust in your people and the process. Instead, it means being observant, continuously seeking feedback, monitoring success or failure, and adapting by making changes as situations warrant. You should

- Reinforce the guiding vision at every opportunity. Examine project decisions to see whether they line up with the vision.

- Continually encourage teamwork and collaboration. Talk to your team members one-on-one as often as possible to keep a pulse on the heartbeat of the project. Watch for signs of stress – rising tempers, fatigue, etc. – and deal with them quickly. Keep abreast of technology so that you can interpret the "tribal language" of your software developers.

- Establish simple rules, but take every opportunity to conduct process reflections: regularly examine what works and what needs improvement. Act with courage to make changes when you feel that they are necessary.

- Work relentlessly to break down the barriers to information sharing. Keep apprised of cultural sensitivities, egos, and other such factors that may impinge upon successfully sharing information. Operate with a light touch. Intervene quickly, but wisely, to solve personnel issues. Motivate and reward initiative, but manage expectations. Recognize and encourage self-organization, but disallow cliques.

Conclusion

The lack of guidance for project managers of agile development projects has been a gaping hole in the software development community over the past several years. The contrast between the world of agile software development and traditional project management has left many managers wondering what their role should be. By viewing the agile development team as a complex adaptive system and the manager as an integral part of that system, we have begun to develop a framework for managers. This framework of practices is meant to overlay the practices of existing agile methodologies such as XP, and provide clear guidelines for the visionary leadership of projects that use them.

These six practices of agile project management do not provide a sure-fire recipe for success. Building and nurturing a successful team is much more like cooking chili than baking a cake – it requires creativity, flexibility, and attentiveness to the unique qualities and interactions of the ingredients. However, we believe that by following these basic practices and adapting them to your own style over time, you will not only find that you add tremendous value to projects but also that you will enjoy the achievement of success and the journey along the way.

CHAPTER SEVEN

The Engineering of Unstable Requirements

James Tomayko, Ph.D.

In a recent cartoon, a manager is seen walking through an area filled with programmers. He says, "You guys start coding and I'll go see what they want." This pretty well characterizes the situation of projects today. There seems to be a common belief that agile development methods reinforce this unfortunate attitude toward requirements. Conversely, my research has shown that an "agile attitude" toward requirements is a very effective means of acquiring them.[1]

I have had 12 teams of from four to six engineers participate in Extreme Programming (XP)[2,3] experiments in the past year. The experiments were primarily aimed at defect reduction and not requirements acquisition;[4] however, observing how these teams go about their work, has led me to

---

Reprinted/derived from an article of the same title printed in the *Proceedings of the International Workshop on Time Constrained Requirements Engineering (TCRE)*, edited by Armin Eberlein and Julio Cesar Sampaio do Prado Leite, September 2002. Used with permission of the author.

several insights into the requirements acquisition process. Others have come to the same conclusions.[5]

The (Old) Method of Up-Front Requirements Elicitation

Current requirements elicitation methods reinforce improper beliefs. Many projects try to follow the waterfall software life cycle and other obsolete software development life cycle models. The requirements are gathered first in one big effort.[6] Frequently, these requirements turn out to be rife with omissions and misconceptions. Correcting them costs time and money. The result has been a movement toward more iterative models.[7]

At first, these took the form of prototypes, both to find missing requirements and to examine the feasibility of solutions.[8] The history of iterative requirements gathering has itself gone through several cycles, of which agile methods are the latest. The trouble is that with each new iterative method the requirements elicitation process appears to become less defined.

I feel that the attitude towards requirements gathered early in the process is incorrect in that ones missed at that stage are considered defects when added later. My observations, and the entire point of iterative processes, is that requirements are seldom omitted, they are just unknown. There is simply no way that the requirements of even well understood problems could be known. Therefore, why even try? Requirements are elicited by agile methods in a more practical way.

Requirements Elicitation in Agile Methods

"User stories" or the like are just the beginning points of both the requirements gathering and development processes in agile methods. Early requirements are simply a place to start. We expect to add more requirements as more is known about the product. Conversely, the method of trying to gather all the requirements before starting development is almost certainly rife with errors and surely takes too long. "I'll know it when I see it (IKIWISI)"[9] has become a well-known requirements elicitation method. In effect, the early version of the product becomes a prototype. Agile methods are designed to appeal to clients that insist on IKIWISI.

Prototyping in agile methods is even more rapid and produces smaller amounts of code than traditional prototypes.[2,4] Developers that use prototype-based life cycle models are familiar with the case of the client falling in love with the prototype so that they want to take it away as the product. Avoiding a situation where bad code and poor documentation characterizes the product makes the developer produce a less robust prototype. As a result, they are not as useful. Agile methods, which have the concept of a "spike"— a rapid development of a prototype that answers a single question about requirements content—avoid this problem of showing the client too much.

In this way, the client is kept from the responsibility of "getting the requirements right." There are no wrong requirements. There are simply some waiting to be discovered.

Difficulties Caused by Agile Methods of Gathering Requirements

This attitude toward requirements makes estimation and software architecture development more difficult, and verification easier, than traditional methods. Without knowing the final form of the product, or marketplace demands, estimation is going to be impossible to get correct.[10] It is little comfort that requirements omissions and changes caused by reacting to the competition make most estimates incorrect right now. Agile methods are likely to be right about the costs involved in the current cycle, but estimating is poorly understood for the unknown requirements of the next cycle.

One thing that can be done is to fund the project one cycle at a time. However, there will be a time when knowing the total cost is necessary, as in contract work. In these cases, customers express the requirements as well as they can, and estimates are adjusted by the probable cost of later changes. For instance, if a project is estimated at $1 million, and prior projects of roughly those same characteristics have had the cost of "changed" requirements at around 20 per cent, then the estimate should be $1.2 million. Of course, as with all estimations, this can not be used without considerable historical data.

The architecture chosen by the team during the early cycles may become just plain wrong, as later requirements become known. Rework of the architecture matches the refactoring principle of Extreme Programming. Most of my XP teams embrace refactoring, claiming that they would do it anyway, even if the requirements were stable. One student identified refactoring as rework, with its attendant negative properties, notably increased cost. Either way, significant refactoring is to be expected in an atmosphere where requirements are relatively unknown. Confidence in the requirements translates to confidence in the architecture.

Advantages of Agile Methods for Correctness

Aside from refactoring and effective prototyping, agile methods have other advantages for a situation in which requirements are unstable. Reliance on test-driven programming, a core principle of XP, means early detection of most minor errors, more certain detection of defects at integration, and early thinking-through of tests for a Graphical User Interface.[5] This is an advantage to any system. For this reason alone, requirements engineering is advanced by the developer knowing right away if a requirement can be tested.

CHAPTER EIGHT

Active Stakeholder Participation

The Key to Your Agile Success

Scott W. Ambler

Agile Modeling (AM)[1] is an agile software development process that describes principles and practices for effective modeling and documentation. One of those practices is *active stakeholder participation*. For an agile project team to succeed, the project stakeholders must not only be involved with the team but, at a minimum, they must also make decisions and provide information in a timely manner. Better yet, they can and should be active participants in the modeling efforts of the team, something that is possible if the team uses inclusive modeling tools.

This chapter expands upon the ideas presented in *Agile Modeling: Effective Practices for Extreme Programming and The Unified Process* (Wiley Publishing 2002) as well as *The Object Primer 3rd Edition: Agile Model Driven Development with UML 2* (Cambridge University Press 2004). Used with permission of the author.

Stakeholder participation is critical to your success because it is your stakeholders who are the source of requirements, information, and priorities – without their participation, you cannot possibly build systems that meet their needs. In fact, a study of 23,000 projects by the Standish Group[2] shows that the top two project success factors are user involvement and executive support, both aspects of stakeholder involvement. The same report points out that only 14% of projects are on time and on budget, indicating that we need to improve the way that we work.

Why is *active* stakeholder participation important? Why not simply develop a requirements document early in the project, get stakeholders to sign off on it, and then have them rejoin the project efforts towards the end of the lifecycle to perform user acceptance testing? There is nothing stopping you from taking this approach – many traditionalists even seem to prefer it – other than the fact that it does not work very well in practice. A study of 1,027 IT projects[3] showed that scope management relating to waterfall practices, including the definition of a detailed requirements specification early in the lifecycle, was the single largest contributing factor to failure (cited by 82% of projects), given an overall weighted failure influence of 25%. In short, it seems clear that "inactive" stakeholder participation is not a very good idea.

In this chapter I explore the following issues that are fundamental to ensuring active stakeholder participation on a project:

- Who is a project stakeholder?

- Rights and responsibilities

- What does it mean to be an active participant?

- Inclusive modeling with business stakeholders

- Dealing with the nay sayers

148

Who is a Project Stakeholder?

A project stakeholder is anyone who is a direct user, indirect user, manager of users, senior manager, operations staff member, support (help desk) staff member, developer working on another system that integrates or interacts with the one under development, or a maintenance professional potentially affected by the development and/or deployment of a software project.

From this definition, you can see that business stakeholders, such as direct users and their managers, are not the only stakeholders of a project. As you know, there is a wide range of people potentially affected by a new system; therefore, to succeed, you must understand and then synthesize their requirements into a cohesive vision. This is one of the things that makes software development hard – each project stakeholder will have their own requirements, their own vision, and their own priorities – but it also makes software development fun.

In this definition, I have chosen to exclude the developers who are working on the project. This may seem strange at first because developers clearly have an important stake in the projects that they work on. Yes, developers are definitely project stakeholders. Why do I continue to distinguish between developers and other project stakeholders? Because I want convenient terms to distinguish them, I really dislike "developer stakeholder" and "non-developer stakeholder." They also have different roles to play on a project.

My definition of project stakeholder and developer may be different than yours, or perhaps you prefer different terms. For example, Extreme Programming (XP)[4] discusses the concepts of customer and programmer, not project stakeholder and developer, and has slightly different definitions because they use the terms differently than AM does.

Rights and Responsibilities

My experience is that a critical success factor for ensuring effective stakeholder participation is for your team members to agree to a "bill of rights and responsibilities" that guides how they will interact with one another. The rights and responsibilities that I have listed in Table 8-1 have been proven to work well in practice and should provide you with a good starting point. Many project teams choose to display these rights and responsibilities publicly, either as a poster on the wall or on the project team's internal web site, and I highly suggest that you do the same.

Table 8-1: Everyone's rights and responsibilities.

Rights
To be treated with respect.
To produce and receive quality work at all times based on agreed to project standards and principles.
To estimate the activities with which you are actively involved, and to have those estimates respected by others.
To be provided iwth adequate resources (time, money, etc.) to do the job that's been asked of you.
To determine how your resources will be invested. For people funding the project, how the funds will be spent and for the people working on the project, what tasks they choose to undertake.
To be given the opportunity to gain the knowledge pertinent to making a project a success. Business people will likely need to learn about the underlying technologies/techniques, and technical staff will need to learn about the business.

Rights

To have decisions made in a timely manner.

To be provided with good-faith information in a timely manner. Sometimes this is just the "best guess" at the time. This includes business infor-mation such as prioritized requirements and detailed domain concepts, as well as technical information such as designs and detailed technical concepts.

To own your organization's software processes, and actively improve these procedures when needed.

Responsibilities

To produce a system that best meets your needs within the resources that you are willing to invest in it.

To be willing to work with others, particularly those out-side of your chosen specialties.

To share all information, inclu-ding "work in progress."

To actively expand your know-ledge and skillset.

151

What does it mean to be an Active Participant?

XP's *On-Site Customer* practice describes the need to have on-site access to people, typically users or their representatives, who have the authority and ability to provide information pertaining to the system being built, to make pertinent and timely decisions regarding the requirements, and to prioritize them. While this level of participation is required to make your software development efforts effective, it often is not sufficient in many organizations, particularly those where politics and not reason are the order of the day. This is why AM evolved *On-Site Customer* into *Active Stakeholder Participation*. Project success often requires a greater level of involvement by project stakeholders – senior management needs to publicly and private support your project, operations and support staff must actively work with your project team towards making your production environment ready to accept your system, other system teams must work with yours to support integration efforts, and maintenance developers must work to become adept at the technologies and techniques used by your system.

It is clear that in order to be successful all project stakeholders must actively work with your team to achieve these goals. There are several implications of this practice:

1   Users must to be prepared to share business knowledge with the team and to make both pertinent and timely decisions regarding project scope and the priority of requirements.

2   Senior managers must first understand, at a high level, the technologies and techniques that your team is using, understand why your team is using them, and understand the implications of using them. With this knowledge, their efforts within your organization's political arena are far

more likely to be effective at the right times in the right ways. Senior managers will not be able to gain this requisite knowledge simply by reading a weekly project status report or by attending a monthly project steering meeting. Instead, they need to invest the necessary time to learn about the things that they manage, and they need to actively participate in the development of your system.

3   Your operations and support organization must invest the resources required to understand both your system and the technologies that it uses. Your support staff must take the time to learn the nuances of your system. To do this, they need to work with your system as it is developed, or your team will need to provide them with training. Your operations staff must become proficient with both the installation and operation of your system. The implication is that both your operations and support organizations will need to be actively involved with your project team.

4   Other developers need to work with your team if your system needs to integrate with theirs. For example, perhaps your system needs to access a legacy database, interact with an online system, work with a data file produced by an external system, or provide an XML data extract for other systems. Integration often proves difficult if not impossible without the active participation of these developers: imagine how difficult it would be to access the information contained in a large legacy database if the owners of that database refuse to provide any information about it.

5   Maintenance developers need to work with you to learn your system. When the intention is to either partially or completely hand-off the maintenance of your system to other developers, it is common to bring in software professionals skilled in maintaining and enhancing existing systems to free up members of the original development

team. Your team must work with these people so that they can take over the system from you. Even when some original team members are still involved, an effort must be made to transfer the knowledge to the new members of the team.

Inclusive Modeling With Business Stakeholders

Traditional software developers like to use many arcane terms and techniques, such as conceptual data models or Unified Modeling Language (UML) class models, which business stakeholders typically find too abstract. Currently, an unfortunate trend within the modeling tool community is something called Model Driven Architecture (MDA).[5] MDA promotes the concept that you should use complex modeling tools to capture detailed business and technical models. Although the idea is interesting, tool vendors unfortunately seem to have forgotten that business stakeholders do not understand the detailed models that these tools support. This is a serious problem because your business stakeholders need to understand what it is that you are modeling if they are to provide the right information to you. The end result is that the tool vendors are building tools that are exclusive in nature: only a small minority of highly-skilled modelers are able to use them. The difficulty in using these tools and techniques is that they effectively erect a barrier to communication that puts your project at risk. It does not have to be this way.

The most radical concept presented in this chapter is the idea that business stakeholders can be actively involved in the modeling process. How is this possible? My experience is that you merely need to adopt tools and techniques that business stakeholders can understand, and then work with the stakeholders to give them the skills that they need to be effective.

The most common modeling tool used in modern business today is the whiteboard. Paper is a close second, although it is nowhere near as flexible as the whiteboard because you cannot easily erase portions of your work. Simple tools such as this are inclusive because virtually everyone can use them. When you stop and think about it, upwards to 90% or even 95% of the modeling that you do is done using these sorts of simple tools, it is quite common to see several people standing up at a whiteboard sketching while they are talking, in order to explore a complex issue.

The second success factor is to adopt simple modeling techniques.[6] How many of your business stakeholders are experts at reading the Barker data modeling notation (or any data modeling notation for that matter), UML class modeling notation, or IDEF business process modeling notation? How many of your business stakeholders can even tell you why you would want to consider using such techniques? How many are

Table 8-2: Modeling options.

Modeling Category	Complex Option	Simple Option
Usage modeling	System use case UML use case diagram	Essential use case User story cards Feature
Domain / conceptual modeling	Logical data model (LDM) Object role model (ORM) UML class diagram	Class responsibility collaborator (CRC) cards Robustness diagram

Modeling Category	Complex Option	Simple Option
User interface (UI) modeling	Traditional UI prototype UI flow diagram	Essential UI prototype
Supplementary	Formal specifications in Object Constraint Language (OCL) or Action Semantic Language (ASL)	Specifications (business rules, constraints, technical requirements) written in prose
Process modeling	Data flow diagram (DFD) UML activity diagram Flow chart	Free-form diagram

really interested in using them? With a fair bit of training, business stakeholders could learn to read and maybe even apply a subset of these modeling notations, but do you really want to invest the time to do so? Does it really make sense that you even need to do so? I think not, particularly when you have both options available to you. Table 8-2 lists several modeling options[6] for common categories of modeling that you can use with your business stakeholders. It is interesting to note that each category includes at least one simple modeling technique.

Dealing With The Nay Sayers

A common reaction to the advice presented in this chapter is that it may work for other organizations but that it will not work in yours. You can make it work if you choose to. Here are several common excuses, and the responses to them, which you may hear when people are presented with these ideas.

We don't have the time to be actively involved

Gaining a high-level of stakeholder participation is not easy – your stakeholders very likely have many excuses for why they cannot provide the level of involvement that your project requires to succeed. If your stakeholders' time is better spent doing other things, your best strategy is to cancel your project and invest your resources supporting these far more important activities. My experience is that when senior management is presented with this option, they will often find ways to motivate your project stakeholders to be more involved with the project. The bottom line is that you require active stakeholder participation on your project, and you can get it if you are willing to fight for it.

There's only one way to do this

Many "experienced" IT professionals will tell you that there is only one way to work – you absolutely must create a conceptual data model before continuing with development – yet, as you see in Table 8-2, there are always simple options available to you. You should question anyone who claims there is only one way to do things, because what they are likely saying is that they only know one way to do it. You always have a choice.

We need better documentation

Many people do not want to use simple tools because they are not very good at writing documentation. It is important to recognize that there is nothing wrong with using complex tools in conjunction with simpler tools. Use a whiteboard when you need flexibility and the input of business stakeholders. If you need documentation, capture whiteboard sketches with a drawing tool or take a picture of it with a digital camera (a much faster approach). Use the right tool for the job: simple, inclusive tools with business stakeholders to identify and analyze requirements; and more sophisticated tools for the few models you actually want to keep.

We want to generate software from our models

Once again, use the right tool for the job. It is quite common for skilled developers to capture design information in a computer aided software engineering (CASE) tool such as TogetherCC[7], Optimal[8], or ERWin[9] because these tools will generate code from the models. There is nothing stopping developers from using whiteboards for business-oriented work and CASE tools for technical-oriented work.

Summary

We work in an industry with a 14% success rate, assuming that you define success as projects being delivered on time and on budget. A low success rate such as this tells me that there is room for significant improvement, and a good place to start is to focus on known success factors. Studies have shown that the top two success factors deal with stakeholder participation on your project. Agile software developers follow practices such as XP's *On-Site Customer* or AM's *Active Stakeholder Participation* to help increase their chance of success. It is possible for business stakeholders to be active participants on software projects, as long as you choose to adopt simple tools and techniques that are inclusive in nature.

CHAPTER NINE

The Heightened Importance of Communication

Scott Ambler

Communication is the act of transmitting information between individuals. Communication is key to your success on agile projects, and it is one of the fundamental values of both Extreme Programming (XP)[1] and Agile Modeling (AM).[2] Frankly, it is critical on non-agile projects as well. For agile projects to succeed, the project team must create and then foster a high-communication environment within which to work; otherwise, the chance of failure will rise dramatically. To foster such an environment, you need to understand the fundamentals of communication – fundamentals that are explored within this chapter.

This chapter is adapted from Chapter 8 of *Agile Modeling: Effective Practices for Extreme Programming and The Unified Process* (Wiley Publishing 2002). Used with permission of the author.

In this chapter, we explore three fundamental issues:

- Factors affecting communication

- Communication Modes

- Effective communication

Factors Affecting Communication

Let's begin by exploring the five primary factors that affect communication:

1 **Physical proximity.** The closer people are to one another, the greater the opportunities for communication. At one end of the spectrum, two people can be working side-by-side and at the other end of the spectrum, two people can be in different buildings.

2 **Temporal proximity.** Whether or not two people are working at the same time affects communication. You may be separated from some of your co-workers by several time zones or simply by different personal schedules.

3 **Amicability.** Cockburn believes that amicability, the willingness of someone to hear the thoughts of another person with good will and to speak without malice, is an important success factor. The greater the amicability, the greater the amount and quality of information that can be communicated; also, less will be concealed. Amicability is affected by the trust that people have for one another and the sense of community that they share.

4 **Tools.** Complicated tools often prove to be barriers to communication, particularly software-based tools that are single-user in nature or which require significant training to use. Simple, inclusive tools – including whiteboards, Post-It™ notes, flip charts, and index cards – are easy to work with and are flexible, making them more likely to be

used in team situations. (See Chapter 8 for additional thoughts on this topic.)

5   **Anxiety.** Individuals may experience anxiety about certain types of communication. Some people love to speak on the phone, while others avoid it. Some people prefer email, while others avoid it because their writing skills are not very good. When a group of people are collaborating, they need to find techniques that they are comfortable with, or at a minimum that they can learn to tolerate for the duration of their involvement with each other.

When people work close together, both physically and temporally, there exists an opportunity for osmotic communication: indirect information transfer through overhearing conversations or by noticing things happening around you. Osmotic communication[3] can often be beneficial – you can subconsciously learn valuable information, such as finding out that someone has finished his or her current task, or that something is not working as expected. Osmotic communication can often be harmful too, particularly if another group of people is being rowdy near you, or if you are picking up false rumors.

Communication Modes

In Chapter 5, Alistair Cockburn[2] describes various modes of communication that people may choose to apply when working together. Figure 9-1, copied from that chapter, shows a graph comparing the effectiveness of these modes of communication with the richness of the communication channel employed. The two arcs are interesting: the left-most one lists communications options for documenting (paper includes electronic media such as HTML that could be rendered to paper) and the right-most arch lists communication options for modeling. The relative value of these options is dependent on the situation: perhaps video conversation (video conferencing) is more effective than face-to-face conversation in some situations but the exact opposite in others.

Cockburn contends that the most effective communication is person-to-person, face-to-face, particularly when enhanced by a shared modeling medium such as a whiteboard, flip chart, paper, or index cards. As you move away from this situation, perhaps by removing the shared medium or by no longer being face-to-face, you experience a drop in communication effectiveness. As the richness of your communication channel cools, you lose the conscious and subconscious clues that proximity provides. You also lose the benefit of communicating through techniques such as gestures,

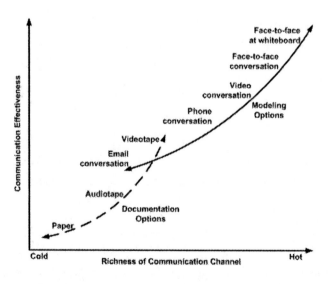

Figure 9-1. Comparing communication modes.

facial expressions, vocal inflection, and timing. Cockburn points out that a speaker may emphasize what they are saying, thus changing the way they are communicating, by speeding up, slowing down, pausing, or changing tones. Finally, the ability to answer questions in real time is important, because questions provide insight into how well the information is being understood by the listener.

What are the implications for your project? First, minimize your reliance on paper-based communication techniques such as status reports, because that is one of the worst ways to communicate. Second, actively strive to make "hot" communication modes, such as face-to-face communication, easy to achieve. The best way to do this is to co-locate your development team with your project stakeholders. This may mean that some people have to move out of their offices for the duration of the project, and it may mean that you need to commandeer a shared workroom as well. Third, recognize that you need to support a variety of communication modes over the length of your project; however, when you are given a choice, you should prefer "hotter" modes because they are more effective.

Effective Communication

Communication is most effective when people are willing to work together to do what it takes to get a job done. This is why AM's principle of *Open and Honest Communication* is important, because if you do not trust the information that you are receiving, or the people who are providing it to you, then your goal of effective communication is lost. AM's principle that *Everyone Can Learn from Everyone Else* is critical to your success, because it defines a mindset that enables communication: someone who believes that he or she can learn something from others is much more receptive than someone who believes otherwise. This principle has its roots in AM's

163

value of *Humility*, a value that proves to be a significant success factor for developers.

Effective communicators realize that the real goal is to share information, and that this information sharing is typically a two-way street. Second, your ability to pick the right mode of communication is critical. As Figure 9-1 implies, whenever you have the opportunity to use a superior form of communication you should choose to do so. For example, don't send someone a diagram via email when you can explain a concept by simply walking them through by sketching at a whiteboard. Third, you need a positive view of documentation. As Chapter 14 shows, documentation can often be versatile and perhaps even simple to create. My fundamental message is that you should write documentation only when it is your best choice and only when it adds the best possible value to your project.

Summary

Effective communication is an enabler of agile software development. It is critical to understand that you have several communication modes available to you and that you want to pick the best communication option for your current situation. Unfortunately, many traditional software methodologies will lean towards "colder" communication modes and inadvertently put project teams at risk. If your project is to succeed, you must foster a high-communication environment for your team, and part of doing so is to actively remove barriers to communication whenever you discover them.

PART THREE

Agile Management Techniques

CHAPTER TEN

Agile Management Techniques

Kevin Aguanno

The agile project management techniques discussed in this book are not new – many have been around for decades, and represent best practices for some types of "traditional" project management. Bringing them all together and packaging them into a single methodology, however, leads to synergies that strengthen the overall approach. For example, short development iterations make customer involvement in development prioritization a much more powerful (and timely) technique for adapting to change. Conversely, frequent customer (re)prioritization makes the iterative development more effective at delivering business value.

Through these synergies, an agile method delivers its true magic – the sum is greater than the individual parts – and can reduce risk, improve quality, shorten timelines, and speed up the return on benefits. (These benefits were discussed in more detail in the introduction to this book.)

Common Agile Techniques

This third section of the book discusses some of the agile management techniques that you can adopt on your own projects. While certain techniques are unique to a particular agile method (such as Extreme Programming's technique of Pair Programming) some are common across most – if not all – agile methods.

Iterative and Incremental Development

The use of iterative and incremental development to structure the work on a project is common to all agile methods. In effect, iterative and incremental development when put together become the primary enabler for most of the other agile techniques we will discuss in this chapter.

While iterative development is common to all agile methods, the use of the technique does not necessarily make a project agile. A number of other techniques must be present before a project can truly be considered *agile*. Some process-heavy methods, such as the full implementation of the Rational Unified Process (RUP) use iterations to organize the development work, yet they are too process-heavy to be considered agile. The RUP tool, however, does have a number of available "agile" plug-ins[1] that customize the method, stripping out (or slimming down) many of the processes so that what remains could be better classified as an agile method.

In Chapter 4 of this book, Pascal Van Cauwenberghe explains in detail the differences between serial (waterfall) development, iterative development, incremental development, and agile development. Refer to his work for details on how to implement iterative and incremental organization techniques on your own development project.

Customer Involvement in Work Planning/ Replanning

One of the interesting characteristics of agile methods is the active participation of a "customer" in frequent, detailed work planning or replanning at the start of each development iteration. What makes this so interesting, is that such close customer influence over the internal workings of the development team has been cited as a major cause of failed projects using traditional methods (often cited as "customer interference"), but is also a major reason why agile methods are so successful. Be warned, however, that this level of customer involvement is a double-edged sword – it can lead to a greater likelihood of meeting the customer's (evolving) requirements, but can also lead to scope creep and blown budgets if not managed well. Agile methods put structure to the management of this close customer involvement such that the likelihood of losing control of the development is minimal.

Concurrent Design/Engineering

Projects that are well-suited to agile methods are development projects where the requirements are either unclear or unstable, or where the design will continually change due to technical uncertainty. If the requirements and design are going to change frequently, then waiting for the "design phase" to end and getting a formal sign off from the project sponsor before proceeding with development will just lead to endless design churn. What is needed is the ability to start development on the portions where the design is reasonably complete, while still working on the design of other portions. In the engineering/ construction world, this practice is called concurrent design or concurrent engineering.

The main benefit here for agile projects, is that it gets the project moving into development mode quickly, and also allows the project still to be very responsive to changing requirements and designs.

169

Feature-Based Design/Planning/Reporting

All agile methods take a feature-based design approach. They may exhibit this approach differently, but underlying their techniques the base approach is still the same. Similarly, agile methods plan their projects around features, not tasks. Finally, agile methods all report progress on feature completion, not on task completion.

Feature-Based Design. In Extreme Programming, feature-based design is handled by capturing feature requirements on note cards (CRC cards,[2] see Figure 10-1). These cards are used as the primary design units. Other processes may use more detailed use cases as their feature-based design approach. Regardless of how this is handled, the basic reason behind the approach is that customers understand (and generally care more about) user-facing features (such as GUI components or reports) while assuming that non-functional requirements (such as security or data search algorithm optimization) should

Class Name:	
Superclasses:	
Subclasses:	
Responsibilities:	Collaborators

Figure 10-1: Extreme Programming uses Class Responsibility Collaborator (CRC) Cards such as this one to record feature requirements and to plan iterations and feature design groupings.

be automatically included in the system. Non-functional requirements are usually noticed when they are absent, but not often thought of in advance by customers. Chapters 11 and 13 deal with the concepts of feature-based design and how they interrelate.

Feature-Based Planning. Once feature-based requirements and design has progressed to a point where there is enough material, you can start your iteration planning. In Scrum, this activity takes place at a Sprint Planning Meeting, where participants review the list of features that need to be built, and prioritize and arrange features into groups that will be built in future iterations. Once features have been assigned to the next iteration, then that iteration can begin, completing the detailed design, development, and testing of the selected features.

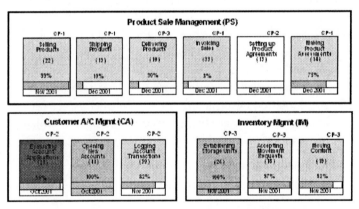

Figure 10-2: A sample status report[3] from the Feature-Driven Development (FDD) method shows one type of feature-based reporting.

Feature-Based Reporting. When status reports are required during or at the end of iterations, feature-based reporting allows you to show progress using an objective measure – the completion of user-facing features. These are features that customers can see for themselves when they examine the end-of-iteration delivered product. No "vapourware" here – features are either complete or they are not. Feature-based reporting leaves no room for "playing with the numbers" to show an arbitrary percentage of completion. Figure 10-2 shows a sample mid-iteration report from the FDD methodology illustrating one way of presenting feature-based status.

Continuous Building/Testing

All agile methods include the concept of continuous testing. Continuous testing allows you to find defects much earlier in the development cycle than waiting for them to emerge when testing is conducted at the very end. Earlier identification means more time to fix defects when it is convenient (most efficient) and more time to fix difficult bugs. Sometimes high-severity defects found late in the testing cycle of a traditional test-at-end method mean significant schedule delays. Continuous testing flushes these defects out earlier, minimizing their impact on the schedule.

To employ this type of testing on your project, you require three main pre-requisites:

- Iterative development,

- Frequent product builds (at a minimum, at end of each iteration; preferably, much more often than that), and

- Automated testing tools (for full regression testing on every build) or many available testers.

172

Empowered Teams

One of the core agile principles[4] is that teams should be empowered to self-organize. This empowerment extends to allowing the teams to choose the processes and tools that they believe will add value to their own objectives and to reject organizational standard processes and tools that do not add value to their project. In practice, such rejection is not always politically possible; however, in cases where organizational standards must be met, teams are given the flexibility to figure out how they will meet the standards in their own way.

Agile Meetings

With the team empowerment of agile methods, long formal meetings are usually the first thing that teams throw out the window. Some agile methods formalize the types of meetings that should still be conducted. In Extreme Programming, these are daily "stand-up" meetings where participants stand around in a circle and share the status of their individual tasks, and to raise any pressing issues. Meetings are kept short by strict time control, avoiding long discussions of issues (these are discussed in separate meetings that follow the main meeting) and by forcing participants to stand so they will not be too comfortable. Scrum uses the same concept, but calls the meetings the "Daily Scrum Meetings."

Frequent face-to-face meetings allow quick exchange of information and the ability to read each others' body language and other non-verbal communications to get at the true messages being conveyed. As Cockburn noted in Chapter 5 and Ambler in Chapter 9, face-to-face meetings allow for high-bandwidth communications between participants. These meetings reduce the risk of misunderstandings and missed interdependencies. Other benefits of agile meetings are discussed by Linda Rising in Chapter 16 in this part of the book.

Agile Contracts

While not truly a common agile technique, contracts need to be written to support the use of agile methods during development work. There are many different ways of approaching agile contracts, each with its own strengths and weaknesses. Agile contracts span the gamut from Time and Materials contracts that place all of the risk on the sponsor, to fixed price contracts that place all of the risk on the vendor. Numerous strategies have been devised for minimizing these risks.[5] Pascal Van Cauwenberghe, in Chapter 12 of this book, explores some of these contracting ideas in more detail.

Conclusion

Using one or more of the abovementioned agile techniques does not automatically give you an "agile" project; however, the use of each technique introduces more and more agility into the project. These techniques allow you to be more responsive to changing requirements, and evolving designs. Additionally, they assist in the attainment of the business case benefits discussed earlier, namely reduced risk, improved quality, shortened timelines, and a quicker return on benefits.

Clearly, each of these techniques should be understood by project managers and be at hand in case they might be of use on a project. Not every technique will necessarily add value on every project, but by understanding the strengths and weaknesses of the techniques, a project manager can decide which techniques to adopt.

CHAPTER ELEVEN

Requirements Documents that Win the Race

Kirstin Kohler
Barbara Paech

Time-constrained projects ask for requirements approaches that are agile: that is, adapted to the project needs and without comprehensive documentation. But how can this be achieved? Our approach provides the steps toward the solution of this question. It supports the identification of the essential content of the requirements document as well as the selection of the appropriate modeling technique. The essential content is determined by conducting a systematic risk analysis, which allows identifying the most important elements of the requirements documentation. For the requirement document to be useful, it must be precise and understandable for all project participants. The appropriate modeling technique is selected by taking the identified content and the context of the project into account. This chapter reports work in progress. It describes the motivation, related work and first ideas.

Introduction

It is well known and widely accepted that a lot of problems in software development are caused by deficiencies in the requirements phase.[20] Nevertheless, a lot of companies lack requirements engineering activities.[17] Especially in projects where time-to-market is critical to success, there is usually not enough time for investments in the requirements engineering process.[16] In order to overcome this resistance against requirements engineering in industrial settings, it is not necessary to invent a new and hopefully better method. Instead, one should focus on making existing methods more attractive.[22] The goal of our work is to make *documentation of requirements* more attractive for time-to-market projects.

Creating and maintaining requirements documents requires substantial effort.[19] This is why it is often neglected, especially when schedules are tight. Whereas Extreme Programming puts the onsite customer on a project, and thereby reduces most kinds of documentation,[5] our experience in industrial projects shows that documentation of requirements is crucial for the transfer of knowledge between stakeholders of the actual project as well as to subsequent development projects. Thus, it cannot be completely disregarded. With our approach, we want to balance the divergent goals of creating good documentation and keeping a tight schedule. Our slogan is "keep the documentation as small as possible but as substantial and useful as needed for the project." Our approach gives advice on how to put this slogan into practice. It supports the following two steps: (1) identify the *essential* part of the documentation, and (2) choose the *appropriate* modeling technique to document them. We reflect the project context[23] in both of these steps, especially in the definition of "*essential*" and "*appropriate*". With our work, we do not invent a new requirements engineering method, but rather provide guidance on how to use existing methods efficiently. So far we have limited the framework according to two dimensions: (1) it supports only documentation of requirements, and (2) it considers only GUI-intensive systems.

Basic steps of the approach

In order to document requirements for time to market projects, it is important to make a trade off between quality and schedule. Gaps or faults in the requirements phase, as a consequence of missing documentation, lead to dissatisfied customers due to quality problems in the end product. In contrast, "high quality" software development including comprehensive documentation takes longer, so customers often choose competing products. The product is of less value due to an unsatisfying market penetration. Narrowing these conflicting dependencies to the scope of requirements documentation means making the tradeoff between no documentation leading to bad quality and complete documentation leading to delayed product delivery. The solution is to keep the documentation as *small* as possible but as *substantial* and *useful* as needed for the project. We accomplish this by supporting the two steps "Identify essential content" (ensures *small* and *substantial)* and "Choose appropriate modeling technique" (ensures *useful).* Figure 11-1 shows the two basic steps of our framework in relationship to the basic ingredients: the project risk, conceptual information model, the project context, and the modeling technique. How these ingredients are integrated in our approach is described in the following subsections, where the steps are elaborated in more detail.

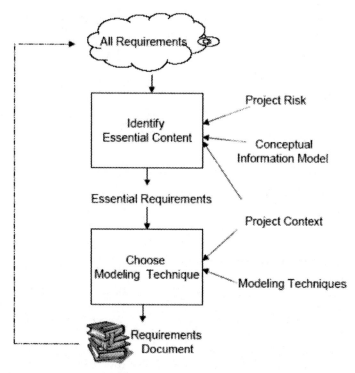

Figure 11-1: Steps and concepts of the approach.

Identify essential content

The basic idea is not to document the complete requirements, but instead concentrate on the most important or essential parts. Finding and separating these essential parts poses a classical filtering problem: separating the requirements that are worth being documented from those that are not critical and need not be documented. In general, a filter separates material or waves according to specific characteristics like grain size or frequency. The materials in our case are the requirements, and we use a conceptual information model to classify the requirements. The filter in our approach separates requirements according to risk. It separates those requirements that are

178

accompanied with a high risk from those that are accompanied with a low risk. The size of the risk (comparable to the size of grains passing the filter) is influenced by the project context. We provide an approach for assessing the risk by considering different risk types, as shown later in this chapter. The next step is to document the requirements; therefore, one has to choose a representation technique.

Choose the appropriate modeling technique.

Requirements documents are a medium of communication and knowledge transfer. In order to gain the most benefit out of them, they have to be precise and understandable for project participants and involved stakeholders (besides other qualities like correctness, consistency, and so on). Choosing the appropriate modeling technique is essential. The modeling technique has to fit to the content that is documented, as well as to the people who will read the document. For example, the navigation of dialogues can be documented by using Constantine's abstract prototypes,[9] whereas the interaction between system and users in terms of function calls might be documented by use cases.[7] Depending on the individual project team members (who might include graphic designers, for example) specification languages like UML might not be suitable. This means that, when deciding about the appropriate modeling language, the content as well as the project context have to be considered in order to make the documentation valuable. Later in this chapter, we will describe how the project context guides the selection of the modeling technique.

The arrow leading back to the start in Figure 11-1 indicates that our approach is not limited to classical waterfall projects wherein all requirements are known at the beginning. The technique should be applied in iterative projects too. It can be applied independent of the process model of the project, and fits at the point where one has roughly understood the requirements (or a subset of them) and has to document them in more detail. Our approach helps to decide which part of these requirements to document and how to document them.

Identify the essential documentation content

We elaborate on the step of identifying the essential documentation content by explaining the three concepts we have built on: the conceptual information model, the project risk, and the project context.

Before filtering the essential requirements, we have to make explicit what we are filtering. What is the totality of requirements we are choosing from? To improve the understanding of a complex subject, physicists and chemists usually introduce models to help with representation. We needed a similar model that allows us to think and argue about requirements, especially in the context of the filtering process. Unfortunately, however, there is not a standard model for GUI-intensive applications comparable to the Parnas' model for embedded systems[19] (at least we are not aware of one after an extensive literature search). Thus, we developed our own conceptual information model for GUI-intensive applications.

Conceptual Information Model

The conceptual information model describes the various elements and abstraction levels for requirements of interactive applications (excluding non-functional requirements). The model is based on Kovitz' understanding[13] that requirements activities lead to design decisions. During the requirements phase, decisions about the effect generated by the software to be developed are made. For interactive applications we identified 12 types of these "design decisions" (see Figure 11-2).

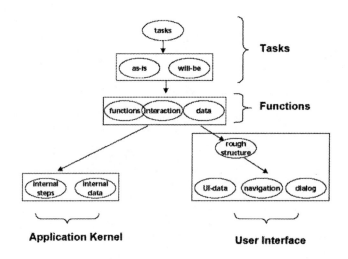

Figure 11-2: Conceptual information model consisting of *12 types of design decisions.*

These can be categorized into 4 groups (decisions about tasks to be supported by the software, decisions about functions implemented by the software, decisions about the application kernel, and decisions about the user interface). Each of these groups is on a different abstraction level. For the sake of brevity, we will not go in the details of this model, but rather we will refer the reader to Kohler and Paech.[11] The elements of the model allow us to argue on a conceptual level about different types of requirements. Therefore, one can explicitly name which type of the requirements should or need not be documented. As a simple example, if a new interface for an existing legacy system has to be implemented, it is important to specify the dialogs and navigation of the user interface, whereas the documentation of the application kernel requirements is less important.

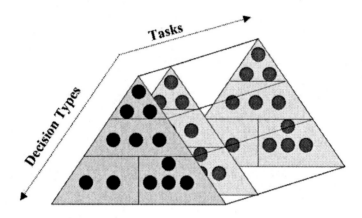

Figure 11-3: Set of task trees. Dots indicate the design decisions of Figure 11-2.

The 12 elements in this model form a tree, in the sense that the elements of lower levels depend on the decisions made before. The decision to support "the task of book ordering" leads to specific dialogs and functions like a "dialog to confirm selection" and "a function to calculate invoice." The tasks span a tree of dependent decisions. The set of all "tasks" to be supported builds a set of trees as illustrated in Figure 11-3. Each triangle in the picture represents one "task tree". This does not mean that the decision to document a lower level requirement implies that the corresponding higher-level requirement must be documented. It must only be clear which tasks a specific functional requirement belongs to.

It is so far an open question of how to identify the essential tasks, and which ones should be documented at all.

Now we come back to the filtering process. Similar to testing of time-constrained projects,[3] we use the concept of risk analysis to guide the selection of the essential requirements.

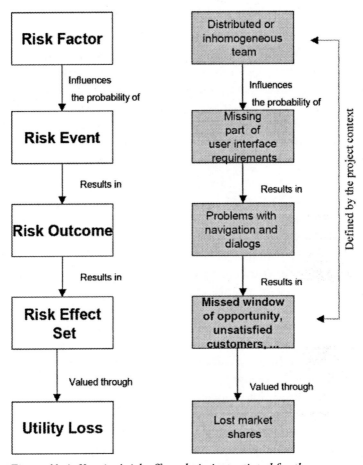

Figure 11-4: Kontios' risk effect chain instantiated for the
requirements documentation.

Risk

We define risk as the possibility of suffering a loss.[10] This means that to asses the risk, we have to know the probability and the loss linked with the risk. We base our risk analysis on a method introduced by Kontios[12] who defined an effect chain consisting of risk factor, risk event, risk outcome, risk effect, and utility loss (see Figure 11-4, left side). Without going into the details of Kontios' method, we explain the elements in the context of the requirements documentation (see Figure 11-4, right side).

The risk event in our example is the missing documentation of requirements concerning the user interface (the design decisions we explicitly decide not to document). Missing documentation of user interface requirements can cause misunderstandings, which lead to wrong, superfluous, or missing navigation and dialogs in the software (risk outcomes). To judge the extent of the risk event and outcome, one has to investigate which risk factors make the event likely (for example, on a distributed team, the probability[24] to cause a misunderstanding due to missing documentation is high) and which risk effects cause a high damage (for example, a late product delivery due to superfluous functionality that might result in a missed window of opportunity and a loss of market share). The project context is essential for both of these questions. The project context defines the risk factors and therefore the probability that the risk event happens. And the project goals that are also defined through the context define the risk effects caused by the risk (the utility loss). Therefore, the risk analysis can be reduced to the questions:

- What factors of the project context increase the probability of a misunderstanding?

- What project goals increase the utility loss caused by a misunderstanding?

The reflections about risk can be transferred to our conceptual information model. For each of the 12 elements of the model one has to consider which context factors enlarge the risk that a missing requirement of this type leads to a misunderstanding. But before this can be done, we have to define how to describe the context. How can one be sure to consider all relevant factors?

Project context

The problem of context description gained importance within the last years in the domain of knowledge engineering, and constructing experience factories for software projects.[4] But due to the fact that this is a young research community, and the relevant factors pretty much depend on the usage of the packaged experience, there is no silver bullet of context description. We used a scheme proposed by Birk[6] and adapted it to our needs in requirement engineering. Table 11-1 contains all factors to consider for a project characterization.

With the information model, the risk analysis, and the attributes of a project context description, we have now all tools at hand to support the filtering of essential requirements. A risk analysis of a given project can be conducted by combining the elements of our information model with the various attributes of the project context. For each project attribute, one has to determine the effect and the probability of a misunderstanding caused by missing documentation.

Our approach supports practitioners not only by guiding them to the risk analysis. In addition, we provide a set of heuristics. By conducting the risk analysis on a generic level (without considering a specific project context) and limited to the four main groups of elements in our information model (tasks, system functions, application kernel, user interface) we identified generic heuristics for the selection of documentation content. They are listed in Table 11-2.

185

Table 11-1: Attributes for the context description.

Attribute	Example
Stakeholders	
Number	Number of people in the development team
Experience	Experience in OO technologies
Roles	Requirements engineer, user interface developer, graphic designer, etc.
Customer	Development for customer X
Suppliers	Usage of COTS products
Distribution of stakeholders	Requirements engineers and developers at the same location, or a distributed development team
Availability of stakeholders	People that developed the former product version left the company. User access.
Product	
Application domain	Web system, embedded system
Lifecycle & history	Reimplementation of an existing product. Maintenance.
Type of product	Consumer product
System size	20 components. 100 KLOC.
Lifetime of the product	The product has to be supported until the end of 2010
Architecture	Client/Server architecture

Attribute	Example
Goals	
Product quality goal	Reliability is more important than usability
Business goals	Time-to-market is more important than usability
Process/Technology	
Development process	Iterative development. RUP.
Techniques	Onsite customer interviews for elicitation of requirements. Prototyping of user interfaces.
Tools	DOORS to manage requirements
Standards	Documentation of requirements according to standard IEEE 1233-1998
Weighting of activities	30% of the total development effort is spent on the requirements phase
Duration of the project	The development of the project will be finished within one year
Work products	Test cases have to be documented

Table 11-2: Heuristics for the risk effect chain.

Risk Event	Risk Factor That Enlarges The Probability	Risk Effect That Enlarges the Damage
Missing documentation of **tasks**	**Lifecycle and History:** Big changes from "as-is" to "to-be" tasks. **Type of Product:** Consumer product with a large variety of different users. Complex user tasks to be supported by the software.	**Business Goals:** Tasks to be supported by the software are critical to the business' success.
Missing documentation of **functions**	**Suppliers:** Parts of the system have to be built by COTS products. Evaluation of COTS products is based upon system functions.	**Business Goal:** Time-to-market is important and forces us to buy COTS products to hit a window of opportunity.
Missing documentation of **application kernel**	**Experience:** Developers are not experienced in the algorithms.	**Product Quality Goal:** The accuracy of the product has to be improved to increase market share.

Risk Event	Risk Factor That Enlarges The Probability	Risk Effect That Enlarges the Damage
Missing documentation of **user interface**	**Lifecycle and History:** No experience of how users will react since this is a new development	**Product Quality Goal:** Usability of the product is required due to mass production and associated high support costs otherwise. **Business Goals:** Usability is important to reduce costs for training and support.

The left hand column lists the risk event. We listed one risk event for each decision type: tasks, function, application kernel, user interface. The second column contains context attributes (risk factors) that enlarge the probability of the risk event. For example, a big change from "as-is" to "to-be" tasks (risk factor) will increase the probability that a missing documentation of tasks causes damage is high.

The right column contains risk effects and their related product and business goals (given by the project context). They define the size of the damage caused by the risk. For example, if time is critical for the business success of the company (risk effect) damage caused by the risk event "missing documentation of tasks" is high. If, for a given project, more than one attribute in a row matches, the risk of omitting this type of requirements in the documentation is high. If either

189

the risk factor or the risk effect is high, the situation has to be judged individually. In that case, Table 11-2 gives a hint for a potential risk.

Our tables help in executing the risk analysis; however, this risk analysis still requires some extra effort. The identification of essential requirements is necessary for project managers to focus development efforts. We strongly believe that an explicit risk analysis is the best compromise between "all or nothing."

Choose the appropriate modeling technique

After having decided what to document, it is now a question of how to document. There is a large variety of modeling techniques available, ranging from natural language to formal languages like Z.[18] One has to choose the modeling technique that fits best for representing the requirements. It has to fit the content that is documented, as well as to the people who will read the document.

During the last few years, a variety of methodologies have emerged that aim to guide the selection of technologies or methods:

- ACRE[15] is a framework containing 12 methods for requirements acquisition that are judged by the authors according to their suitability in different projects. The framework is limited to the 12 methods, and does not cover modeling techniques for documentation. Furthermore, there is a limited number of project characteristics covered by the framework; for example, the characteristics do not consider the needs of specific applications like interactive or embedded systems.

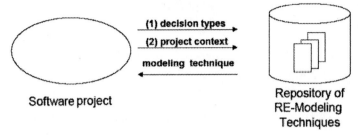

Figure 11-5: A repository of requirements engineering techniques for the selection of the appropriate modeling technique.

- As part of the PROFES project[6] the concept of PPDs (Product-Process-Dependency-Models) was developed. PPDs describe the impact of a specific technology (like inspections) on a specific product quality goal (like reliability) when applied to a certain process. PPDs also contain a description of the context. Although this approach seems to be very promising, it is very generic because it is suitable for all kinds of software engineering techniques and not especially tailored for our purpose of requirements documentation.

- In *Agile Software Development*, Cockburn brought up the concept of the Crystal Family.[8] He proposes to choose the appropriate development approach dependent on the three characteristics: number of people, criticality of the software, and project priority. We believe that this approach does not consider enough project characteristics.

We propose a two-fold approach for the selection of the appropriate modeling language. As illustrated in Figure 11-5, we assume the existence of a repository containing a characterization and description of all available requirements engineering modeling techniques. By specifying the essential content in terms of its design decision types, and by specifying the project context, the appropriate modeling technique can be determined. We will elaborate on this by referring to the underlying concepts: the decision types, and the project context description:

- By defining the essential content, one already has selected a subset of **decision types**, as defined in the conceptual information model. The type of decisions determines a subset of suitable modeling techniques because not every modeling technique is suitable to describe all types of design decisions. Kohler and Paech[11] provide a tabular overview of models used in common processes, like RUP[2] or Usage Centered Design,[9] to document design decision types. Typically, after this selection process, there is still more than one modeling technique left to choose from. Figure 11-6 illustrates this with an example. Based on the decision type "user interface," three techniques (use-cases, storyboards, and abstract prototypes) are selected by function S1, which represents the selection based on the decision type.

- To further narrow down the appropriate modeling technique, the **project context** should then be considered. The output of function S1, together with the project context, are inputs for a second selection function, S2. In S2, for each of the specified techniques, the project context attributes are compared to the attributes of the technique description. The technique with the best match is the result of this final selection mechanism. In the example of Figure 11-6, the project is characterized by a distributed team consisting of software engineers. Therefore, use cases are selected as an appropriate modeling technique. Storyboards require special drawing skills and are more difficult to exchange and discuss between different development sites.

The context attributes describing the stakeholders and the process and technology (compare with Table 11-1) support this part of the selection process. Most important of these context attributes are the stakeholders. Their experience with special modeling techniques and their individual roles (testers, graphic designers, etc.) have a very high impact on the acceptance of the modeling technique. This is supported by empirical findings from McPhee and Eberlein[14] who showed that the usefulness of requirements engineering techniques is correlated with the familiarity of stakeholders with that technique. In addition other "non-requirements engineering" tools and techniques that are already established in the process may influence the selection process. For example, if UML class diagrams are in use to document the systems design, one should also use them to document the input/output data of the user interface.

So far, our approach of choosing the appropriate modeling technique consists of initial concepts. This is especially true when considering the relationship between context attributes and the selection of the modeling technique. This challenge needs further investigation.

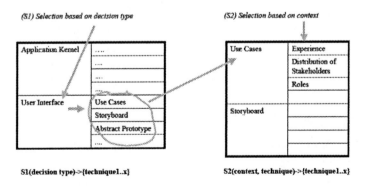

Figure 11-6: Selection of the modeling technique based on decision type and context.

Summary and Future Work

Our approach fits the recommendations for documentation of agile software development given by Cockburn[8] who states "Don't ask for requirements to be perfect" and "Capture just enough." Whereas Cockburn does not give any advice for how to find out what is "enough," we give concrete guidance on the selection process of critical elements. In addition, it substantiates the demand for adaptiveness as postulated by the agile community.[1] In that sense, we make the "agile requirements process" more concrete. Therefore, we built our approach on two practices: the systematic consideration of risk, and the consideration of the project context to drive the documentation in time-constraint projects.

So far, we have provided the skeleton that is now ready to be fleshed out with more details to guide practitioners in their requirements engineering processes. Our future work will concentrate on the following topics:

- We want to validate the context attributes through expert interviews, similarly to Vegas[21] who validated a characterization schema for testing techniques. By doing this, we will further adapt our characterization scheme for the needs of requirements engineering.

- We want to provide more heuristics similar to those listed in Table 11-2. They should not only support the risk analysis for the selection of decision types, but also for the selection of a subset of task trees as illustrated in Figure 11-3 to determine which tasks must be documented and which can be omitted.

- During future projects, by collecting empirical data to investigate the dependency between project context characterization, the selection of the content, and the selection of a modeling language. We want to better understand the relationship between context attributes and the choices that have to be made based on these attributes. Knowing these dependencies would be a first step to automatically support the selection process.

- And of course we want to evaluate the complete approach to empirically prove, that our approach is beneficial for the requirements phase of time-constrained projects.

CHAPTER TWELVE

Succeeding with Agile Fixed Price Contracts

Pascal Van Cauwenberghe

When I talk about Agile Software Development methods[1] and Extreme Programming,[2] the remark I get most often is "That will never work!" The only reply I can give is "It works for me." The second-most often heard remark is "I can't do that, I have to do fixed-price contracts!"

Projects start with the first customer contact through to sales, project execution, delivery, after-care and ... the next project. Everything you do for the customer—everyone who works on the project—must work together as an integrated whole.

I will describe my approach and techniques here. All of these techniques have been applied on successful fixed-price projects. How do I know they were successful? Because, given the choice, everyone involved would do the next project the same way.

A fixed price contract

A fixed-price contract between a vendor (me) and a customer defines the scope, features, planning, timing, deliverables and price of a project. Pretty much everything is fixed.

Why do customers so often demand these fixed-price contracts? There are many good reasons:

- Customers need to know scope, timing and price to choose between bids in a multi-provider bidding process.

- Customers think that they take no functional risk: if the vendor does not deliver what was agreed, the customer can always refuse to pay, or even sue! Of course, if the customer really needs the deliverables on the given date, then suing does not solve their troubles.

- Customers think they take no financial risk, as the fixed price is known at the project start. However, many "fixed price" projects cost more than initially agreed upon. We'll see later how this can happen.

- Customers prefer a defined, planned and sequential project flow that gives them a warm, safe feeling of control—that is, until near the end of the project, when these projects so often "suddenly" start to fail.

Fixed price contracts seem to protect the customer at the expense of the vendor. This type of contract is almost universally hated and feared by custom software vendors because of their high financial and functional risk and their low success rates. According to the "Standish Group Chaos report,"[3] 72% of IT projects fail to deliver what was originally specified, in the agreed time and budget.

Do I have what it takes?

What does it take to be the successful project manager of such a project? I will enter into a fixed price contract only if

- **I know the domain of the application.** If I have worked in this domain, I am more likely to understand my customer and know the most likely functional risks. I will be able to assist my customer in drawing up and evaluating the requirements of the system.

- **I know the technology.** I am not going to experiment with new or "cutting edge" technologies on this project. We will only use tried and true technology that my team knows well.

- **I know the team.** Team performance depends for a part on the talent and experience of its members. Performance depends a lot more on how well these people work together. I need a *team*, not just a bunch of people brought together for this project. It takes time to build a team. When I introduce new people into a team, I always have at least two experienced team members for every newcomer. Pair programming is an excellent technique to get new team members up to speed quickly.[4]

- **I have done projects of this size before.** Multi-year projects are different from multi-month projects. Managing a large team is different from managing a few developers.

I am willing to do fixed price projects only if the project is in line with my experience, where I have a lot of risks under control, and there are as few unknowns as possible. That leaves plenty of risks and unknowns to provide me with a full working day.

Don't just respond to RFPs

Customers often look for a provider for a fixed-price project by sending out a "Request For Proposal" document. The RFP contains a description of a problem to be solved. Providers who wish to implement a solution, have to respond with a written proposal containing a specification, timing, planning and price. The customer then chooses the provider with the best proposal, according to their own criteria.

It all sounds very simple and logical; however, this customer has, possibly, been helped to write this document by one of my competitors. As a result, RFPs, which should be open-ended, typically have a specific solution in mind: my competitor's solution. And, in any case, these RFPs are always incomplete. Just responding with a proposal document is not very likely to win me the deal. Even worse: I might win the deal, but if I base my specification, planning and estimate upon this biased and incomplete RFP, my project will most likely fail.

Michael Bosworth's "Solution Selling"[5] tells you how to sell projects in such a way as to set you up for success. I go and talk to the customer, ask questions, get some more information, get the answers that are not in the document, establish a rapport, and try to steer them away from the solutions already envisioned with my competitor during the drafting of the RFP ("re-engineering the vision" as Bosworth calls it).

If the customer will not talk to me, answer my questions or clarify their wishes now, I do not make a proposal. I do not have enough information to work on. Even if I could win the project, how likely is it that we will communicate better during the project?

It works both ways

A fixed-price contract is a contract between two parties for their mutual benefit. Both parties have rights and responsibilities and these must be divided fairly between the two parties. If I feel that both of the parties are not being treated fairly, I do not enter into the contract.

More important than the contract is the working relationship of the customer and the vendor:

• Is there a good level of communication?

• Do both parties trust each other?

• Are both parties willing to perform their part of the job?

• Does everyone realize the commitment they are making? Do both parties have the necessary time, knowledge and authority to do their job well?

• Is there a willingness to solve the problems that will inevitably arise?

• Is everyone committed to making a success of this project?

One of the most important tasks during the sales process is to set up this working relationship. If you fail to do that, you've just added a huge risk to your project.

• **Test your mutual understanding.** Ask for feedback to verify that you are communicating well. E.g. "I understand that you require capability X. Did I understand that correctly?"

• **Test commitment and keeping of promises.** Agree on "mini-deadlines" during the sales process, where each party needs to perform some action or provide some information. See if you can easily come to an agreement. See if everyone keeps their commitments.

Real business requirements

I write the specification together with the customer. If they do not have enough time to discuss, review and improve the specification, I do not bid for the project: if the project is not important enough to specify and plan well, it is not important enough to implement.

Each item of the specification, each feature (or use case or user story) must comply with the following criteria:

- The description of the feature must be fully understood by the customer and by the development team. The description uses a vocabulary that is familiar to the customer, no technical *mumbo-jumbo*!

- The feature must add some business value. The customers must understand why this feature is included, what value it will provide.

- The feature must be verifiable by the customer. At some point I have to ask the customer "Is this requirement met? Yes or no?" If we have defined the acceptance criteria beforehand, I can be confident that I will get a "Yes".

I leave the technical details out of the customer's specification, as they are only used within the development team.

Requirements as stories. Don't sweat the details

I do not specify each requirement in great detail. Do I need all of these details to estimate and plan correctly? Not always.

For example, this requirement is from the planning of a fixed-price project: "The user can view 5 types of reports about orders. These are shown in a separate browser window.

Cost 10 points. The customer shall specify the parameters, layout and data to be shown before <the latest date that implementation of this feature must start>."

How do I know five types of reports is enough? Usually, projects in this domain require about five different reports. How do I know it will cost ten points, if I do not even know the parameters, layout, data or queries? I know the kinds of reports that are useful in this domain and I have implemented them several times before. From previous projects I know that it typically takes around 8-10 points to complete these reports. What do we gain by this technique?

- The specification becomes smaller, easier to write, easier to understand and verify by the customer.

- As there is less work to do on the specification, we can get on to the implementation part earlier, and thereby deliver value sooner.

- The customer can delay decisions. At that time they will know more about the project, and will be able to specify more precisely what they need.

This technique only works under the following conditions:

- I have a pretty good idea of what is required without all the supporting details

- I have a constructive, trusting relationship with the customer. I must trust that they will complete the requirements in time and not make unreasonable requests. I must trust that there will be no problems when it comes to accepting the implementation based on this incomplete specification. The customer must trust me to implement this requirement following the spirit of the contract, not just following the contract to the letter.

- I have a Project Buffer to handle unforeseen problems. For example, they might really require six reports, or the queries are unusually complex.

This is the same technique as "User Stories" in Extreme Programming, where requirements are detailed when and if the details are needed.

Estimating

One of the most risky tasks of the whole project is the estimation of the required effort to implement the project. Estimate too low and you lose money. Estimate too high and you lose the sale. How can I estimate the "right amount" of effort to balance the likelihood of winning the project versus the risk of losing money?

It is very simple. If I have done similar projects, of similar size, with the same team and the same technology, I know how much effort those have required and how much functionality my team can deliver per month.

I use the "Extreme Programming" estimating technique explained in the "XP Game:"[6]

- Divide the requirements into features

- Give each feature a score between 1 (easy) and 6 (complex) points. Do this by comparing the feature with features in previous projects.

- Make sure the feature scores are consistent.

- Add up all the scores. You now know how many "points" of effort you need to implement the whole project.

From previous projects, you know how many "points" your team (with this technology, in this domain) can implement (on average) per month and you know the deviation.

For example, I know my team can implement 18 +/- 2 points per month (of 20 working days). That's my team's "velocity."[2] I also know that all the features add up to 70 points. Therefore,

- On average, we will be done in (70/18)*20 = 77.5 working days

- Worst case, we will be done in (70/16)*20 = 87.5 working days

- Best case, we will be done in (70/20)*20 = 70 working days

Let the customer order the requirements

I have this long list of features in the specification. But in what order do I implement the features? I let the customer decide.

When the customer and I lay out the project plan, the customer gets to choose the order. It is a simple process. First, you implement the crucial features. Just ask the customer "which one is the most important of them all?" This one goes first. Then implement the next most crucial requirement, and so on. Once all of the crucial requirements are implemented, start on the *important* requirements. How does the customer choose? By comparing the value each requirement will bring. It is usually possible to compare two requirements and decide which one is more important.

Can I always implement stuff in the order that the customer chooses? How do I handle any dependencies, requirements that have to be handled first to reduce risk, or dependencies between requirements? These sequential links should not be many if we have really tried to keep each feature independent from the others. In the few cases where there are dependencies or risks, we can increase a feature's priority and adjust the planning accordingly.

There are several advantages to this technique:

- We reduce the risk because the least important requirements are tackled near the end of the project, where there is the most schedule pressure.

- The customer can give feedback on the most important features first, at the time when there is the most leverage.

- The customer sees value being added to the system from the early stages of the project. The customer might even be tempted to use the system before it is finished, thereby learning to handle incremental delivery.

This technique is also used in the Extreme Programming "Planning Game"[2] and SCRUM's "Product backlog." [7]

Planning

Use a project buffer to plan

I have to admit that I cannot specify, estimate, plan and execute a project perfectly, and I know I will make mistakes before and during the project. There are factors related to the customer that cannot be controlled, such as how well will the customer respects commitments, how well have needs been specified, and how high the odds are that the requirements will change? There are also "forces of nature" that I have no control over: people will get sick, computers will throw tantrums, and other jobs will need to be done urgently.

All of these foreseen events, and many more unforeseen ones, are the "risks" of the project. I try to enumerate and quantify the risks, the odds of their happening, and the cost of avoiding or mitigating them. And then I add some more for unforeseen risks.

"Critical Chain" planning[8] explains how you use optimistic estimates to plan and put the difference between optimistic and safe estimates in a global project buffer. People mis-estimate effort. For the Critical Chain planning method, this is a feature, not a bug. When we underestimate effort, we take some days out of the buffer. When we overestimate, we put some days back in to the buffer. In the end, a lot of our mistakes cancel each other out.

Many small projects are better than one big project

It is a well-known fact that project success rates are higher for small projects than for big ones.[3] Small projects are easier to oversee, require fewer people, handle fewer requirements, have smaller estimation errors, and lead to tangible results faster. I prefer smaller projects, lasting a few months, requiring only a handful of people. But what if my customer has a really big need? Do I need to take on that extra risk that a big project brings?

When facing what appears to be a big project, I always try to reduce the size of the project to a level with which I am comfortable. Does the customer really need all of those requirements? We must prioritize the requirements: what is crucial, what is important, what is nice to have? If we just meet the crucial requirements, could the customer use the product? If not, what do we need to add? What would be good enough for a first, useful release?

Often, customers are surprised when I do this; however, there are many advantages for them:

- Project cost is reduced if we can drop or postpone some features

- Users get the software earlier than expected

- Project risk is reduced as we work on fewer requirements and concentrate on the high value features

- Customers can evaluate the outcome of the project sooner

- Customers can delay their decision about dropping requirements from the first release. Closer to the release date, the customers will have more information with which to make a better decision. This allows the customer to "Decide Later."[9]

As a vendor, I realize some advantages too:

- My risk is reduced, as I have to estimate and handle fewer requirements, get feedback sooner and have a smaller team.

- I can prove myself and gain the trust of the customer by delivering something worthwhile. Most of the tips in this text rely on a constructive, open and trusting working relationship with my customer. A first small, successful project is the perfect way of earning that trust and building that relationship.

- If the project fails, both parties' loss is small.

When breaking a project into smaller projects, it is imporant to remember that I do not want projects that are too small, either. Projects of only a few days are very hard to get right, as there is no room for compensating for missed estimates or problems.

Put dropped requirements into a follow-up project

Dropping lower-priority requirements to a future project phase seems too good to be true. What if the requirements that were dropped were crucial to the project? What if they were useful?

If the dropped requirements were really crucial or useful, the customer will just have to define a follow-up project to implement these features. This is a new project, with a new specification, new planning (we can reuse the estimates of the features that were dropped), and a new contract. I can start this follow-on project as soon as the current project is complete.

Why push new requirements to a new project rather than accept them as changes to the current project? Customers get the same features; vendors bill the same amount. These are a number of reasons:

- When implementing the additional requirements on the current project through change requests, we have one project that is late and over budget. With "exchange requests," where we exchange features with a new follow-on project, we have two projects that are on budget and on schedule. I know which project I would rather be managing.

- Unless really crucial requirements have been dropped, the customer can use the software on the date planned.

- Usually, the customer will learn that some of the original requirements were not really crucial and can be dropped altogether after the exchange. Projects are often shorter and less costly with exchange requests than with change requests.

Let the customer use the software before the follow-up project

After the first project, if there are no crucial requirements left to implement, just some useful or "nice to have" requirements, I advise customers to use the software before defining a follow-up project. They will get lots of useful feedback, which will allow them to define a far better follow-up project. Then, they can add and drop requirements based upon actual use. They will have learned what works and what doesn't.

Warning: The Money Trap

What is the "Money Trap?" Simply put, "Money received now is worth more than money received later."

Breaking the project into several small projects, and letting the customer use the software before starting the next project, delays the implementation of some project features, thereby delaying a vendor's ability to charge the customer for implementing those features. For example, if the customer delays a follow-up project by six months to use the software, a vendor will be worse off, because its income has been delayed for six months. Even worse, the customer might realize that the follow-up project is not really needed. Forget *that* income!

For customers, it is all good: they get to change the specification, they get to drop requirements that are discovered to be unimportant, they can postpone decisions until they have more knowledge and experience, they never pay more than necessary, and projects are never late. All of this makes for happy customers. Happy customers have a habit of awarding projects to vendors who make them happy. Forget the small loss you make now, invest in a long-term relationship with your customer.

In my experience, the customer often gets lots of useful ideas for improvement and extension by using the software.

Thus, the follow-up project is sometimes larger than it would have been if they had not used the software first. So, in the long run, I earn more. Investing in quality and in your relationship with the customer pays off, if you can afford the initial investment.

Don't allow change requests!

Change Requests are a well-known tool used by most project managers. If a customer wants something that is not in the original specification, a project manager can fill in a "Change Request Form" that describes the change. Based on the information in this form, the vendor's project manager can estimate the extra work and cost required. If the customer agrees with the estimate, the extra time is added to the planning, the extra work is performed, and the cost of this work is added to the final bill.

Change requests have some advantages:

- They allow customers to steer the scope of the project, using the knowledge they have gained during the project, and to correct any mistakes made during the initial specification phase.

- Vendors get to bill more than budgeted, which makes the vendor's CEO and CFO happy.

But, there are many drawbacks:

- Changes disrupt the orderly flow of a project, making the development team less efficient. Team members get demoralized when feature lists and planning are in a state of flux and completion dates slip.

- Change requests make it more difficult to schedule and synchronize with other projects, as there is no way to predict when this project will be finished.

- The disputes preceding the change request ("It's in the spec! No, it's not! Yes, it is…"), and the haggling over estimates and extra cost, poison the relation of the vendor with the customer. All of this nasty commercial negotiation stuff should have been finished before the project started.

- Change requests invariably lead to dissatisfaction of the customer as the budget and timing creep upwards. How does a project get to be late and over budget? One change request at a time. Welcome to the "challenged projects" category!

The problem with change requests is that their negative effects only show up after a delay. Responsibility for the project at the customer side is typically shared between a project manager (with authority over functional matters) and the finance manager (with authority over budgets). The project manager agrees with every small change request and is happy to see more functionality added. The finance manager only sees a large budget overrun at the end of the billing period. The end users only see that the product is not delivered on time. By the time the negative effects appear, it is too late to do anything about it. And so, a lot of yelling and recriminations ensue, which makes everybody unhappy.

Use Exchange Requests instead

It is clearly not possible to always prepare perfect specifications before the start of a project: we make mistakes, we forget things, and we learn during projects, and the business environment changes. How can we be agile and react to changing circumstances, yet keep to our agreement?

I work like this: each time a customer and I need to change a specification, we make a Change Request and estimate the required effort and cost. When approving the change request and estimate, the customer can add the new features to the project only if they first remove unimplemented functionality requiring at least the same effort. For example, the customer can add feature X (cost 5 points) if they first remove features A (cost 3 points) and B (cost 2 points).

What are the advantages of this technique?

- We keep the budget and timing constant. The development team and the customer have the satisfaction of finishing a job on time, on budget.

- We are able to change the specifications flexibly to deliver what the customer needs, not necessarily what was requested. If we have revised the specifications, then the new features were more valuable than the old ones, or the customer would not have swapped them in. This means we deliver something that is at least as valuable as what was agreed upon.

- We put more thought into changes to the specification. The customer has to think very carefully if the new feature is really worth more than the features being taken out; therefore, we expect fewer, but more useful, changes to the project.

- We shorten the feedback loop between functional changes and their effects upon budget and timing, so that they are immediately visible. The customer project manager becomes more responsible for budget and timing.

I call this procedure an "Exchange Request." It sounds so much like like "Change Request" that most customers do not notice the difference.

Simple, honest and correct tracking

During the course of a project, I need to track my team's progress. Are we behind or ahead of schedule? Will we be able to deliver as promised? Do we need to take some corrective action? It all sounds very complicated and time-consuming. There are all of these wonderful, expensive and complicated tools I can use. Do I really spend a lot of time tracking? Of course not. The team and the customer only need to know two things:

- Will we be able to deliver as promised?
- If not, what can we do to get back on track?

A simple and effective method is to have a "burndown chart" or "backlog chart."[8] This essentially plots the amount of effort left versus time. Each time a feature is finished, we reduce

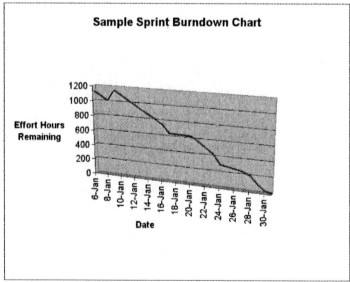

Figure 12-1: A sample Sprint Burndown Chart as seen at the end of a project.

the "amount of effort left" by the effort estimated for that feature. Each time the customer accepts a feature, we reduce the "amount to test". With this method, we can easily see how we are doing. This chart is easily updated and should be visible to all project participants, as an "information radiator."[10] If anyone asks "Are we there yet?" they just have to look at the chart. (See Figure 12-1.)

It is important to only count fully completed, tested and "ready for acceptance" features. This keeps me from deluding myself with statements like "the feature is 80% finished". A feature is either done (acceptable or accepted for the customer) or not done. This guarantees that the tracking represents real progress.

The plan is just a plan; the truly important thing is the delivery of the project. I do not care about deviations, as long as the goal of delivering is not jeopardized. For example, if I have two features, each estimated at five days, I do not worry if one takes four days and the other takes six days. Sure, I did not follow the plan, but I am still on target to deliver as planned.

As long as the actuals remain within acceptable tolerance levels, there is no need to act. As soon as the actuals reach the limit, I will start to plan ways to bring the project back on track. When the actuals exceed the tolerance limit, it is time to act. Critical Chain uses a similar method (do nothing-plan-act) when the project buffer is consumed 1/3 (plan) and 2/3 (act).

Do not shield the team

Some people think the project manager should shield the team from every outside influence that might impede their progress. For example, I have often heard that "developers should not talk to the customer, lest they (both) get confused." On the contrary, involve the team in discussions with the customer about functionality, allowing them to avoid and mitigate risks and to solve problems. The job of the project manager is not to solve all problems and shield the team, but to ensure that the problems get solved.

Do not shield the team. Help them to avoid and to solve problems.

Being the onsite customer

Extreme Programming mandates an "onsite customer," someone who is available full-time and has the authority and knowledge to make decisions about functionality and priorities. For the development team, this is an ideal situation: they only have to deal with one person, they can clarify any requirement when needed, and they can ask for business decisions to be made quickly.

How often do I get a representative from the customer organization to act as an "onsite customer?" Sadly, not very often. But when it happens, the development team can work a lot faster.

In most cases, I will have to act as the onsite customer. I know the domain, I have the experience and I have gained a lot of information about the customer organization during the sales and specification process. I expect to be able to answer most of the developers' questions. I have already prioritized the requirements with the customer, so that should not be a problem. I expect to be able to take many decisions, as I have negotiated most of these issues with the customer beforehand. And if I am unable to answer the question or make a decision, I can always ask the real customer.

Thus, we get a situation where both the developers and the customer can work effectively:

- The specification does not have to be very detailed, and thus it is easier to create and to understand.

- Most of the team's questions get answered quickly. Most of the decisions are made quickly. Few are deferred.

- The customer does not have to be available all the time, but the customer does have to be available regularly to answer my questions or make some decisions.

The most important thing is to know when I do not know the answer or cannot make a decision. Better to take some time deferring to the customer than losing the team's time by sending them down the wrong path.

Frequent releases, incremental delivery

When working on software development projects, I like to release the software often. Typically, the software will be released once per week to the customer, as agreed during the sales process. The team gives a demonstration of the new features, then the customer uses these releases to do acceptance testing. The customer then gives feedback within a defined delay; the team acts upon this feedback before implementing new features. What are the advantages of releasing so often?

- The development team gets the hang of releasing the software, with all the messy stuff related to installation, database upgrades, and backward compatibility.

- The development team focuses on delivering high quality complete features. Each time the customer accepts a feature, the team gets a little buzz of satisfaction.

- The customer can test and accept features incrementally. Each week, some new features are available for testing. All the testing work (and its valuable feedback) is not delayed until the end of the project.

- The customer can give useful feedback from the beginning of the project. They learn a lot from seeing and using the actual product. This knowledge can be used to improve the rest of the project.

- The customer has a real sense of progress.

- The finished features you remove from the totals in your "burndown chart" are accepted by the customer. The chart will therefore better reflect the amount of work actually done.

I make sure to negotiate with the customer to ensure that they will provide this regular and timely feedback. This level of feedback requires considerable commitment and effort from the customer. All of these commitments are put into the contract:

- How often the customer must be available to answer questions.

- When the customer will receive new releases.

- The response time for acceptance test feedback and decisions to be made.

- The dates certain information must be provided by the customer.

The aim is not to over-regulate communication between the customer and the development team, but to agree on maximum communication latencies. If the feedback and communication latencies become too large, we cannot steer the project.

I divide the whole project into (maximum) one-month increments. I try to define each of these increments so that it delivers some coherent functionality, organised around a "theme." The project is not complete until all the increments have been delivered. This technique helps the customer to learn to handle incremental development, since after a while, as the features and the increments roll in regularly, the customer gets more confidence in the vendor and the process.

During testing, the customer will often discover that these increments are good enough and complete enough to be used by end users. Thus, the customer might suggest deploying the increments to users. This enables the customer to get the return on investment earlier than expected.

Looking back to learn

After each project, we need to take some time to look back, to learn lessons and to prepare for the following project. Project Retrospectives[11] provide a useful format to learn from our experiences.

This is also the time to compare the estimates and actuals, so that we can improve the accuracy of our estimating. Also, if we have encountered some new risks and handled them, we should preserve this useful knowledge.

Thinking about project management

Many of the situations that I have described have the form "If you do X it will bring benefit in the short term but has disadvantages in the longer term" (for example, the use of "Change Requests") or "If you do Y you will see negative effects in the short term and positive effects in the longer term" (for example, "Let the customer use the software before the follow-up project"). These will sound very familiar to those who practice "Systems Thinking."[12,13]

Experience and examining these situations as systems has taught me that it is important to act upon the causes of problems in such a way that the long-term effects are positive. I am not just working on this project, but will be working on many more. I can drive my team really hard and exhaust them to deliver on the current project, but then they will be in no shape to deliver the next one. By winning some time on this project, I lose more time on the following project.

The tricky problem is that it is hard to "do the right thing" when I am under pressure to deliver. I am always tempted to take the shortcut, to do what brings me the short-term gain, or to fix the symptom without fixing the cause. The way I counteract this is to impose "rules" upon myself.

Them's the rules

The rules that I have just described force me to work so that I attack causes and not symptoms of problems; they force me to consider the long-term good of my team, my customer, and myself. When under stress, I follow the rules, which avoids the temptation to sub-optimize for the short term.

All of these previously-discussed rules are guided by some "meta-rules:"

Always keep the goal in mind—delivering value for all stakeholders

Everything we do, every decision we take must have this one goal in mind. We do whatever we need to do, within the constraints of the other rules, to reach our goal. The task of the project manager is to ensure that the team never loses sight of its goal.

The rules are the rules. You cannot play the game, unless you accept the rules.

I am strict about these rules: if you want to play in or with my team, you have to follow the rules. If the customer cannot or does not want to follow the rules, we do not start the project. If a team member does not follow the rules, they are off the team.

Rules can be broken if that's the only way to solve a problem.

Sometimes, I have to be a bit flexible and bend the rules if this is the only way we have to solve a problem, and if, after examining the situation, we agree that this will help us to reach our goal. For example, one of my rules is "No Overtime," because I know the negative effects it has on long-term productivity. I am quite willing to break this rule and work two hours longer to finish something or to meet some deadline. If that is not enough, we have to look at another way to solve our schedule problem; more overtime will not fix the cause of the schedule slip but it will lower team productivity.

Every rule can be changed, but not during a project.

No rule is perfect. Some rules become obsolete, others must be updated, and new rules are learned. The rules should capture the knowledge you gain. But I cannot run a project if the rules change out from under me or if there is constant discussion about the rules. Regularly scheduled reviews (like the project retrospectives described previously) are the ideal moment to evaluate and update the rules.

Be honest with the customer, with the team, with myself.

Honesty is the best and easiest strategy in the long run. If I have a problem, I should not hide it, but solve it. I can only solve the problem if I know and admit I have one. Hiding problems from the customer or the team does not work: they find out eventually, most likely when the product must be released. Why not ask for their help in solving the problem?

Why would I want to do fixed-price projects?

We have seen all the advantages that fixed-price projects can bring to my customers, at least if we implement the project correctly. What is in it for me, besides all of this hard and risky work?

- Because of the fixed schedule, I can more easily plan different projects.

- Because of the fixed schedule, my costs are predictable.

- Because of the fixed budgets, my income as a vendor is predictable.

- Some customers are more likely to spend time thinking about their real requirements, making tough decisions to avoid threats to the budget or schedule.

Conclusion

With all of these tasks, the job of a project manager looks quite hectic. It's not, unless it is done badly. A good project manager is proactive and solves most problems before they become apparent, which still leaves enough problems to fill a full working day. If problems grow and fester, the job becomes a lot harder.

We can apply "agile" techniques to handle risk instead of avoiding all risks. These techniques can be used to add some flexibility to a fixed-price contract, without losing its advantages. These techniques can only be applied if there is sufficient trust and commitment from the customer. The vendor has to earn that trust and commitment by delivering upon promises, and by gradually increasing the involvement of the customer. Building on that trust, we can go from projects where budget, time, and value are fixed to projects where budget, time, and minimum value are fixed.

Customers who have experienced these gains by agile methods do not want to work any other way again. They also prefer not to work with other vendors again.

CHAPTER THIRTEEN

Process Agility and Software Usability

Toward Lightweight Usage-Centred Design

Larry L. Constantine

S oftware and Web applications development can seem like a strange game. At one end of the playing field, in scruffy jerseys of assorted color and stripe, are the unruly rabble representing the methodless chaos that all too often passes for programming in many organizations; at the other end, we see the advancing phalanx of the heavyweight team, a bright letter *U* (for Unified) emblazoned on the chest of each hulking goliath. These true heavyweights of modern software development—the Unified Process and its supporting player, the Unified Modeling Language—have shrugged off scholarly scrutiny and competition alike to lead the league in goals scored.[1]

Adapted from an article in the August/September 2002 issue of *Information Age*. Reprinted with permission of the author.

Between the contrasting extremes of libertarian license and methodological muddling, the centerfield of the process playing field is currently dominated by the real crowd pleasers of modern software development: a small group of relatively young, fast-moving players—the so-called lightweight processes with names like XP, Crystal, Scrum and FDD. To be both correct and *au courant,* however, we should follow the lead of a group of the leading coaches and promoters of these processes who met in February 2001 at Snowbird in Utah to discuss their current interests and future prospects. Wishing to shed the negative connotations of the term *lightweight,* they agreed thereafter to refer to their sundry methods as "agile" processes. Agile it is, then. After all, who would want to risk being thought of as the 98-pound weaklings of software and Web development?

Agile Players

Managers and developers who want to play today's game need to understand not only the league leaders like RUP, the Rational Unified Process, but also the agile competitors. A complete comparison of all the agile processes would be beyond the scope of this chapter; there are just too many and they differ in too many details. In any case, Martin Fowler has already provided a concise but detailed overview.[2] In this chapter, the emphasis is on a management and decision-making perspective with a focus on some of the pluses and minuses common to the agile processes.

The archetype of the agile athletes of software development is XP, short for eXtreme Programming.[3,4] Undoubtedly the best known and arguably the most successful of the agile processes—it is the subject of over a dozen recent books—in many respects, XP typifies the entire diverse bunch. Like nearly every other methodology—light, heavy, or middleweight—XP and its agile teammates are really tossed salads that mix tricks and techniques with a mish-mash of methods, models, and management formulas, all dressed with tools, practices and even a bit of philosophy. Some advocates argue that, because the various pieces were all concocted to complement each other, you have to buy the whole assorted package of any given method, but many practitioners simply pick and choose the parts that seem to work for them and toss out the bits they do not like or do not believe.

The hallmarks of XP, as with most of the agile processes, are that it is more people-oriented than process-oriented, and that it emphasizes flexible adaptation over full adherence. Along with the need for agility, the stress on effective teamwork puts a premium on good management and leadership skills. Success with most of the agile approaches requires particularly close, hands-on management aimed at smoothing the process and removing impediments.

Oddly enough, one of the more controversial aspects of XP teamwork is also one of the established best practices of software development: pair programming. Also known as the dynamic duo model, pair programming puts two programmers in front of a single screen. By providing instantaneous inspection for every line of code that gets written, the technique radically reduces bugs, improves programming style, and cuts the overall cost of programming. Pioneered by C/C++ guru P. J. Plauger and popularized by yours truly,[5] pair programming is a proven technique with a solid track record.

Philosophy is also a big part of nearly all the agile methods. XP itself is built around a set of core values: simplicity, communication, testing, and fearlessness. Yes, fearlessness. To this list, Scott Ambler, a recent banner-waver for model-driven agile processes, has added the value of humility.[6] Jim Highsmith's Adaptive Software Development,[7] which has also been classified with the lightweight processes, is more framework and philosophy than prescribed practices, especially compared to such precisely delineated approaches as XP or Peter Coad's Feature Driven Development (FDD).

The rules of the agility game are relatively simple. Work in short release cycles. Do only what is needed without embellishment. Don't waste time in analysis or design, just start writing code. Describe the problem simply in terms of small, distinct pieces, then implement these pieces in successive iterations. Develop a reliable system by building and testing in increments with immediate feedback. Start with something small and simple that works, then elaborate on successive iterations. Maintain tight communication with clients and among programmers. Test every piece and regression test continuously.

Although some programmers and their managers may think of agile methods as a license to hack, it should be clear that following its philosophy and practices takes genuine discipline. I have heard some managers refer to XP as structured hacking, and that may not be far from the truth.

The Pros

Perhaps the biggest selling point of the agile processes is their weight—or lack thereof. There is simply far less to them than to the leading heavyweights, which means potentially less time to learn and master the process. That does not mean that agile processes are easy, any more than it means that agile process can substitute for programming skills and developmental discipline—but it does mean that there is less to explain about the processes themselves.

Reduced overhead is another strong point. Unlike the more heavy duty processes that emphasize diverse deliverables and numerous process artifacts, the agile processes concentrate on code. Design is on-the-fly and as-needed. Index cards and whiteboard sketches take the place of a slew of design documents, and brief, standup exchanges replace protracted meetings.

Early results are yet another point of appeal of agile processes. With short release cycles that produce a fully-functional system on every iteration, agile methods enable clients to begin using a simplified working core with limited but useful capability early in a project.

For clients, managers, and developers alike, a major potential payoff comes from the ways in which agile methods reduce the defect injection and leakage rates: the number of bugs created in the first place and the number that sneak past successive phases of development. More reliable code means more up-time, cheaper development, and less support and maintenance.

The simple philosophies of the agile processes appear to translate fairly well into practice. Despite—or because of—the streamlining, agile processes seem to have worked well for a variety of real-world projects. The success stories far outnumber sob stories (but of course!), at least for well-trained teams working on appropriately limited projects.

What goes round

What are the risks and shortcomings of the agile methods? Readers who have been around long enough or have a sufficient grounding in the history of programming may be experiencing a strong sense of déjà vu. Some thirty years ago, IBM was touting so-called chief programmer teams,[8] small, agile groups headed by a strong technical lead who could hold the implicit architecture in mind without resorting to much explicit design. Applications were constructed with thorough inspection and testing through successive refinements. The objective was to have working code at all times, gradually growing it through successive enhancements into a full-scale working system.

Like XP and its agile teammates, chief programmer teams also seemed to enjoy early victories for awhile, but the model ultimately foundered on the shoals, caught between the Charybdis and Scylla of charisma and scale. Led by gifted technical managers and applied to problems of modest size, the approach worked well, but there were only so many Terry Bakers in the world and not all problems could be sliced and diced into the right pieces for speedy incremental refinement.

The same issues challenge the agile methods today. There are only so many Kent Becks in the world to lead the team. All of the agile methods put a premium on having premium people. They work best, if at all, with first-rate, versatile, disciplined developers who are highly-skilled and highly-motivated. Not only do you need skilled and speedy developers, but you need ones of exceptional discipline willing to work hell-bent-for-leather with someone sitting beside them watching every move.

Scale is another problem. When I surveyed colleagues who are leading lights in the world of light methods, they agreed that the agile processes do not readily scale up beyond a certain point. While a few of XP efforts with teams of 30 developers have been launched, the results have been mixed. Alistair Cockburn claims that his family of methods known as Crystal[9,10] has been used for larger projects, but the general consensus seems to be that 12 to 15 developers is a workable upper limit for most agile processes. The tightly coordinated teamwork needed for these methods to succeed becomes increasingly difficult beyond 15 or 20 developers.

All the agile methods are based on incremental refinement or iterative development in one form or another. The basic premise is that it is easier to add capability to a compact base of well-written existing code than to build a complete application in one fell swoop. Within the prescribed short release iterations of agile processes, a small team can only do so much. Systems that total some 250 thousand lines of code may be achievable over many such iterations, but a million lines is probably out of reach. Moreover, some projects and applications cannot, for all practical purposes, be broken into nice and neat 30-, 60-, or 90-day increments.

What's the use?

Informants in the agile process community have confirmed what numerous colleagues and clients have reported to me. XP and the other light methods are light on the user side of software. They seem to be at their best in applications that are not GUI-intensive. As Alistair Cockburn expressed it in email to me, this "is not a weak point, it is an absence." User-interface design and usability are largely overlooked by the agile processes. With the possible exception of DSDM and FDD, users and user interfaces are all but ignored. To be completely fair, neglect of users and user interface design is a failing shared as well by the bulk of the big-brother behemoths in the heavyweight arena. Nevertheless, it is significant that no representatives from the human-factors, interaction design, or usability communities were invited to participate in the formation of the Agile Alliance.

Some agile methods, like XP, do explicitly provide for user or client participation in pinning down requirements and setting scope through jointly developed scenarios, known as *user stories.* It is noteworthy that user stories are typically written by customers or customer representatives, not necessarily by genuine direct end-users. Anyone familiar with usage-centered design[11,12] understands the importance of this distinction. Users outnumber customers and are the critical source of information for user interface design. Clients legitimately make decisions regarding scope and capabilities, but as often as not they do not really understand genuine user needs. Moreover, user stories are concrete scenarios, detailed and believable vignettes that, like conventional concrete use cases, tend to assume many aspects of the yet-to-be-designed user interface.

Despite the availability of user stories, when it comes to user interface design the agile processes maintain their emphasis on minimalist design process and rely on repeated refinement to pound the user interface into shape, favoring somewhat simplistic forms of iterative paper prototyping rather than model-driven design or thorough forethought. Particularly with XP, which relies so heavily on testing, GUI-intensive projects pose particular problems. Testing of user interfaces is labor intensive and time consuming; automated user-interface testing is difficult if not impossible except at the most elementary level. True usability testing requires repeated testing with numbers of users under controlled settings. User or client reactions to paper prototypes are no substitute and can even be completely misleading. What people will say they like (or claim is workable) when they see a paper sketch will often prove unworkable in practice.

The most critical shortcoming of nearly all techniques that are based on iterative expansion and refinement in small increments is the absence of any comprehensive overview of the entire architecture. For internal elements of the software, this shortcoming is not fatal, because the architecture can be refined and restructured at a later time. Refactoring[13] can, in many cases, make up for the absence of a complete design in advance. User interfaces are a different story.

For user interfaces, the architecture—the overall organization, the navigation, and the look-and-feel—must be designed to fit the full panoply of tasks to be covered. When it comes to the user interface, later refinement of the architecture is not as acceptable because it means changing the system for users who have already learned or mastered an earlier interface. Even small adjustments in the placement or form of features can be problematic for users. Whereas refactoring of internal component structure need not necessarily have any manifestations on the user interface, redesigning the user interface architecture is unavoidably disruptive for users. Maintaining a consistent and comprehensible look-and-feel as new features and facilities are added to the user interface becomes increasingly difficult as the user interface evolves through successive releases, as the history of many large commercial products attests. Periodic rework of the user interface as a whole to overcome the entropy of inconsistent expansion imposes a huge burden on users. For these reasons, the user interface is one aspect of the system that absolutely must be designed, designed completely, and designed right before its code is written.

Iterative prototyping is an acceptable substitute for thorough user interface design only when the problems are not too complicated, when there are not too many screens with too many subtleties, and where a rather pedestrian and uninspired solution will suffice. Software with intricate user interface problems or for which usability will be a major factor in product success demand a more sophisticated, model-driven approach to user interface design. This is where usage-centered design enters the picture.[11]

Agile Usability Processes

When Lucy Lockwood and I began developing usage-centered design in the early 1990s, we did not set out to create a lightweight process. Our philosophy has always been simply to use whatever tools and techniques helped us design more usable systems in less time. We draw diagrams only when we have to or when drawing them is faster than not drawing them. We should not be surprised, then, to learn that usage-centered design is increasingly mentioned in company with the other agile processes.

Where usage-centered design parts company from most of the agile processes is in the emphasis we place on modeling and on driving the user interface design and development by models. Scott Ambler's Agile Modeling *nee* Extreme Modeling[6] is an exception to widespread model-phobia among the lightweight approaches. In usage-centered design, the profiles we build of roles users play in relation to the system directly inform the task model we construct to capture the nature of the tasks to be supported by the system. The task model—collections of interrelated use cases in simplified, abstract form—directly drives how information and capability are collected and arrayed on the user interface.

In its most agile incarnation, usage-centered design works some of the same card magic that powers XP.[14] We model task cases on index cards, thus keeping them short and sweet and facilitating easy collection and distribution. We shuffle the cards to prioritize them in terms of business and end-user importance. We sort them into related groups that help us construct complete usage scenarios and that guide the collection of user interface components into screens, pages, or dialog boxes.

The same task cases that steer the user interface design are grist for the programming mill that grinds out the objects and methods that power the software. In detailing task cases, we focus on user intentions and system responsibilities in order to help distinguish genuine needs of users from mere wants and wishes. In short, usage-centered design probably qualifies as an agile process, even if it was not contrived with that in mind. Moreover, it supplies a critical piece missing from other methods—an effective and efficient scheme for designing highly usable interfaces. However, usage-centered design makes no claim to being an end-to-end process for cranking out software. Rather, it is an adjunct to an effective agile process, the missing link back to users that can turn an incomplete process into one that can reliably deliver good solutions for users, not just good code.

For success as an agile process, usage-centered design requires close collaboration and communication with users, domain experts, and clients, but especially with genuine users and qualified experts in the application domain. If users and domain experts are not actual participants in the design process, then they need to be readily available for quick review and validation of the design team's work. The JITR (Just-in-Time-Requirements) technique,[15] in which users and/or domain experts are immediately available to answer questions and clarify issues as they arise, is another approach that works for accelerated, agile design.

In outline, the most "extreme" or agile incarnation of usage-centered design follows a simple process of card-based modeling and decision-making. The use of index cards not only speeds and simplifies the process, but the limited visual "real-estate" of index cards forces parsimonious modeling. The chief disadvantage of card-based modeling—that models are not software compatible without transcription—is not a major problem in agile development where direct communication and face-to-face discussion is substituted for documentation and diagrams. While the use of cards to carry information does not preclude drawing a picture for clarification, it does not require it either.

We have long argued that collaboration, as in Joint Essential Modeling,[11] yields superior results more quickly. As with other more elaborate and detailed variations on the usage-centered theme, the agile activities outlined below are best carried out within a team that includes both designers and developers plus at least one user or user surrogate (such as a domain expert).

Inventorying roles. Construct an inventory of the roles users can play in relation to the planned system by brainstorming directly onto index cards.

Refining roles. Review and refine the inventory on cards, then briefly describe salient aspects of each role on its index card. Keep track of questions and ambiguities about user roles that arise along the way. If you are not working directly with users, these will need to be clarified through discussions, observations, or interviews.

Prioritizing roles. Sort the user role cards to rank them in order of priority for project success. Consider deferring support for low priority but challenging user roles.

Inventorying tasks. Construct an inventory of task casesto support the identified user roles by brainstorming directly onto index cards, beginning with the highest priority roles. Keep track of unanswered questions and unresolved ambiguities about user tasks to be clarified through discussions, observations, or interviews with users.

Prioritizing tasks. Sort the task case cards to rank them, first by anticipated frequency or commonality, then by overall priority for project success. Next, sort the task case cards into three heaps: required (do first on this release), desired (do if time on this release), and deferred (for later release cycles). Mark the cards by their assigned heap.

Describe tasks. For required task cases—along with any desired ones that appear to be critical, complex, unclear, or interesting—write out the narrative body of the task on the index card. The narrative should cover the "success case" (normal flow of events) in essential form (abstract, simplified, technology-free) using the standard two-column format of user intentions and system responsibilities. Extensions, alternatives, or "failure" cases of the narrative can be added on the back of each card later. If not working collaboratively with users or user surrogates, clear up remaining questions and issues through discussions, observations, or interviews with users if needed.

Organize tasks. Cluster task case cards (all of them) into co-operating groups based on the likelihood that they will be enacted together within a common scenario or sequence or timeframe. Create duplicate cards for tasks that fall in more than one cluster, but clearly identify them as "copy cards."

Paper prototype. Treat each cluster as the tentative set of tasks to be supported by an interaction context (screen, page, dialog, or the like) in the user interface, and then sketch an initial paper prototype for that part of the user interface, concentrating on the required task cases, but considering others. (All task cases are considered to ensure that the overall user interface architecture is sound.)

Refine prototype. Inspect the prototype with users and clients using scenarios derived from the task cases. Revise and refine the paper prototype based on inspection results.

Interface construction. Begin programming of the user interface or presentation layer based on the paper prototype and associated task cases.

As in nearly all agile methods, the assumption here is that development proceeds through successive release cycles. Successive iterations will pick up additional roles and task cases to guide refinement and expansion of the user interface. On each successive iteration or release cycle, then, the user roles, tasks, and co-operating clusters are reviewed and refined as needed before the next set of paper prototypes is sketched, inspected, and refined.

Not all programming has to await design of the user interface. In an accelerated development process based on agile usage-centered design, design and programming of internal and back-end components that are not directly dependent on the form and details of the user interface design can proceed in parallel with the above process. Furthermore, once task cases are identified, these can be harvested for possible programming implications independent of the user interface design. When the revised paper prototype is done, each interaction context within it and its associated task cases become grist for the programming mill, whether extreme or "normal."

Architecture? What Architecture?

Except for the grouping of tasks into co-operating clusters, the abbreviated outline above still omits any systematic consideration of the overall architecture of the user interface. The denizens of XP dismiss all such architectural design as BDUF, or Big Design Up Front. But some minimum up-front design is needed for the user interface to be well-organized and to present users with a consistent and comprehensible interface. Experience in a number of short-cycle projects, particularly on the Web[12] has clarified what is the minimum architectural consideration for agile usage-centered design of user interfaces.

The minimal up-front design for user interfaces is not very big. You need to establish three things:

1   an overall organization for all the parts of the user interface that fits with the structure of user tasks

2   a versatile common scheme for navigation among all the parts;

3   a visual and interaction scheme that provides a consistent look-and-feel to support user tasks.

The overall organization is already covered, although barely, by sorting task cases into co-operating clusters. The navigation scheme requires thinking through how best to enable users to move among different views or interaction contexts and how these will be organized into collections and presented visually to users. The third minimal requirement means constructing—and refining through successive iterations or release cycles—a kind of abstract style guide that describes the visual and interaction techniques to be used throughout the application. Examples and more discussion of navigation architecture and visual and interaction schemes, are available in other publications.[12]

Mid-field Scrimmage

Between the world of hack-and-slash programming and that of obsessive-compulsive docu-mania is a middle ground offering hope for beleaguered managers, over-burdened programmers, and under-served users alike. With this in mind, I left readers of my final column for the *Software Development* Management Forum with one piece of simple advice. If you are ready to leave behind both ochlocracy and bureaucracy in software development, then best join the agile few and heed the words of the venerable William of Okham. "It is vain to do with more what can be done with less."

CHAPTER FOURTEEN

Agile Documentation

You need a lot less documentation than you think

Scott W. Ambler

The Agile Modeling (AM) methodology[1] defines a collection of values, principles, and practices for effective modeling and documentation. Yes, contrary to what you have heard, agilists not only model but they also write documentation. The goal of this chapter is to examine how you can take an agile approach to your documentation efforts.

Let us start with understanding the relationships between models, documents, source code, and documentation, something depicted in Figure 14-1. From Agile Modeling's point of view, a document is any artifact external to source code whose purpose is to convey information in a persistent manner. This is different from the concept of a model, which is an abstraction that describes one or more aspects of a problem or a potential solution addressing a problem. Some models will become documents, or be included as a part of them, although many more will simply be discarded once they have fulfilled their purpose. Some models will be used to drive the development of source code, although some models may simply be used to drive the development of other models. Source code is a sequence of instructions, including the comments describing those instructions, for a computer system. Although source code is clearly an abstraction, albeit a detailed one, within the scope of AM it will not be considered a model because I want to distinguish between the two concepts. Furthermore, for the sake of discussion the term documentation includes both documents and comments in source code.

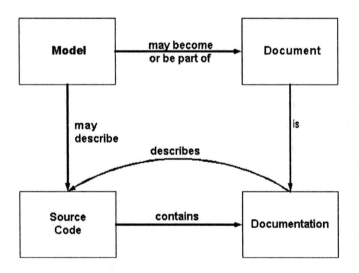

Figure 14-1. The relationship between models, documents, documentation, and source code.

This chapter explores the following topics:

- Appropriate reasons to create documents
- Inappropriate reasons to create documents
- Documentation trade-offs
- The essence of traveling light
- When is a document agile?
- When should you update a document?
- Effective hand-offs
- Increasing the agility of documentation

Appropriate Reasons to Create Documents

Agile developers recognize that documentation is an intrinsic part of any system, the creation and maintenance of which is a "necessary evil" to some and an enjoyable task for others, an aspect of software development that can be made agile when you choose to do so. There are four valid reasons to create documentation:

1 **Your project stakeholders require it.** The creation of documentation is fundamentally a business decision, you are investing the resources of your project stakeholders in the development of the documentation; therefore, they should have the final say on whether their money is to be spent that way – this should not be a technical decision. If your project stakeholders request a document from you, perhaps at your suggestion, and understand the trade-offs involved (more on this later), then you must create the document. It is important to note that Extreme Programming (XP) is very explicit about documentation

243

being a business decision[2] but that the Rational Unified Process (RUP) does not appear to share this philosophy, a concept that RUP teams need to adopt to apply Agile Modeling effectively.

Although it sounds strange, it is not unreasonable that you should create documentation only when your project stakeholders ask you to. Your project stakeholders include a wide variety of people, including all of the clients of your system, and therefore they should have a reasonably good idea what they want. Maintenance developers, or someone representing them if they are not in place yet, will request system overview documentation. Users and their management will likely request user documentation. Operations staff will request operations documentation. Yes, you will need to work closely with them to determine what they actually need, someone is going to have to decide to pay for the development and subsequent maintenance of the documentation, and you may even need to explain the implications of what is being requested, but this is doable.

2   **To define a contract model.** Contract models define how your system and an external one interact with each other: some interactions are bi-directional, whereas others are uni-directional. These models make the interaction(s) explicit to everyone involved. Contract models are often required when an external group controls an information resource that your system requires, such as a database, legacy application or information service. The Agile Modeling practice *Formalize Contract Models* states that a contract model is something that both parties should mutually agree to, document, and change over time, if required. It is important to understand that the development of a contract model should still be verified by your project stakeholders – it is their money that you are spending, and

if they choose to go at risk and not have the contract model in place then that is their choice.

3   **To support communication with an external group.** It is not always possible to co-locate a development team and it is not always possible to have project stakeholders (or at least the ones you need at the time) available at all times. When you need to work with an external group of people you need to find ways to communicate with them, and shared documentation is often part of the solution in combination with occasional face-to-face discussions, teleconferencing, email, and collaborative tools. It is a mistake to use documentation as your primary means of communication because it is far too easy to misunderstand something that has been written, but it is a good supporting mechanism. Effectively, this is documentation as your option of last resort.

4   **To think something through.** The act of writing, of putting your ideas down on paper, can help you to solidify them and discover problems with your thinking. What appears clear and straightforward in your mind can often prove to be very complicated once you attempt to describe it in detail, and you can often benefit from writing it down first. This, in effect, is an extension of the practice *Model to Understand* into the realm of documentation.[3]

Inappropriate Reasons to Create Documents

My experience is that developers in non-agile environments are often forced to create documentation for less-than-ideal reasons, often based on political reasons and sometimes due to sheer ignorance, and therefore may not have been allowed to be as effective as they possibly can. Questionable reasons for creating documentation, and how to combat them, include:

- **The requester wants to be seen to be in control (although is not actually doing anything of value).** When this occurs, I try to redirect their request, and suggest that they provide constructive feedback about the working software that my team has built. This enables them to be seen adding real value to the team, not just political value.

- **The requester wants to justify their existence.** To address this problem, ask the requester what they intend to do with the document, why they need it, why creating that documentation for them is more important than other work that my team needs to do, if there are more efficient approaches, and so on. If they do not have valid answers, you can safely deny their request.

- **The requester doesn't know any better.** Many people have been following documentation-centric processes for years and are not familiar with the concept that you can successfully produce software in an evolutionary manner without mounds of useless documentation. Therefore, you will need to reeducate such people in agile concepts.

- **Your process says to create the document.** Although this should not be the case with agile processes, the best strategy to address this problem is to explore whether the creation of the document actually provides value to your efforts.

- **Someone wants reassurance that everything is okay.** The solution is to make people understand that documentation says nothing about th etrue status of a project, that the only valid measure of a software development project is working software.[4]

- **You're specifying work for another group.** Documentation is one way to communicate but it isn't the best way (see Chapter 9). Try to find alternative approaches, such as occasional meetings with the other group, or the use of collaborative tools, to reduce your reliance on documentation.

- **Your development contracts are routinely subject to re-bidding.** So what? If your primary goal is to develop software then focus on doing so, and you are much more likely to perform adequately enough to keep the contract.

Documentation Trade-offs

Agile developers recognize that effective documentation is a balancing act, the goal being to have just enough documentation at just the right time for just the right audience. To accomplish this you must address the following issues:

- **Software development versus documentation development.** Any time spent creating documentation is time spent not developing new functionality for your users. At one end of the spectrum are projects where no documentation is written at all, whereas at the other end, no software is written at all. Neither extreme is likely to be appropriate for your situation. Follow Agile Data's Sweet Spot philosophy[5] and find the middle ground that is right for you.

- **Software developers have the knowledge, technical writers have the skill.** An effective approach is for the developer to write the initial version of a document, and then hand it off to a technical writer for clean-up. This has the advantage that the developer does a "knowledge dump" and the technical writer reworks the material to present it effectively; however, this has the disadvantage that the developer may not know how to get started, or even what to write about. An even better approach is to have the technical writer and developer work together to write the documentation, learning from each other as they do so.

- **What is required during development is often different than what is required after development.** During development, you are exploring both the problem and solution spaces, trying to understand what you need to build, and how things work together. Post-development, you want to understand what was built, why it was built that way, and how to operate it. During development, you are much more willing to tolerate rough drafts, sketches, and greater inconsistency – it is your own work after all – whereas post-development you typically want more formal documentation.

- **Willingness to write documentation versus willingness to read it.** You can write documentation but it does not mean that people are going to read it – if this is the case, why are you writing so much?

- **Do you document as you work or when you are finished?** An effective middle ground is to take notes of important decisions that you make, often something you can do in your source code, and to retain copies of the critical diagrams and models that you create during development. In other words, travel as light as you possibly can but no lighter.

- **Internal versus external documentation.** Do you place all of your documentation in your code? Do you write "self-documenting" code for that matter, or do you place all of your documentation in external artifacts? You need to find an effective middle ground. When your audience is made up of developers, the best place to put the majority of the documentation is in the source code. However, the audience for documentation is much wider than just developers and they will require some external documentation written to meet their exact needs.

- **Project-level versus enterprise-level documentation.**
  Some documentation may be needed outside of your
  project team, to be made available at the enterprise level.
  Centralized administration teams need to be customer
  focused to be truly agile, they must provide real business
  value for their efforts, and actively strive to understand
  how and why the resources that they manage are used by
  their customers.[6]

- **Quantity versus quality.** What would you rather have, a
  200-page system document that is likely to have a
  significant number of errors in it but a lot of details, or a
  20-page, high-level overview?

The Essence of Traveling Light

One of the greatest misunderstandings people have about the
concept of traveling light[7,1] is that it appears that you do not
create *any* documentation. The reality is that nothing could be
further from the truth. What traveling light does mean, at least
in the context of Agile Modeling, is that you create just enough
models and just enough documentation to get by. On
extremely rare occasions, that may mean you create no models
whatsoever – perhaps on a very small project – or even no
documentation. But for the vast majority of projects, you need
to create some models and some documents.

How can you ensure that you are traveling light? A
good rule of thumb is that you should not create a model or
document until you actually need it – creating either too early
puts you at risk of wasting your time working on something
you do not actually need. Traveling light also requires you to
think about what you are doing. An air traffic control system
will likely require greater documentation than a web site. As
the project progresses you will find that your initial estimate of
your documentation needs changes with experience: perhaps

you will need more, or perhaps less. Highsmith[8] likes to use the analogy of hiking: packing too light or too heavy can lead to disaster, at worst it kills you and at best forces you to turn back and rethink your strategy. Imagine crossing a desert with insufficient water – you are traveling too light. Now imagine trying to cross the same desert with a 100-pound pack strapped to your back – now you are traveling too heavy. Imagine building a mission-critical e-commerce application without providing any documentation describing how to operate it – your project effectively fails because you have traveled too light. Now imagine building the same system with thousands of pages of documentation that you must update and validate every time you change the system – you fail again because you are traveling so heavy that you cannot respond quickly to changes in the marketplace. Traveling light means models and documentation; too little or too much documentation puts you at risk.

When is a Document Agile?

The easy answer is that agile documents, like agile models, just need to be barely good enough. Unfortunately, because "just barely good enough" is in the eyes of the beholder, you need a little more guidance. A document is agile when it meets the following criteria:

- **Agile documents maximize stakeholder investment.** The benefit provided by an agile document is greater than the investment in its creation and maintenance, and ideally the investment made in that documentation was the best option available for those resources.

- **Agile documents are lean.** An agile document contains just enough information to fulfill its purpose and no more. When writing an agile document, remember the principle *Assume Simplicity*, that the simplest documentation will be sufficient, and follow the practice *Create Simple Content* whenever possible. One way to keep agile documents lean and mean is to follow pragmatic programming's[9] "DRY" (don't repeat yourself) principle.

- **Agile documents fulfill a single purpose.** If you do not know why you are creating the document, or if the purpose for creating the document is questionable, then you should stop and rethink what you are doing.

- **Agile documents describe information that is less likely to change.** The greater the chance that information will change, the less value there is in writing about it. Information may change before you are finished, and the resulting documents will be difficult to maintain over time.

- **Agile documents describe "good things to know."** Agile documents capture critical information, information that is not readily obvious such as design rationale, requirements, usage procedures, or operational procedures.

- **Agile documents have a specific customer and facilitate the work efforts of that customer.** System documentation is typically written for maintenance developers, providing an overview of the system's architecture and potentially summarizing critical requirements and design decisions. User documentation often includes tutorials for using a system written in language that your users understand, whereas operations documentation describes how to run your system and is written in language that operations staff can understand. Different customers, different types of documents, and very likely different writing styles. You must work closely with the customer, or potential customer, for your documentation if you want to create something that will actually meet their needs. When you do not have the customers actively involved, you are at risk of creating too much documentation or unnecessary documentation, and hence becoming less agile. You will often discover that when you involve the customers, they often have a very good idea of what they actually need, and can often provide examples of what works (and does not work) well for them.

• **Agile documents are sufficiently accurate, consistent, and detailed.** I have no doubt that you have successfully learned something, perhaps how to use a spreadsheet program, for example, by working through a book describing an older version of the software. Why did you not buy a new book? Usually, the answer is that the older book was good enough, and the updated version was not worth the $40 price to you. The point is that documents are read by people, and that people do not expect or need perfection. Agile documents just need to be *good enough*.

• **Agile documents are sufficiently indexed.** Documentation is not effective if you cannot easily find the information contained in it. Would you purchase a reference manual without an index or table of contents?

When Should You Update Documentation?

My recommendation is to follow the Agile Modeling practice *Update Only When It Hurts.* Agile documents, like agile models, are just good enough. Many times a document can be out of date and it does not really matter. For example, I live on a street that does not appear on my road map, yet I am still able to find my way home. Documents are used by people, and those people are probably very good at coping with less-than-perfect situations.

You should update documentation when:

• Your project stakeholders have authorized the investment of resources required to do the work.

- You have contract models that describe systems that have been updated.

- The documentation is part of the system, such as operations and user manuals, and the system is being re-released.

- The customer of the documentation is being inordinately harmed, including a significant loss of productivity, because the documentation is not updated (e.g. it hurts).

Yes, it can be frustrating having models and documents that aren't completely accurate, or that aren't perfectly consistent with one another. This frustration is offset by the productivity increase inherent in traveling light, and in not needing to continually keep documentation and models up to date and consistent with one another.

Effective Documentation Handoffs

A documentation handoff occurs when one group or person provides documentation to another group or person. Unfortunately, documentation hand-offs are a reality in some situations – often your development team is so large it cannot be co-located, perhaps a subsystem is being created by another company (implying the need for a contract model), perhaps important project stakeholders are not readily available to your team, or perhaps regulations within your industry or organization require the production of certain documents. As we discussed in Chapter 9, documentation is a very poor way to communicate but, if you must, the following strategies can help to increase the effectiveness of handoffs:

- **Avoid documentation handoffs.** As you migrate to an agile software development process, you will constantly run into people who are not as agile, people who see nothing wrong with documentation handoffs. Point out that there are better ways to communicate – face-to-face conversations, video conferencing, telephone conferencing – that you should consider before writing documentation, and whenever possible try to find a better way that fulfills your needs.

- **Support handoffs with other means of communication.** If you cannot avoid providing documentation to someone else, you should at least strive to support the handoff with face-to-face communication or other approaches. This may enable you to write less documentation, therefore allowing you to focus on other activities, and will help you to avoid some of the common disadvantages of documentation, such as misunderstanding the material.

- **Avoid documentation handoffs.** Chances are good that the people you are interacting with do not like writing and receiving documentation either – at least it does not hurt to ask.

- **Write agile documentation.** See the next section, *Increasing the Agility of Documentation*.

- **Avoid documentation handoffs.** I cannot stress this enough.

Increasing the Agility of Documentation

If you cannot avoid writing a document, how can you at least write it in an agile manner? The following strategies should help:

- **Focus on the customer(s).** Identify who the potential customer for your documentation are, what they believe they require, and then negotiate with them the minimal subset that they actually need.

- **Keep it just simple enough, but not too simple.** Follow the Agile Modeling principle *Use the Simplest Tools* and the practices *Create Simple Content* and *Depict Models Simply* when creating documentation. The best documentation is the simplest that gets the job done. Do not create a fifty-page document when a five page one will do. Do not create a five-page document when five bullet points will do. Do not create an elaborate and intricately detailed diagram when a sketch will do. Do not repeat information found elsewhere when a reference will do.

- **The customer determines sufficiency.** As the writer of documentation, it is your job to ensure that it has true meaning and provides value. Your customer's role is to validate that you have done so.

- **Document with a purpose.** You should only create a document if it fulfills a clear, important, and immediate goal of your overall project efforts. Do not forget that this purpose may be short term or long term, and that it may directly support software development efforts or it may not.

- **Prefer other forms of communication over documentation.** Highsmith[8] believes that the issue is one of understanding, not of documentation; therefore, you should not overrate the value of documentation. Documentation supports knowledge transfer, but it is only one of several options available to you and it often is not the best option.

- **Put the documentation in the most appropriate place.** Where will somebody likely want a piece of documentation? Is that design decision best documented in the code, added as note on a diagram, or best placed in an external document? The answer to this question should be driven by the needs of the user of that information – where are they most likely to need that information? You should also consider issues such as indexing, linking, and accessibility when writing documentation because you do not always know who will eventually become its customer.

- **Wait for what you are documenting to stabilize.** Delay the creation of all documents as late as possible, creating them just before you need them.

- **Display models publicly.** When models are displayed publicly – on a whiteboard, corkboard, or internal web site – you are promoting transfer of information and thus communication through the application of what Cockburn[10] refers to as an "information radiator." The greater the communication on your project, the less need there is for detailed documentation because people already know what you are doing.

- **Start with models you actually keep current.** If you have chosen to keep your UML deployment diagram, your user interface flow diagram, and your physical data diagram up to date throughout development then that is a good sign that these are valuable models that you should base your documentation around. Models that were not kept up to date likely were not because there was little sense in doing so, so not only are they out of date but they are not of value anyway.

- **Write the fewest documents with least overlap.** One way to achieve this is to build larger documents from smaller ones. For example, I once worked on a project where all documentation was written as HTML pages, with each page focusing on a single topic. One page described the user interface architecture for our system, a page which included a user interface flow diagram and appropriate text describing it. The table of contents pages for the system documentation and the support guide both linked to this UI architecture page. The advantage was that this information was defined in one place and one place only, so there was no opportunity for overlap.

How Does This Work?

Your project team should ruthlessly focus on creating documentation that provides maximum value to its customers. You should create documentation only when it is the best option available to you. When you have better options you should naturally choose one of them instead. The simplest documentation that gets the job done is your goal. Like an agile model, an agile document just needs to be good enough for its intended audience. So how does this work? How could it not work? Although agile software development processes value working software over comprehensive documentation, that does not mean that you will not develop any documentation. You should just develop documentation that makes sense. Just as knee-jerk documentation is wrong, knee-jerk non-documentation is just as wrong. Think first, then act.

The true goal of software developers is to develop software that meets the needs of their users. How relevant is maintaining mounds of documentation to achieving that goal? Not very. Yes, you need some documentation, but not a lot. You want to maintain a minimal amount of artifacts appropriate for your situation, and no more. At the same time, you want to invest the bare minimum effort in the artifacts that you do maintain. It does not make sense to do more work than you need to, and that means you will update your artifacts within the tolerances of your project.

CHAPTER FIFTEEN

Extreme Testing

Why aggressive software development calls for radical testing efforts

Ronald E. Jeffries

Very rapid development of high-quality applications software is quickly becoming an expected norm. How can you and your team ride that wave and deliver the goods? Extreme Programming, the rapid application development practice formulated by Kent Beck, may be the answer. This humanistic discipline combines simplicity, communication, feedback, and aggressiveness to produce high-quality software very quickly.

To develop software rapidly, you start simply, and evolve quickly from release to release. This is the standard

This chapter originally appeared in the March/April 1999 issue of *STQE*, the software testing and quality engineering magazine. It has been reprinted with permission of the author.

"incremental development" approach recommended by many. But to go fast and win, you have to live through change after change after change. Feedback is vital, and the most basic and critical feedback is that of Extreme Testing—the best way to survive extreme change.

Testing is not just for testers anymore. With Extreme Testing, you can develop software more quickly, with more confidence, and with higher quality. We will get to the details of Extreme Testing shortly, but first let me tell you a little story of how it works.

More than two-thirds of the way through the development of a famous payroll project (see also Chapter 18) the customers asked for a very tricky change. We had been storing and displaying entitlements—the money you get—as positive, and deductions as negative. It made sense to us.

But the payroll people wanted both entitlements and deductions handled as positive—a lease car deduction of $110, for example, not ($110). This request was scary because the system saves hundreds of internal values and displays them on demand. This request affected everything.

Part of the change was not very challenging. There were "bins" of money, and the system already knew which ones were entitlements and which were deductions. We just changed things so that deduction bins were always subtracted from entitlements when they were combined.

The devil, as always, was in the details. There were lots of places where entitlements and deductions were added, using procedural code rather than bins. Each of these additions had to be changed to include some subtraction. Similarly, there were tests for negative that had to be changed to positive, and so on. After a couple of days of getting the base support in place, a team of two of us went ahead and started changing things.

Over two-thirds through the project, would you want to change this critical assumption? With Extreme Testing, it was almost easy!

We had, at that time, around 2,000 Extreme Tests. We had Unit Tests testing the behavior of each class, and we had Functional Tests computing hundreds of paychecks and validating thousands of values. We just started running all of the tests.

Most of them worked, but hundreds did not. Each of these failures was due to a comparison or arithmetic operation somewhere and each such operation was affecting a lot of tests. The two of us worked through the tests one at a time, while the rest of the team pretended to ignore the tests being wrong. In one week, we had all the tests back where they had been, and had stumbled across and fixed a number of unrelated problems as well.

That was when we knew that Extreme Testing was magic: we had fearlessly changed an essential assumption of the system, well into development, and in a week, *we were certain that it had worked!* Over the life of the system, we have found few defects, if any, that were due to this extensive change.

Extreme Testing is all about confidence. **Unit Tests** let developers evolve the system rapidly and with confidence, and **Functional Tests** give customers and developers confidence that the whole product is progressing in the right direction.

Unit Tests

Rapid development implies rapid change to the code base. We need to build small increments of business value very quickly. This means that we cannot invest up front in general purpose support software: we have to let it evolve into being.

We are always learning. Developers have to learn how to build the system, and customers have to learn what they really want. We can connect and overlap these two learning processes by building the software and changing it quickly as we both learn.

This is "just in time" software development. To go this way, we embrace the fact that the things we build will need to change. We approach development to make it easy to transform yesterday's code into what we need tomorrow. To accomplish this, we make sure that our code is "well-factored."

While a complete description of good factoring is beyond the scope of this chapter, I will just say that well-factored means that the code does everything "once and only once." Because it only does one thing, it is easy to change that one thing. Because that thing is done in only one place, it is easy to find what to change. It is what (in the olden days) we used to call modularity.

Changing well-factored code is easy. If at some point in the future we see our needs more clearly, it is very likely that the change we will need is localized, if our code is well factored.

Even so, all this rapid change adds risk. We need to be sure of two conditions: that the new capability works, and that we have not broken anything that used to work. Both of these require testing.

Extreme Testing specifies two key actions to validate each of these two conditions:

1   To be sure that new features work, write Unit Tests for every feature. Write them before you release the code, preferably before you even write it. Save all the unit tests for the whole system.

2   To be sure that nothing else is broken, run all the Unit Tests in the entire system before any code is released—and ensure that those tests run at 100 percent!

Let me emphasize that last point. Whenever Extreme Programmers release any code at all, every unit test in the entire system must be running at 100 percent!

That shows us not just that the new feature works, but that the changes have not broken anything anywhere. Set aside your doubts, for a moment, about whether your programmers would do it, or whether you could afford to do it. We will come back to that.

Just bask in this essential truth: if you had tests for everything, and they always ran at 100 percent when new code was released, you would have incredible certainty that you had not broken anything—no matter how complex the change you had made. Would that be worth having? You are interested in testing, or you would not be reading this. You *know* it would be worth having!

Functional Tests

For rapid incremental development to be successful, team confidence must be high. Unit Tests give the developers confidence. Customers and management need confidence too, to keep putting up the money and time. Their confidence comes from seeing the system actually perform these buinsess functions.

Since each increment adds specific business value, include tests that check each increment to see whether the value is there. In Extreme Programming these are called Functional Tests.

In a payroll system, for example, an early increment might call for giving employees their regular base pay for days worked, with no special entitlements, and taking a straight tax deduction.These employees still have to be read in from the database, their pay rate determined, and so on.

Functional Tests for this can just check a small number of employees. Each employee has his pay rate checked for correctness, with the pay amount calculated for the days worked, the tax deducted, and the net amount.

In a later increment—with overtime, shift premiums, sick days, comp time, and with federal, state, and local taxe calculations included—we have to check many more employees and more values for each employee in order to cover all the cases.

There are several key dimensions of Extreme Functional Tests:

Customer-owned. To get confidence from the tests, the customers must understand them, and should provide the values tested.

Comprehensive. We tell our customers that they only have to test it if they want it to work. Invest wisely, however—do not just shotgun a million values; rather, pick values where the test will have meaning if it succeeds *and* if it fails.

Repeatable. The rules of pay will not change—except to get more complex over time. Every time you do a new increment, write new tests, and upgrade all the old tests, making sure they work too.

Automatic. You cannot have comprehensive repeatable tests if you have to manually check the results. Have a testing facility to set up and run the tests, check the results, and report them.

Timely. If the tests do not show up until weeks after the development is done, it just slows things down. Everyone's mind is on something else by then, and it is disruptive to think back in time. Get Functional Tests for an increment running (although probably failing) by halfway through the increment. Developers improve and release code during the increment, and get feedback as they go. Rapid feedback enables rapid development.

Public. The developers need rapid feedback, as we have seen, but customers and management need to see progress as well. With all this testing, things will probably go well, and everyone will know it. But if things are not going so well, declines in test scores will alert everyone to the problem. Let's face it: under pressure, developers may start to ignore test scores. The testing group, the customers, or management may need to step in and put things back on track.

Test Reporting

Now that we have all these tests, how do we report on the results? Here, as everywhere, Extreme Programming offers a simple answer. No reporting has to be done on Unit Tests—they are always at 100%. For Functional Tests, the interesting questions are

- How many Functional Tests are there?

- Have the customers validated all of the answers?

- How many tests are running correctly?

- What is the trend?

    There may be hundreds of Functional Tests. Using Extreme Testing, we test run all of them, every day, on the integrated system. We can display the scores in a graph, as shown in Figure 15-1.

    Here we see the testing status at the end of each development increment. This represents about three weeks' work, with perhaps ten or twenty user stories (think mini-use cases or scenarios) implemented by ten developers. A story should encompass about three days of "perfect engineering time," spread over six to nine real days.

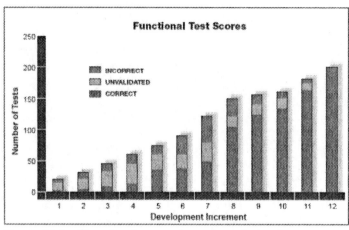

Figure 15-1: Functional test status at the end of each development increment.

In one simple graph, we get the overall picture of quality for the project. The bottom part of each bar means the test is getting the right answer, the top part of each bar means wrong, and the middle of each bar means that the customers have told us what system outputs to test; however, if they have not yet provided a validated answer to compare against.

A simple graph like this one can tell almost the complete story of quality, in a single glance. Early on, the widening middle band says we were having trouble getting validated answers. Then, as validated answers started to come along, we learned that the system was making a lot of errors. In increment eight, quality took a big step upward, and has improved ever since. Finally, in increment twelve, all the data values are validated, and there are just a few tests to fix to be at 100%. We see that this has been a healthy project, and we can have great confidence in the quality of the system.

Extreme projects update graphs like these on a daily basis, posting them prominently on the wall for everyone to see. Developers, customers, and management all see the truth of the project's progress, all the time. While the project may keep detailed graphs for various suites of tests, we find that the bulk of the benefit comes from this one graph.

But Can You Do It?

Your reaction to all this is probably that it sounds good, but *could* you do it and could you *afford* to do it? Here are some questions and answers based on actual experience with Extreme Testing in development.

Will the developers actually write Unit Tests?

Teams who try working with Extreme Programming's extensive up-front Unit Tests will never go back. New work goes much faster when you have tests to show you when you are done. Refactoring and other revisions go much faster when you have tests to show you that you have not broken anything. Software release goes much faster when you run the tests before every release, because if anything breaks, you know almost exactly where the problem is. Developers who work with tests get to spend more time working with new code, and less time trying to find obscure bugs in old code.

Yes, but how do I get them to try it?

Getting others to use the testing tools can be a challenge. Most teams are willing to try an experiment for a few iterations, and most will experience enough early success to keep going. You may find it desirable to have a coach with the team, at least during the early days of trying any of the Extreme Programming disciplines.

Doesn't writing all that extra test code slow things down?

Instead of being concerned that testing preparation is going to cause delays, picture the days you will have to spend debugging when a problem first shows up during integration testing, after everyone has been releasing code for days or weeks. Imagine your developers saying that some part of the system is so fragile that it cannot be enhanced in the direction you need to go. And think of the fear of dealing with some part of the system that only one programmer understands, after he or she has gone.

Won't the tests either take a long time to run, or not get run at all?

If you do not run your tests, you do not know if the system works. If the tests run too slowly, you have the wrong tests, or the wrong testing facility. Keep the tests comprehensive, but lean and efficient.

Yes, You Can!

Extreme Programming is extreme in simplicity, in communication, and in aggressiveness. To make it work, we are also extreme in the amount of testing we do. This combination lets us develop software rapidly, confidently, and with a lot of fun in the process. It will work for you, too.

Author's Note

Since this text was written, Extreme Programming terminology has changed a bit. Today, we would refer to Customer Acceptance Tests, or just Acceptance Tests, rather than Functional Tests. We do not use the term Extreme Testing that was introduced here, but Extreme Programming is even more strongly focused on testing than it was at the time this text was written. One notion that followed is that of Test-Driven Development, which is now considered to be a core practice of Extreme Programming.

CHAPTER SIXTEEN

Agile Meetings

Putting frequent, short meetings to work for your team

Linda Rising, Ph.D.

I know what you are thinking: "Oh, boy, another person writing about meetings. Just what I need!" Believe me, I hate meetings as much as you do. In fact, I consider meetings the biggest time sink in organizations today. I cannot believe that I am writing about having *more* meetings. But please bear with me. Let me share some stories about how frequent, short meetings helped a few teams solve significant problems. Suspend judgment for just a bit...

My first experience with having frequent, short meetings came as part of our organization's trial with agile

This chapter originally appeared in the May/June 2002 issue of *STQE*, the software testing and quality engineering magazine. It has been reprinted with permission of the author.

processes. In particular, we were using Scrum. Although there is considerable overlap among the many agile processes practiced today, one component that set Scrum apart—the one that provided the most benefit for our teams—was the frequent, short meeting. You may or may not be interested in learning more about Scrum, but the meetings can be used by anyone, whether you are following an agile process or have your software development process certified at CMM Level 5. Any team working toward a common goal will benefit because the practice improves communications.

No one likes meetings, least of all those of us in the software community who are already under considerable schedule pressure. I believe this resistance to meetings exists because they are usually poorly run and often scheduled for no reason other than because it is time for the weekly or monthly staff report. The only reason our teams agreed to sign up for a trial with Scrum was sheer desperation. They knew things were not working well, and they were astute enough to know that communication was a contributing factor.

The Meeting

As an integral part of the Scrum methodology, teams meet frequently—daily or every other day. The meeting usually lasts fifteen minutes, occasionally longer, but never more than thirty minutes. This provides enough time to address obstacles, but does not allow time to define solutions. Problem-solving discussion is held later, where only those who are involved in the problem attend. Having the meeting focus on raising but not solving issues is definitely a factor in making these meetings effective.

During the meeting, the Scrum Master (usually the team leader) asks three questions of each team member. Each team member answers those three questions. That's it. Meeting over.

Here are the three questions:

1   Relative to the Backlog (list of incomplete tasks), what have you completed since the last meeting?

2   What obstacles got in the way of your completing this work?

3   Relative to the Backlog, what specific things do you plan to accomplish between now and the next meeting?

This meeting achieves several goals. The most important is focusing effort on the Backlog items. It does not help to accomplish tasks that have nothing to do with the list at hand. Removing items from the Backlog is the focus of the team. But it is also important to communicate the priorities of Backlog items as you go. Some items in the Backlog are more important than others. The team needs to be reminded of the priorities to make sure the most important things are done first. The meeting keeps everyone informed of progress and obstacles, which allows the team to share in the success and pain of others. The protocol enables the team to resolve obstacles as quickly as possible. Finally, the meeting makes it possible to track the progress toward delivering Backlog functionality. Fred Brooks in his still relevant book, *The Mythical Man-Month,* said, "How does a project get to be a year late?" The answer: "One day at a time." The meeting identifies any obstacle immediately, and everyone knows about it.

Having frequent, short meetings keeps everyone on track. It is no secret that many of us are addicted to work. We put in long hours, look so virtuous, and seem to be getting so much done. We look productive, but often waste time on less important tasks. We are well intentioned, but working in isolation can make it difficult to set priorities that best serve the team. It was always an eye-opening experience to see how many developers had a tendency to wander off in the weeds—intent on solving some problem that they felt was important but that, even if solved, would not reduce the Backlog. In many situations, the Scrum Master had to corral these cowboys and convince them that solving their very important problem was not going to help the team make progress. Sometimes, well-intentioned people wanted to create a homegrown tool that would (in the eyes of its creator) solve a recurring problem for teams in the future. It was astounding to see how many closet tool writers we had, and how many experienced old hands underestimated the effort it would take to produce a truly useful tool for cross-project use.

A couple of warnings:

1 **Stick to the meeting plan.** It is tempting to get caught up in problem solving. Don't do it! The Scrum Master must be a strong facilitator and restrict comments only to answers to the three questions.

2 **Only active participants are involved.** It is acceptable to invite a manager or customer, but these outsiders may not speak. Sorry, but rules are rules! The manager or customer can hear the progress but may not comment. This prevents any side discussion that will distract the team and waste precious time for those not essential to the discussion.

Case Studies

The following case studies report two of my experiences with frequent, short meetings. The first team was made up of software developers who followed the tenets of Scrum pretty closely. The second team was made up of testers. Their process could be only loosely described as "related" to Scrum. This shows that you can achieve the benefits of frequent, short meetings regardless of your team's product and regardless of whether you're following an agile process.

From Reluctance to Enthusiasm: The Month-Long Trial

This first team had a problematic history. It was a support team made up of people from several projects who were given the task of creating an integrated set of tools. It was unclear where this team should be in the organizational structure, and they were passed around from one department to another. Each new "home" provided a new team leader and a new management hierarchy. The members of the team were experienced, tough, independent thinkers used to solving problems on their own. Unfortunately, as a team, they were going nowhere fast and losing ground with each reorganization. Finally, they came to rest in a new department with a team lead who wanted to succeed.

The new team lead called for a project checkup to understand what was going on. The checkup uncovered several problems, most of them related to poor communication. This team was not especially enthusiastic about trying a new development method, but decided to pilot Scrum and the frequent, short meetings for one month.

Daily meetings seemed too much to tackle, so they set a schedule of Monday/Wednesday/Friday one week, followed by Tuesday/Thursday the next week. The meetings involved all developers, including telecommuters—some from different time zones.

I remember the first meeting well. We had to round up some team members who grumbled all the way, "I don't have time for this! I've got work to do!"

Once we started around the table, problems quickly surfaced. One person said "I've been having trouble getting the database access to work." Another team member responded, "What? I didn't know you were working with the database! I thought I was doing that! We need to talk after this meeting!"

The next person complained "I've had trouble finding someone who knows about the code libraries we created on the Intelligent Network project." A helpful offer: "Hey! I used to work on IN. I can help you with that. Come on over to my office after the meeting."

Detailed problem solving does not happen in the meeting, of course—only an offer of help and an agreement to get together after the meeting. For example, someone would say "I ran into a problem." Typical responses would be: "I had that problem a couple of weeks ago. I can help with that. Let's talk offline," or "I know the people working in that area. I'll help you get in touch with them," or "I'm having the same problem myself. Let's get together after the meeting and talk about it."

What would have happened if the meeting had never taken place and the problem was never voiced? The person with the problem would have probably struggled long and hard before asking for help. Or maybe that person would have created a workaround or another tool that would have contributed nothing to the list of required deliverables.

As problems surfaced and were met head-on, the team began to come together. I could feel it and I could see that the team felt it, too.

Along with this, the team started to have hope. Suddenly, they had a way to get their arms around the problems they had been fighting. They were excited and energized—all in one short meeting. When is the last time you felt that a meeting accomplished *anything*—let alone a team transformation? It is hard to believe, but after only one meeting, this transformation was well under way.

At the next meeting, most people were there early and were eager to hear what the others were doing. It was a 180-degree turnaround from reluctance to enthusiasm. These people could immediately see the benefits of the meetings and what they meant for their project.

As the meeting progressed, there was a shift in emphasis. At the beginning, everyone was there to complain. but after a few team members had reported, everyone became a helper—a problem solver. Instead of lobbing a nasty roadblock at the team, people began to ask for help. Instead of taking aim at someone who was in trouble, people began to take a real interest in seeing what they could do to help out. When one team member shared an obstacle, the resources of the entire team were brought to bear on that problem. The entire team immediately owned every problem.

The fact that the team solved all or most of their own problems helped clarify the Scrum master's role for me. I originally thought that this role would be hard to fill. I throught that the Scrum master would need to facilitate a tight meeting, keep everyone on track, and solve problems on the fly. But for these meetings, a good facilitator allows the *team* to solve the problems and only jumps in when an issue must be raised to a higher level. Even if the team is not using Scrum, this experience applies.

The team began to bond and team members displayed increasing involvement in and delight with others' successes. Frequent, short meetings helped the team "synch up" and allowed in-house members to know exactly what remote team members had accomplished. The team completed a successful on-time delivery. The pilot was declared a success and, as far as I know, this team is still enthusiastically having frequent, short meetings.

Advice and Observations

The Network Tools team in my example was less than thrilled about trying a new development method. However, after only one meeting, they were singing the praises of Scrum. Here are some observations and advice from the team that extended indefinitely its one-month pilot with frequent, short meetings:

- The Scrum Master must have the skill to run a short, tightly focused meeting.

- Stick to the three questions. It is easy to get off the topic and extend a ten- to fifteen-minute meeting into a half-hour.

- Some people are not very good at planning their workload. The Backlog keeps people on track and aware of expectations. Answering the questions helps people structure their work and address tasks in a more organized fashion.

- There is an increase in volunteerism within the team. We are taking an interest in each other's tasks and are more ready to help each other out.

- The best part of the meetings has been the problem resolution and clearing of obstacles. The meetings allow the team to take advantage of the group's experience and ideas. As Gerald Weinberg has said, "None of us is as smart as all of us!"[1]

Improved Communication: Short Meetings during Testing

My second example comes from a test team that was working on preliminary testing and bug fixing for a feature when they tried frequent, short meetings. The team was scheduled for four testing runs in eight days, so they planned a meeting before each test run. The team was on the critical path for delivery. It was imperative that the product be delivered on time.

The big problem this team was facing was hit-and-miss communications. Important information was sent out via email but seemed to always be missed by at least one person on the team. Team members were on so many email distribution lists that their mailboxes were full. They received dozens of emails a day and could not keep up with them, so they usually did not try. As a result, unless they happened to see someone who could remind them of an update, they sometimes went about their work without knowing critical information. In addition, the testers sometimes worked strange hours, and team members did not often see one another or communicate plans for a test session or the results. This caused problems when software updates were not ready or fixes had been added.

During the meetings, team members could ensure that the proper software update was being used for the next scheduled test run and that the fixes that had been added were announced. The team redefined some testing procedures to make things go faster. The meetings allowed all the testers to hear what was planned and to volunteer to work the next test time. The meetings also served to remind everyone of problems with the current software version, as well as events scheduled for the next day. Decisions about the kind of testing to perform in the next test run were made by the group, instead of just the tester who worked on that run.

During one meeting, the team lead had to make a phone call to help decide whether to go ahead with the next scheduled test run. Without the meeting, without the phone call, without the information, the tester would have worked an entire shift on an obsolete software version—a complete waste of time.

I saw the regularly scheduled meetings provide the team with an efficient way to share information and track progress. The meetings kept everyone together. The team met its goal—the update was ready for integration testing at the end of the trial.

279

Advice and Observations

For you skeptics who might think my experiences are an anomaly, let me share some results that have been reported by others. The December 2001 issue of *IEEE Software* featured several articles on agile processes that addressed the topic of frequent, short meetings. Here is an excerpt from one team that used frequent, short meetings:

> We also incorporated the daily stand-up meeting into the team. Each team took fifteen to thirty minutes to review their progress, and each person took a couple of minutes to talk about what he or she was working on that day and the previous day. The focus was not only on improving visibility but also on encouraging communication between team members. The qualitative results were immediate. Some engineers found it difficult to explain why they spent so much time on issues or why they looked at things that weren't high priorities on the team's list of tasks.[2]

Here is an excerpt from another team—one that did not use frequent, short meetings:

> We never introduced these [frequent, short meetings], and I believe it was a major mistake. Quick, daily, face-to-face meetings keep developers informed about what others on the team are doing. They help stop people from stepping on each other's toes. They keep the team lead informed about who's ahead and who's behind. They air new ideas and prevent people from duplicating work.[3]

Conclusion

In his novel *The Deadline*,[4] Tom DeMarco observes that projects *need* ceremony, and suggests that projects *use* ceremony to focus attention on project goals and ideals. This is certainly one of the roles of frequent, short meetings. The agenda is the same for each meeting: ask the three questions of each participant. This small ceremony is the way most teams at our company begin each day. If you were standing on the second floor of the building where product development takes place, you would see clusters of teams gathering between 8 and 9 o'clock in the morning—team members standing with a cup of coffee, listening intently to the answers to the questions and then—*poof!*—the meeting is over and everyone is back in their offices, working with a clear sense of where the team is heading.

This is such an easy process improvement. Try it with your teams. Frequent, short meetings have a small cost and a tremendous payback. Every day or every other day, get the whole team together, form a small circle, and have the team leader ask the three questions.

Make sure that asking and answering these questions is the only thing that happens. This should take fifteen to thirty minutes—and it is a good way to start the day.

PART FOUR

There Are No Silver Bullets

CHAPTER SEVENTEEN

There are No Silver Bullets

Kevin Aguanno

At the most basic level, we all understand that any process we create cannot apply equally to every single project without adaptation. Projects are unique, the details of specific situations are different, organizational cultures are different, and the skills makeup of a team varies with the addition of each team member. There is no single method that is perfect for every project.

So far in this book, we have examined the specific problems that agile methods address, and the history of how they evolved to meet those problems. We have also examined the common elements behind nearly all agile methods that differentiate them from traditional methods. Finally, we have examined a number of specific agile techniques that are common to many agile methods. Everything we have presented so far in this book paints a rosy picture of a new, "agile world."

The picture is almost too perfect. Nothing is completely good – there has to be a negative side to these agile methods as well. This section of the book looks at some of the weaknesses of agile development methods, and includes a chapter by Gerold Keefer, who is known for presenting some of the best-researched rebuttals of the claims made by agile method proponents.

One Size Does Not Fit All

As we noted above, no single method fits every project. Organizations that have standardized on a common development method have experienced failures when projects were just not suited to the method. These failures point out the inefficiencies that result from force-fitting a method onto a project that the method was not made to address.

I can illustrate this point with an example from my own work experience. I once ran a project for a large corporation that had very rigorous project and technical governance processes. Our software development process had to go through numerous rounds of architectural reviews, budget reviews, and risk reviews (and this is only a partial list!) While the overall process could be described as following governance "best practices," the cumbersome processes destroyed any chance of delivering a short or inexpensive project.

One process step, a review and approval by the Architecture Review Board, required that the project manager prepare a presentation in a standard format that addresses a long list of technical details. This presentation has to be submitted by the first Tuesday of each month for review by the Board before the project manager presents the material before the Board meeting on the last Thursday of each month. The net effect of this single process step amounts to a one-month delay on project schedules while waiting for a design approval.

For our short Web development project, estimated to take five weeks, the one-month design review almost doubled the duration of the project *for just one governance process step out of more than a dozen* that the project would have to endure. Clearly, in this environment, the governance processes have destroyed the chances of delivering a quick project. In fact, efficiency is the first characteristic that flies out the window when governance processes become too rigid and too complex.

You can usually tell a lot about the biggest failed project an organization has ever had by the complexity of its current governance processes. In most organizations, the current governance process is a reaction to the largest failed projects in recent memory. People want to avoid such large failures in the future, and modify their processes to prevent such failures from happening again. The thinking is usually "If only we had done *more...*" This gets translated into *more* reviews, *more* documentation, *more* risk analysis, and *more* planning that results in *more* costs, *more* delays, and *more* bureaucracy.

For the few organizations that have tried to break out from these overburdening governance models and become more efficient, the solution has often been creating parallel governance models: one set of processes for large, complex, high-risk projects that require extra planning, reviews, and oversight; and another set of processes for small, simple, low-risk projects that can execute quickly and start delivering value sooner, if the processes did not slow them down. The need to react quickly in the marketplace is often cited by executives as one of the reasons that they outsource a lot of development work. Outside developers do not have to follow all of the same restrictive processes as developers within an organization. Often, the differences are dramatic.

Learning from these situations, corporate governance experts have suggested that organizations adopt multiple processes, each suited to a different project type. Software development groups have taken this concept and applied it to their world, recommending different types of software development processes for different types of projects. In effect, treating software development methods as tools in a toolbox – you need to know how all the tools are used so that you can select the right tool for a specific situation.

Each Method has a Different Focus

Each development method was created for a specific reason, often to address a specific situation. While methods have evolved over time, these differentiations are still evident, and should influence your decision when choosing the right method for your project.

For example, Scrum is designed to be a way of organizing the overall structure of a development project (whether it is software development or the development of any other new product) to reduce the risk of not delivering business value. As such, details of how to perform the technical work within the iterations are not dictated by the method – the teams are allowed to choose whatever technical methods they prefer for developing the product.

Extreme Programming, on the other hand, is designed as a software development method and includes specific recommendations on how the team is to conduct its technical work, such as refactoring, pair programming, keeping the design simple, using test-driven development, etc. XP can even be used as the technical method within a project where Scrum is being used to manage the overall project.

Some are More Scalable than Others

When choosing an agile method for your own project, you also need to consider the size and complexity of the project. This can be measured in many ways, but one that we can use here for illustrative purposes is the number of team members. Agile methods do not all scale equally to larger teams.

Many years ago, psychologists studied team dynamics in an effort to uncover the optimal team size. The most famous of those studies was published by George Miller in 1956. It concluded that the optimal team is composed of seven people, plus or minus two.[1] Agile proponents often cite this study[2] when describing their ideal team sizes. Others generally note that agile methods are best suited to small teams.[3]

Scrum adopts Miller's ideal team size of seven. Ken Schwaber, Scrum's founder, notes that

> Teams as small as three can benefit, but the small size limits the amount of interaction that can occur and reduces productivity gains. Teams larger than eight don't work out well. Team productivity decreases and the Scrum's control mechanisms become cumbersome.[4]

To cope with projects requiring larger teams, Schwaber suggests that subteams be formed, and that they are each assigned their own "manager." Then, to coordinate between teams, he suggests a "Scrum of Scrums" technique be used. Schwaber sums up his thoughts on large teams by noting that "large teams generate too much complexity for an empirical process."[5]

Rob Thomsett, a noted Australian expert on agile project management notes that "Large and superlarge projects are completely different from smaller projects. Extensive research has shown that the dynamics of large projects (long time frames, high internal and external complexity, etc.) result in poor estimation, mis-managed expectations, and other dysfunctional results."[6] The best advice for large projects or large teams is to break them down into smaller sub-projects orsub-teams.

Cockburn, in his Crystal Methods, creates a scalable methodology that applies more structure as team sizes grow (see Table 17-1). He notes[7] that his methods are not well-suited for very large projects, since there is insufficient subteaming, and that they are not meant for use on projects where the output of the project could jeopardize human life, since there is insufficient verification. These two criticisms could apply to all agile methods.

Table 17-1: The Crystal Methods provide different levels of structure depending upon project size and complexity.

Method Name	Team Size
Crystal Clear [8]	3 to 6
Crystal Yellow	Less than 20
Crystal Orange [9]	Less than 40
Crystal Red	Less than 80

In a study[10] on agile methods commissioned by the U.S. Department of Defense's Data and Analysis Centre for Software (DACS), the authors compared the scalability of various agile methods. Table 17-2 is adapted from that study.

In Chapter 18 of this book, Gerold Keefer notes that large XP projects are more prone to failure, and provides evidence to support his claims. I have personally used Scrum on a very large project (approximately 200 team members in 17 cities) and found that, while it can work, the management overhead skyrockets as the number of team members and locations increases.

On the whole, quick projects and small teams are supported by all agile methods. Beyond this, you will need to carefully examine the individual methods to see how best they will scale to your particular situation.

Table 17-2: *Prescriptive characteristics of various agile methods.*

	XP	Scrum	Crystal	FDD
Team Size	2-10	1-7	Variable	Variable
Iteration Length	2 weeks	4 weeks	Less than 4 months	Less than 2 weeks
Distributed Teams	No	Adaptable	Yes	Adaptable

Cultural Factors should Influence Method Selection

You should also consider how agile methods will fit within your organization's culture. Agile methods require a number of characteristics to be present within your culture:

Trust. You need to be able to trust the team members enough to allow them to select their own work methods and give them enough authority to become self-organizing.

Openness. Agile methods rely on open, honest, and timely communication between team members. These will not work if people are hiding bad news or will not share their information for political or cultural reasons.

Responsibility. Team members need to take ownership for the success of their whole team during each iteration. This is truly a team effort, not every man for himself. Team members need to feel that they all share in the success or failure of their team's work.

If you work in an organization filled with inter-divisional rivalries and Machiavellian politics, then do not try using agile methods – you will be less than pleased with the results.   Instead, use traditional methods, but try to adopt some agile techniques into the traditional methods as discussed in Chapter 20 of this book.

Cockburn notes[11] that as the criticality of the project deliverables increases, there is less tolerance for personal stylistic variations in the work products and working habits.   In other words, as the work gets more serious, the organizational culture will dominate the project, possibly reducing chances for innovation.

Finally, consider each agile technique in light of the organizational culture.   Some techniques, such as feature-based planning may be readily accepted by your organization. However, other techniques, such as paired programming, may not be well accepted due to cultural issues.   I have witnessed a case where paired programming was not well accepted by developers because they felt that it was just another way of "spying" on them and assessing their productivity.   In an organizational culture of strained relationships between workers and management, a technique such as paired programming may not be seen for its real benefits, but for how it may be misused by management to further oppress the workers.

And Don't Forget about Past Experiences

Projects are performed by people.   Cockburn developed the Crystal Methods as a human-centric project approach in recognition that you need to make sure that project team members feel empowered and that they have the required knowledge, skills, and tools required to get their jobs done. Similarly, Scrum focuses on reducing risk by structuring the communications between project stakeholders (reviews, requirements, team meetings, etc.) to maximize the opportunities for learning from each other's past experiences.[12]

Agile methods empower team members to select the techniques and approach that they believe will add the most value – regardless of organizational standards. This empowerment only works if teams are made up of experienced people. New college graduates with no real-world experience may not have the backgrounds to know which processes will add value and which will not. We aim to ensure that teams avoid common pitfalls and learn from their past experiences by sharing their ideas with other team members.

While this sounds good in theory, it sometimes does not work in practice; usually, these failures happen because poor past experiences have prejudiced individuals (or the organization as a whole) against certain agile techniques. For example, if an organization has suffered a recent project failure that was (in part) attributed to self-organized teams who got out of control, then the mere suggestion of this technique will raise serious objections from management. Similarly, if a team member has worked on a project that failed due to unclear requirements, poor scope management, and poor change management then the team member may prefer locking down requirements and design points early on in the project using detailed scope and design documents – you may *not* be able to sway him or her to another approach, given the pain caused by the failed project.

To get around these biases, you may need to try another approach. Chapter 20 presents the concept of Stealth Methodology Adoption, which describes how to package agile techniques to make them more palatable when introducing them to an organization or to a team.

You Must Consider the Controversies Surrounding Agile Methods

While there are many good reasons to be considering agile methods and techniques on your project, you should not blindly accept them without first understanding the possible negative consequences. Sometimes it is difficult to differentiate facts from hype, and a questioning mind may draw out those who are fanatical supporters of a method or technique who do not look at its application pragmatically.

In Chapter 18, Keefer presents a very critical look at some of the claims made by proponents of Extreme Programming. While his analysis is focused on that one method and some of its composite techniques, many of his comments apply more broadly to other agile methods as well. While he recognizes some of the benefits of using these methods, Keefer warns that other benefits are not supported by scientific research. In fact, Keefer notes that some published studies disprove supportive claims.

Aside from Keefer's specific criticisms, there are a number of more generic concerns with agile methods. Some critics claim that agile techniques are not really new at all; rather, they are simply a repackaging of practices that have been performed for years. This may be true; however, repackaging can often make something easier to understand, easier to relate with other practices, and will sometimes draw the renewed attention of those who failed to use the practices under their old guise. Two other common criticisms are that

- Many self-organized and empowered teams tend to optimize for their specific project, thwarting organization-wide initiatives; and

- Agile development efforts may not have adequately structured design and quality review processes to ensure the safety of products built using the methods.

Self-Organizing, Empowered Teams Tend to Locally Optimize

One of the underlying principles of the agile movement is the creation of self-organizing teams who are empowered to select whatever tools and processes that they feel help them meet their objectives.[13,14] This principle, while appearing laudable on the surface, can lead to problems when looking at issues broader than an individual project.

The root of the problem is that agile teams tend to optimize their processes, designs, schedules, and tool usage to best meet their own project's objectives. While this helps ensure that the individual project succeeds, it puts broader objectives at risk.

The first casualty from local optimization is usually enterprise project management initiatives. Enterprise project management is the emerging practice of managing portfolios of projects to optimize cross-project resource use, multi-project interdependencies, and the overall investment in these initiatives. Local optimization of a given project ignores the needs of other projects that may be dependent upon specific timelines, quality objectives, or software interface specifications of the subject project. If a project optimizes, it is only concerned about meeting its own objectives, putting other projects at risk. David Hussman discusses the problems of local optimization in more detail in Chapter 19.

Safety Concerns

While agile methods do stress testing as a core competency, there is still strong criticism that agile methods are not well-suited to the development of life-critical or mission-critical systems. Critics are concerned with the lack of detailed up-front design and complete, rigorous design reviews to ensure that no requirement (or unusual circumstance) has been forgotten.

There have been many examples of how software failures in life-critical systems have caused human deaths. *Baseline Magazine*, a publication aimed at Chief Information Officers (CIOs), published an issue (March 2004) focusing on problems arising from software quality. The feature article[16] includes a list of examples of software failures leading to tragic deaths, including a software application for calculating X-ray dosages that had a bug leading to fatal double dosages for some patients, software failures in infusion pumps leading to lethal dosages of morphine to patients, and a software application that led to the 2003 cascading power shutdown across most of the northeast USA and eastern Canada causing a number of deaths.

Projects with a rapidly-evolving design concurrent with development (as in the iterative and incremental development of agile methods) risk having fundamental design flaws work their way into a system. The development team may simply not think of a design point, or consider a possible error scenario that needs to be accommodated. Critics point out that more rigorous design-driven methods require rounds of independent detailed design reviews and certifications before development begins – reviews that have a higher likelihood of catching any missed design points. In the aforementioned *Baseline* article, the authors cited a US Food and Drug Administration (FDA) investigation into the radiation-dose calculation software provider. The FDA found that the root causes of the failure included "a lack of good software specification and documentation procedures to guide and control the software-development and change process." Agile methods risk raising the same issues, unless specific modifications are made to the agile methods to allow for formal, independent detailed design reviews.

Another safety aspect comes up when considering how agile projects do testing. Continuous testing works well for some software projects, but may not work well for all projects.

Some projects such as space shuttle launch systems can only be simulated during testing. In this case, individual components can be tested, and some integration testing can be done, but a complete system test is too expensive or too time-consuming to be executed continually. (Imagine how many shuttles you would lose during development!) Instead, test harnesses are built for these systems that mock interfaces to components that are too expensive or time-consuming to test regularly. While this might be the best that we can do, a harness is only a substitute and may not fully emulate the behavior (error conditions, outages, and other anomalous behaviors) of a real system.

Some projects may be governed by laws or other obligations (such as FDA regulations, or standard contractual terms) that require detailed up-front design and independent reviews. As a result, some projects may be forced to modify agile testing practices. While some agile techniques may still be deployed on most development projects, care must be taken to address safety concerns and rules (whether legal or contractual).

There is No Silver Bullet

While agile techniques and methods may add a lot of value to some projects, they may not apply well to some others. Consider each technique or method as a tool in your project management toolkit. Know how each tool is used and when to use it. To paraphrase an old saying, do not run around with a hammer thinking that everything looks like a nail – select the right tool for the job. Consider the strengths and weaknesses of each method, and how the use of each method would impact your particular project. Do not forget to take individual and organizational experiences (biases) into account.

Do not feel that you need to adopt a whole agile method as a complete unit. Often, you can make great improvements to a project simply by adopting a few agile techniques into your existing methods. If you encounter resistance to these new techniques, try the Stealth Methodology Adoption approach described in Chapter 20.

CHAPTER EIGHTEEN

Extreme Methods Lead to Extreme Quality Problems

Gerold Keefer

Since I first published contents of this chapter as a whitepaper back in February 2002, it has received significant attention both from software development practitioners and experts, and has been successfully presented at several conferences. In the meantime, the impact of agile software development methods, with Extreme Programming being still the most prominent among them, has certainly further increased. However, it is my observation that there has been a growing recognition that adopting agile methods is not always easy, and that preparing a smooth transition from traditional methods is essential. This pragmatic approch is coupled with the acceptance of the benefits that some traditional methods can provide to projects. In essence, the debate is now not to be agile or not agile, but rather what is the recommended level of agility (and what are the specific supporting practices) for different types of projects.

The updated materials in this chapter include new facts and research results that further solidify my concerns with Extreme Programming:

1   It is a set of practices that are only in very rare cases applicable –and applied–"by the book."

2   It relies to a high degree on the skills of individuals and their tacit knowledge.

3   It does not explicitly manage quality in the sense required by any major quality standard.

4   It does not scale up to larger projects.

5   Some practices, such as pair programming, have not been validated for their efficiency and are promoted based on anectodal evidence.

The following facts have been updated or newly introduced:

1   Not only the first, but also the second Extreme Programming project was cancelled.

2   Kent Beck's flattened cost of change curve phantasia is dismissed even inside the agile movement.

3   Several empirical research results question the usefulness of pair programming.

4   Initial empirical research results question the feasibility of test first programming.

5   Reports from larger Extreme Programming projects indicate that the anticipated scaling problems are indeed valid.

Beyond justified criticism, however, there are agile lessons to be learned:

1   Any process that is actually applied is far superior than a perfect paper process that is not applied.

2   Traditional planning processes do not sufficiently address operational planning.

My answers to those lessons are "Mutual Programming", a method to accomplish development work effectively and efficiently by employing developer duos, and "Task Stack Planning," an operational planning method that bridges the gap between traditional planning approaches and short-term planning solutions like Scrum.

Motivation

Following my positive experience with software development in a large telecommunication software project, whereby I inspected and unit tested the code of my partner and vice versa, I came across websites that recommended programming in pairs as a practice of a software development method called "Extreme Programming." I thought this practice to be similar to what we did in my project, and I recommended it to others. About three years later, I was hired as the quality manager of a project that involved thirty developers, and was one of several subprojects in a large SAP migration.

On this project, one contractor team consisting of seven programmers intended to use Extreme Programming to develop a Java framework for others to use. At that time, I was unbiased towards Extreme Programming, because I simply did not know much about it. What I did know was that a project of that size required substantial planning, analysis, and architectural groundwork up front. This conflicted with the view of that team, which lead to ongoing debates. The chief architect and I clearly favoured a more traditional software engineering approach, and the customer's project leader stood somewhere in the middle, seeing advantages in knowledge transfer to his staff when using pair programming. During the risks analysis that I conducted, conflicting software development philosophies were consequently identified as the topmost risk. In general, we experienced very slow progress from this team during the development of an architectural prototype. Eventually, the team leader confessed that they would not be able to deliver the required work products and apologized for the wasted time and resources. Initially, it took an application based on the new framework 40 minutes start up and the memory consumption was unacceptable, clearly exceeding our performance and resource constraints.

During the last few years, I noticed an ever-growing influence of Extreme Programming on mainstream software development. This growing popularity is fuelled by support from respected people like Tom DeMarco and recurrent claims that put Extreme Programming to the level of alchemy, such as one article reporting on an organization employing Extreme Programming that moved from CMM Level 1 to CMM Level 4 within five months.[34]

Developers were reading Extreme Programming books, and Extreme Programming became a widespread conference topic. Once, when I approached the local university campus, the first question I heard was "Extreme Programming is great – isn't it?"

Later on, I became involved in many heated debates in Usenet newsgroups, most notably comp.software.extreme-programming, about the validity of the claims and practices of Extreme Programming, and I investigated deeper. Quite soon I learned that most of the claims were based on weak grounds.

My motivation for writing this chapter is to put together the information and references I have about the facts of Extreme Programming and how they relate to traditional Software Engineering practices. I will state reasons, albeit no scientific proofs, why I consider Extreme Programming to be harmful for reliable software development and why it provides not many answers to the significant questions that contemporary software development methods have to answer. Secondly, the Extreme Programming hype(and the hype of the other "Agile Methods") is so dominant that even if we wanted to ignore it, we no longer have that option.

The practices of Extreme Programming have been explained in many publications. In this chapter, I will not try to explain them; instead, I will directly address the harm, as well as the benefits, that I see accompanying agile methods.

Bias

Everyone who followed my comments and thoughts on the Extreme Programming newsgroup will agree that I have my opinions about major aspects of Extreme Programming firmly set. In other words, I am biased. I consider it appropriate to define my bias before we move further.

My degree is in telecommunication engineering and I clearly favour an engineering approach to software development. During the past five years, I have been involved in quality assurance and testing consulting tasks within my company. I moved into quality assurance shortly after experiencing all the pitfalls of a non-quality oriented development environment:

- Reliance on verbal communication.

- Intuition-based decision making.

- High dependency on individual skills.

- Insufficient planning.

- No sound approach to system verification and validation.

Those practices lead to

- rework as a norm,

- error prone systems,

- non-maintainable systems,

- frustrated staff, and

- few heroes.

Out of those experiences, I am convinced that for large or complex software projects, explicit management of quality is imperative for reliable success.

Benefits

I will not paint a completely negative picture. Extreme Programming (and other agile methods) have made some positive contributions to the world of software engineering.

The Extreme Programming approach to testing

My prediction is that, in the long run, Extreme Programming will enjoy more respect as a vehicle for the widespread introduction of testing than for anything else. This is underlined by the fact that recent Extreme Programming publications and discussions focus on testing aspects of the method.[40] I have substantial doubts about how Extreme Programming addresses testing in detail, as described by others.[8] One concern is that 100% test automation in most cases is not feasible, and frequent releases will therefore add manual test effort.

Another complaint is the focus on test cases that show presence of features and not presence of defects. The first empirical investigations show that those concerns could be valid: "Test-first pays off only slightly in terms of increased reliability. In fact, there were five programs developed using test-first approaches with a reliability over 96% compared to one program in the control group. But this result is blurred by the large variance of the data-points."[41] However, there is no denying the fact that it brought testing basics to companies that had no real testing in place before, which explains some of the Extreme Programming success stories.[42]

The seminal testing reference books were written[5,22] decades ago, but Extreme Programming was the trigger that initiated the rapid and widespread adoption of some of these practices. Would you have succeeded in convincing anybody to put 30 or 40 percent of the project resources into testing before the arrival of Extreme Programming?

The visualization aspects

Besides the benefit of frequent testing, I see remarkable benefits in preparing a common project vision for all stakeholders involved. The first measure in trying to achieve this is the system metaphor. Despite the fact that I consider it as naïve to assume that you can replace the system architecture by a system metaphor for anything else but trivial systems,[3] the idea to express the system visually is good, and is something I have been proposing for a long time.

Despite the fact that I am not very ecstatic about using 3x5 index cards to write down stories, I feel very positive about the visualization aspects of using a project whiteboard. Transferred to the corporate intranet, these ideas are very useful.

Dubious Values and Practices

While using Extreme Programming practices produces several benefits, there are also a number of dubious claims made about the value delivered by some of its other practices.

The "80% benefit with 20% work" rule

I have seen too many 80/20 software systems. At the core, those systems give a false impression of reliability, safety, or security to the user. As these systems fail, not only is the systems' credibility gone, but also a part of the credibility of software technology as a whole. Professor Alan V. Oppenheim of the Massacheusetts Institute of Technology stated,[25]

> I realized many years ago when doing a major project on my home that you can paint 90 percent of a room in 10 percent of the time. The walls are easy. It is careful attention to the trim and other fine details that makes the difference.

This is in line with the observation that the C3 project[1] (also described later in this chapter)was initially highly productive, but got cancelled after it did not meet the expected schedule.

The embrace change value

Change is good; however, a sound system cannot be developed in an environment of constant transition—this will undermine its conceptual integrity. The impression that changes are easy with software is one of the major reasons for software troubles.

Fuelling this impression with dubious cost of change calculations[3,43] does not help. In fact, there is no credible published industry data that contradict the consistently-reported observation that the effort for a change increases (in a non-linear way) with system size. There are clear indications that this is also true for Extreme Programming projects: "As the application grew in size and complexity, the sort of functional unit that was simple and easily estimated in earlier iterations became more complex and harder to complete within a single iteration."[44] Considering this, and the fact that even inside the agile community the flattened cost of change curve reported by Kent Beck is largely dismissed, it can be stated that despite some misguided fantasies, "the exponential cost curve is still safely in place."[43]

The practice of refactoring

Hand in hand with the practice of embracing change, we looked at the practice of refactoring: after initial coding, the code gets beautified and the design improved. Although it is a good idea to keep source code as readable as possible and the design sound, there is not much point in fixing afterwards what can be done properly from the start. It is also unclear how the initial high-level design is created. Jukka Viljamaa from the University of Helsinki states:[45] "Fowler claims that refactoring makes redesign inexpensive. This seems rather an exaggerated statement if anything else but the lowest level of design is concerned." Considering the fact that Extreme Programming requires a functioning unit test suite all the time, refactoring will lead to considerable extra effort in adapting this test suite. Moreover, any code change is an opportunity for error injection, requiring yet additional regression testing.

The simplicity value

Simplicity is a universal and highly respected design principle. However, in most cases it is a complex process that finally comes up with a simple and elegant solution. "As simple as possible, but not simpler," said Albert Einstein, who is often quoted by Niklaus Wirth,[14] who feels that this approach is fundamentally superior to Extreme Programming's "the simplest thing that could possibly work." The Extreme Programming approach does not address the need for abstraction and generalization that even Extreme Programming experts report[44] about: "So we, like good XPers, know that we should *do the simplest thing that could possibly work* and we developed a single invoice format." And the result later on was that "There was an inordinate amount of code thrown out because it was hardcoded – I mean parameters that needed to be moved to the database."

The practice of pair programming

Extreme Programming publications make statements such as "There have been several studies conducted on the topic of pair programming. [...] These studies show that pairing causes no loss of productivity at all, while significantly decreasing defect rate, code size, and job dissatisfaction."[36] in reality,[21] the facts are:

1   There have been three studies on pair programming: One in a maintenance environment on a 45 minute task[24] and two in student settings.[23,24,30,31,33]

2   In all three studies the total effort pairs spent on their assignments was higher than that of solo programmers.

3   At least one study[23] suggests that "pair programming is rather expensive technology" and

XP-like pair programming appears less efficient than it is reported by J.T. Nosek and L. Williams et al. Only in one case (Program 4) reduction of average development time for XP2 (to 77% of the time needed by XP1) was similar to that reported by J. T. Nosek (reduction to 71%) but still it is far from the level of 50% mentioned by L. Williams et al. Moreover, in case of Program 4 one of the students misunderstood the assignment and this distorted the results.

4   A recent study by the University of Karlsruhe compared the efficiency of pair programming to solo programming. The study concluded that "If we combine this result with the result of the reliability analysis, we have to say that the single programmers developed programs with comparable quality but with fewer cost as compared to developer pairs."[46]

There is a growing body of evidence suggesting that pair programming is not superior to solo programming with code reviews. The evidence also suggests that the benefits of pair programming over solo programming without code reviews are not consistently reported. A recent economic analysis revealed that, even when taking the most positive empirical data on pair programming into account, pair programming does not pay off.[47] A similar study[48] came to a contradicting result under the overly-optimistic assumption that the agile process will yield zero defects.

Table 18-1: Research findings on the Pair Programming speed factor (elapsed time one developer / elapsed time pair). Values <2.0 indicate that Pair Programming was more expensive than solo programming.

Experiment	Elapsed Time Factor
Nosek	1.4
Williams	1.8
Nawrocki	1.0
Müller	1.0 (with constraints)

In addition, there are several reports that indicate that pairing leads to faster exhaustion.[10] On the other hand, no one will deny that pairing in certain situations, such as in educational settings or during debugging sessions, makes good common sense.

The practice of having an on-site customer

Everybody will welcome a customer like the one Extreme Programming proposes on its projects. The problem is that in real-world situations such a person hardly ever exists and several experience reports underline this.[16,44] The first Extreme Programming customer in history left the C3 project due to burn out and could not be adequately replaced:

> Marie was able to transfer to a less stressful job and her place was taken by a very bright and dedicated man named Paul Kowalski. [...] In due course, we realized that Paul didn't know how to be an XP customer. It should not have been a surprise; we had done nothing to teach him. We didn't know how to teach him, since we didn't know how Marie had done it.[16]

The practice of having no documentation

Extreme Programming made it into the headlines partly by proposing "no documentation." Later on, this slogan was changed to "documentation only as needed," and oxymorons like "XP is not anti-documentation; it just recognizes that documentation has a cost and that not creating it might be more cost-effective."[12] Who would not like to be "cost-effective" and avoid the cumbersome task of documenting software systems? However, considering maintenance and usage aspects, proposing "no documentation" is clearly professional malpractice, and is based on the assumption that teams will stay together until the very end of the product life, which is not likely to happen in most cases. Here is a lecture note from MIT's 6.170 laboratory in software engineering (fall 2001) that neatly underlines this:

> My personal opinion is that JUnit, the jewel in the crown of XP, itself belies the fundamental message of the movement – that code alone is enough. It's a perfect example of a program that is almost incomprehensible without some abstract, global representations of the design explaining how the parts fit together. It doesn't help that the code is pretty lean on comments – and where are there comments they tend to dwell on which Swiss mountain the developer was sitting on when the code was written. Perhaps high altitude and thin air explains the coding style. The 'Cook's Tour' is essential; without it, it would take hours to grasp the subtleties of what's going on. And it would be helpful to have even more design representations. The 'Cook's Tour' presents a simplified view, and I had to construct for myself an object model explaining, for example, how the listeners work.

The practice of having 40-hour weeks

I would welcome this practice, although it compromises Brook's "as few minds as possible" rule. What I am critical about is that those who propose the practice seem to avoid it frequently.[16,28] This sounds like a reputation booster to unfairly attract attention.

The practice of collective code ownership

It has been reported that collective code ownership works fine in some environments. However, the idea is based on altruism and therefore severely limited in scale and depends on suitable team settings. If the team culture gets disrupted by internal or external causes, the collective ownership will become non-ownership in due time.

311

[Editor's note: the Extreme Programming concept of collective code ownership is in conflict with the recommendation of its agile cousin, Feature Driven Development. FDD recommends that individual developers own specific code modules as a means to control code quality and avoid "churn."]

The "everything-is-in-the-code" attitude

At its heart, Extreme Programming is a code-centric approach. "The design is in the code," "the code documents itself," or "the requirements are documented with code for test case execution" are repeatedly heard assertions. The reality of this attitude is a return to garage duo programming that Fred Brooks tells us about in his classic book.[6] Brooks estimated that the effort to transform such programs into a generally useful software system takes nine times the effort initially required to have a running program. A precise estimate would depend on the specific environment, and there may be environments that are happy with only the code, but in general a software system is more than code. Extreme Programming does not describe how to create work products beyond code.

The "test cases are requirements" recommendation

Some of the proponents of Extreme Programming consider acceptance test cases to be sufficient as a substitute for documented requirements. Documenting requirements is hard work even in a natural language. It is highly doubtful if expressing them in Java or C++ will be an improvement to that situation.

The people orientation

Extreme Programming sees itself as a "humanistic discipline of software development."[39] Project problems are mainly people problems, as Gerald M. Weinberg once pointed out: "No matter what the problem is, it's always a people problem."[35] However, it is highly doubtful that you can solve people problems with a process. If that were possible, you could establish the right process up front, and avoid all future problems.

This is a false impression Extreme Programming seems to create. Even worse, there are indications that Extreme Programming leads to a tendency to blame the people, not the process.[13]

There are also practioners' reports stating that self-directed teams, as proposed by Extreme Programming, are dysfunctional in many real-world settings.

The non-specialization recommendation

Like every other industry, we have and will have specialization in software development. Due to the high technology turnover, the depth of specialization is certainly limited. However, software development has passed the time when everyone was supposed to know everything. Peter Drucker recently pointed out that "effective knowledge is specialized."[38] Due to ambiguous statements on this issue from the Extreme Programming experts,[16] the impression is that they are unclear about their own position on this point.

The bottom line is that substantial tacit knowledge and social maturity are mandatory for some of the mentioned values and practices to work. I was pretty much amazed, for example, as one of the Extreme Programming experts explained how to prioritize customer requirements. The description was about six pages long. It indicates that, in real life, the explicitly stated simple practices are heavily supported by tacit knowledge and wisdom.

The C3 Project Revisited

The Chrysler Comprehensive Compensation System (C3 in short) may well be the most often-cited software development project in history, and it was the "proof by example" of the Extreme Programming inventors. Of the 20 participants,[1] five subsequently published a current total of three books[3,4,18] about extreme programming, and a myriad of articles.[2,15,16,30] Numerous other articles and books reference the project as well.[7,30]

Despite the heaps of information provided, I have ceased the search for a clear picture about what really happened in C3. The exaggerations are obvious. In one journal article[15] it is stated that the project "was to scale up to pay hundreds of thousands of people every week." In another article, there is talk about "The recently completed Chrysler Comprehensive Compensation System (C3) experience." I found the most credible information from Beck[1,2] and Hendrickson:[16]

- January 1995: C3 was launched under a fixed price contract with a joint Chrysler and contractor team.

- Since March 1996: C3 was conducted in Extreme Programming style after Kent Beck arrived, according to Ron Jeffries. At that time the fix price contractor had failed to deliver a working product and the project was in a mess. It is reported that there was no sound testing in place.

- August 1998: C3 was paying a pilot group of around 10,000 people.

- February 2000: C3 was cancelled after being nearly four years in Extreme Programming mode.

Other facts are credibly reported:

- C3 experienced a high productivity in the first 30 weeks after Kent Beck arrived and significantly scaled down the staff.

- C3 was supposed to serve as a payroll application for a total of 87,000 employees and was supposed to be operational by mid-1999.[1]

- C3 was at no point in time used to pay more than around 10.000 employees, but has proven to be capable of paying another 20,000.

- It is reported[16] that the first person to play the customer role in the Extreme Programming method left the project due to burn out after a few months and could not be adequately replaced.

- Extreme Programming was retired as a development method after this project at the DaimlerChrysler Company.

Considering the fact that, for a long time, all of the major Extreme Programming experts were involved in the project and they programmed in Smalltalk, which is considered to be most suitable for Extreme Programming due to its dynamic typing, the project outcomes are not particularly convincing.

The VCAPS Project Revisited

The exaggerated reports on the success of the C3 project culminated in an article on December 2000 (8 months after C3 was cancelled) in *The Economist*. The article stated that

> XP was invented in 1996, when Kent Beck, a software developer, was called in by an American car maker, Chrysler, to rescue a project which had proved so frustrating that it had been scrapped. As Mr. Beck

worked on this venture, known as Chrysler Comprehensive Compensation (C3), he formulated a set of directions for keeping code 'elegantly written.' The C3 system now provides correct monthly payroll information for more than 86,000 employees.

These exaggerations where repeated by the report on the second XP project in history, the Vehicle Cost and Profit System (VCAPS) project at Ford, that according to Kent Beck[49] went pretty well: "They report dramatic success." "10 programmers, working productively indefinitely." However, this project was also cancelled later. At least the wording found to describe the failure have been carefully chosen: "VCAPS died with its boots on."[50]

Missing Answers

So far Extreme Programming has failed to give answers to a range of important questions that contemporary software development faces:

How does Extreme Programming work with fixed scope, fixed price, and fixed schedule contracts?

Extreme Programming works similar to a subscription. As a customer, you subscribe iteration by iteration. This certainly gives you a clear picture about costs and functionality for the next few weeks, but what about total project costs, total project effort, and the overall project schedule, something a customer could be interested in?

What about changing interfaces to other projects?

If you welcome change all the time you will have to change interfaces all the time. This is fine as long as you change internal interfaces. As soon as you have to change the published external interfaces, you are in trouble. Bob Wyman, a former Senior Product Manager for Applications Programmability at Microsoft, pointed out:

> Even if you're not publishing to millions of programmers, you may still be defining interfaces that will be used outside your organizational scope (perhaps by dozens or hundreds of other programmers) and the managers of those other projects will not tolerate your screwing up their projects because you wanted to make the interfaces 'better.'

What about non-functional requirements, like performance or security?

One cannot arbitrarily change non-functional requirements in the course of a project. Performance or security has to be analysed and designed before implementation, at least to a certain degree. Functional and non-functional requirements influence each other, which limits the amount of change your system can bear.

What about distributed development settings?

The "one room setting" is supposed to be the ideal Extreme Programming environment. It is common sense that high levels of noise and frequent interruptions that are the consequence of such a setting lead to a decrease in quality. There is credible empirical evidence supporting this.[9] Nearly all of the larger companies that I know subcontract parts of their development to remote locations, which makes such an environment impossible. There are certainly people courageous enough to try Extreme Programming in such settings, although with limited success.[11]

What about integration of COTS?

Most of the software systems implemented today are not developed from scratch. Commercial Off-The-Shelf software (COTS) products are integrated during the development effort. Extreme Programming gives little advice on how to handle those situations.

What about large projects?

If typical beginner's mistakes in software development projects with less then 10 person years of effort are avoided, the results are quite satisfying. The real challenge is dealing with large-scale projects that often experience substantial budget and schedule pressures due to their complexity. Those projects get cancelled frequently.

Alternatives

Following my criticism of Extreme Programming, I was routinely asked what I would propose as alternatives to Extreme Programming practices. Here are some of my answers:

- In contrast to Pair Programming, I see much more sense in practicing what I call "Mutual Programming."[51] In this practice, a pair of developers reviews each others' work products for quality. If one partner is finished with coding, the other partner inspects and tests the code, and vice versa. Compared to Pair Programming, there are several advantages including applicability in remote settings, measurement of effectiveness, and better ergonomics.

- In contrast to launching a project without a reasonable amount of requirements, I recommend sound prototyping as a cost effective way to investigate functional and non-functional requirements of the system, as well as possible solutions. Requirements turnover cannot be avoided, but it needs to be managed.

- In contrast to "no documentation," we have to think about how we can automate more of the documentation work and thereby avoid the routinely experienced inconsistencies. Work product documentation with XML is a promising approach to achieve this.

- In contrast to hoping that somebody capable of filling the customer role will appear on the horizon, how about setting up a concise requirements specification?[27] This specification may not be complete, and might not get completed until the end of the project. If a critical mass of requirements have been specified, then it serves its purpose.

- In contrast to relying on testing alone, establish a sound review or inspection process for your work products. Reviews and inspections have repeatedly shown to be more cost effective than testing.

You will find a wealth of useful Software Engineering knowledge in the SW-CMM and its successor the CMMI-SE/SW.[19] There is no need to practice all of it in each and every project. Use this material as a reference and adapt it to the specific needs.

What to do about large projects?

A first recommendation is to read Brooks' book *The Mythical man Month,* and then avoid large projects whenever you can. A second recommendation is to look after the CMMI Level 2 and 3 key process areas. Particularly *Requirements Management, Configuration Management,* and *Project Planning.* (For a scalable project management method, see my Task Stack Planning approach.[52]) Implementing those KPAs results in a development task that has lost the constant flux that makes software difficult to handle in a traditional engineering way, and the unbound temptation for change—a major source of trouble—is limited. A sound risk management process such as the one I have described elsewhere[20] is also mandatory for large projects.

On top of this, I recommend something I have been promoting for half a decade with not much success. The idea is pretty old, and was written down by Sun Tzu around 500 BCE:

> The Book of Army Management says: On the field of battle, the spoken word does not carry far enough: hence the institution of gongs and drums. Nor can ordinary objects be seen clearly enough: hence the institutionof banners and flags.
>
> Gongs and drums, banners and flags, are means whereby the ears and eyes of the host may be focused on one particular point.
>
> The host thus forming a single united body, is it impossible either for the brave to advance alone, or for the cowardly to retreat alone. This is the art of handling large masses of men.[37]

In large software projects, we routinely experience a wide range of views. In traditional engineering projects, the visibility of the product under development, such as a bridge or building, allows for the continuous refocusing of the participants' views—a very powerful and passive tool of Quality Management.

In order to transfer this beneficial situation from traditional engineering fields to software engineering, we must seek key metrics for the project, and constantly present them in graphic format to the stakeholders involved. This will give our software a face. A beautiful one if we are doing well, and an ugly one if we are performing badly. Pearse has written about one rather simple example of this idea employed at Hewlett-Packard.[26]

Conclusions

As a victim of the Byzantine German tax system, I am critical about rules and bureaucracy that routinely get bypassed by the privileged few. I certainly know about the shortcomings of formal software development approaches, such as the CMM/CMMI or ISO. However, in order to successfully develop software, we have to limit the degrees of freedom our nice languages, tools, and personalities offer and select from all the practices and techniques available. Formal quality models are useful guides.

I used to participate in competition swimming. Consequently, one of my favourite spare-time activities is going for a swim at the local pool. It is much more convenient to train when lanes are in place, which limits the degree of freedom, but increases the total capacity of the pool by putting some order in place. A software process should do the same: avoid collisions and still let individuals perform.

There is no denial to the fact that certain individuals and teams are capable of producing quality software without a solid process or explicit quality assurance. However, this is not the norm. General recommendations have to target what can be expected on average. On average, teams will not be able to reliably develop software using the twelve Extreme Programming practices alone. I was pretty much amazed as one of the Extreme Programming experts explained how to prioritise customer requirements. The description was about six pages long. It indicates that in real life the explicitly stated simple practices are heavily supported by sophisticated, implicit knowledge and wisdom. Good for you if this knowledge is at hand; in all other cases, you are lost.

If your project is small, fast delivery of "something running" is top priority, your business environment is volatile, the professional level of your developers is high, and the technical constraints are rather shallow, Extreme Programming might be an option for you. In most other cases, Extreme Programming is a method that is likely to introduce a high degree of unnecessary risk.

In February 2001, a tourist got caught in an avalanche in the Swiss Alps near the village of Ayer. In the rescue effort that followed, six people of the rescue team were caught in a second avalanche and two of them died. Asked about what to change in the future, a senior member of the rescue team later recommended to hold a short meeting before the start of each rescue mission that would define the course and the limits of action for the respective situation.

Considering the fact that the survival rate of avalanche victims declines rapidly with progressing time,[29] it seems that even if time is by far the most dominant factor for your project, and the environment is highly volatile, you should still plan thoroughly.

CHAPTER NINETEEN

Synchronizing Agile Projects

David Hussman

Having embraced Extreme Programming (XP) as a developer and a coach, I have seen the success XP brings to projects, as well as the smiles it brings to the developers' faces. But how does XP address dependencies between projects? How does the customer team react to the news that the developers are waiting on functionality that is being implemented by a different team, which may or may not be using XP? Does an organization using XP on multiple projects need some kind of "super customer team" to help synchronize development efforts? How realistic is it to believe that all projects at a larger company will embrace XP or some other agile process?

After witnessing problematic interactions between multiple XP projects more than once, I found myself starting discussions around this topic with other XP practitioners. When I found out that there seemed to be more questions than answers, and I was not alone in my observations, I decided that an attempt should be made to raise the topic to a larger audience for discussion.

The Environment

While working as a consultant for a company which has spent a great deal of effort exploring XP as a corporate development process, I found myself looking for information describing the synchronization of planning for one or more XP projects. Having done a bit of searching, as well as having asked one or more XP coaches, I discovered the information I wanted was not in great supply.

I had found some information in "Planning and Running an XP Iteration" by Cara Taber and Martin Fowler.[1] Although the article describes one way to scale XP for a large team, the situation at my engagement was different (yet I do not think it is or was unique).

Once the move to embrace XP had taken hold at the company, XP was finding success on more than one project. Though the planning game helps steer projects toward success, the persons responsible for overseeing the organization of more than one project, or team, are faced with bringing projects together, scaling existing projects due to success or demand, and dealing with possible overlap between multiple projects.

The company's struggles were further magnified when two or more successful XP projects were sharing dependencies. Although XP promotes communication and cooperation, when several teams have found success with differing designs, asking the teams to look toward that which is best for the company raised interesting questions.

It seemed possible that the very project dedication and ownership cultured by XP had now inadvertently become a problem. When this situation arose, it appeared that the rules of the planning game, as well as the traditional XP roles, needed to embrace change.

The First Encounter

To help describe the problem, I have selected two development efforts in which I was either a developer or a coach during this past year. The first of these involves using XP to build a framework used to build other applications.

In an effort to find a general solution to a large business problem, a small group of developers within the organization created a framework that provided the ability to quickly build efficient applications. At the same time, several other teams within the company, which I will refer to as the application teams, were addressing similar problems using a disconnected collection of solutions. When the framework was found to be a more effective way to deliver functionality, many of the application teams started to rely on the framework as an integral component in their designs.

Not expecting this response, the framework team suddenly found that they were not able to respond to the increased demand for new features and other development support. Having heard that XP might help organize their efforts, the framework team decided to give it a try. Although XP helped the team to clarify requirements and define team velocity, the team was still confronted with an ever-growing development task list.

Communications Breakdown

Even though the framework team was successfully using XP, the application teams were not able to wait for features to be implemented. Now that the applications teams were dependent on the framework, they started implementing features, and extending the framework, rather than waiting for the framework team's response to feature requests.

325

It was around this time that the framework team started to focus on the core of the framework. Without a clearly defined customer, the framework team had promoted the technical lead to the customer role. Although XP planning was working well for the framework team, the application teams and their project managers had become more and more frustrated with the lack of response to their requests for new features.

At the same time, the framework team had become frustrated by the amount of time they were spending supporting the application teams. The framework team felt that they should be working on the deeper problems within the framework. Not unlike the classic problem that exists between those that create requirements and those that implement the requirements, the two teams had reached an impasse, and communications had broken down.

A Proposed Solution

In an effort to get the two teams working together again, a group of individuals from both the framework and the application teams met with a group of XP practitioners to see if there was a way in which XP could be used to help. As the group talked, it became clear to everyone that the real problem was not about technology, it was about process. More specifically, it was about scheduling and expectations. The success of the framework came with an increase of requests from the application teams as well as the support teams. Fear was growing that the company was building upon a framework which needed modification if it was to handle the increased demand.

The Customer's Customer

A group consensus was reached that all parties would benefit by creating a customer team for the framework developers. This customer team would interact with the customer teams for the applications. As is the case with every XP project, a good customer is essential. Due to the fact that the framework had to support a variety of applications, address a complex domain, and grow beyond its internal issues, the new customer team would need a diverse and knowledgeable composition of players. It was decided that the team should contain players who understood the needs of the applications, possesed domain expertise, and understood some of the problems that existed within the framework. It was during this meeting that Figure 19-1 was created as a communications tool.

The Modified Process

For all XP projects, a more informed and organized customer team will most often present a clearer road map to the developers. In this spirit, the group discussed how the new customer team would make its players available to the many persons that would request changes to the framework. The application customer teams would still be responsible for gathering and prioritizing requirements for their individual projects, but to rekindle communication and provide a simpler focus to the framework developers, only the framework customer team would own the responsibility of creating, organizing, and presenting stories to the framework developers.

A variation was added to the iteration planning for the application teams. While tasking and estimating a story, the application development team was empowered to suggest that a task or a story be addressed within the framework. At this point, the application customer team may choose to remove the story from the table. This done, they could now choose to present the story to the framework customer team, or ask the application development team to proceed based on their estimates for the task or story. If the application customer team chooses to bring the task or story to the framework customer team, the framework customer team prioritizes the request.

The modified process was designed to solve two problems. The first of these was to allow the framework developers to stop focusing on scheduling and defending the features they were choosing to implement, and spend more time focusing on building the framework. Also, by sending all framework requests through the framework customer team, one group will have a better understanding of the features most desired by all application teams. This would hopefully provide a broader vision during feature selection and prioritization.

The second problem to be solved had to do with the scheduling issue previously mentioned. The application customer team was now responsible for making scheduling decisions for the applications based on information from the application development team and the framework customer team.

The Right Stuff?

In a perfect XP world, all parties would be using XP and the planning would be used across all applications. But as we know, there are no perfect worlds, and I wonder how many companies will choose to have a single planning game for all development efforts. The determination of whether the solution proposed here will work will be evaluated over the months to come. For now, at least the groups are working together and there is some vehicle for managing expectations as well as providing exposure to the framework development schedule.

A Broader View

To further the discussion, let's examine a more general version of the first encounter. What happens when there is a need to synchronize concurrent XP projects within an organization? When applications do not have any shared dependencies, or when there is one large XP project, this problem is

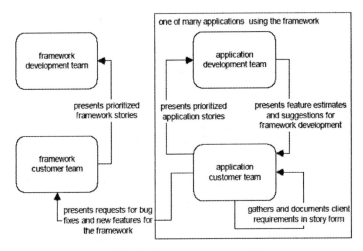

Figure 19-1: A modified XP process incorporating a customer team made up of representatives from dependent sub-projects.

unimportant. Once XP projects, which were initiated independently of each other, become dependant on each other, planning and design across the projects becomes problematic.

Imagine a company where several teams, somewhat disconnected from each other, are using XP and finding success. All projects are proceeding well, velocities are high, and quality is good. As each team's design materializes, the designs are distinctly different. This is fine until it is decided that the projects must be deployed together or merge to solve a business problem. At this point, with a significant portion of development completed, each team is vested in their design.

With significant development completed, and more than one solution working well for any of the individual projects, who decides which of the projects will be modified to work within another project's architecture? More importantly, what criteria will be used to make this decision?

329

The Company Customer

Now that we have moved toward emergent design, and away from big design up front, is it acceptable to create another form of the customer team to promote synergy among the XP projects? In the agile process community, where "the architecture group" is no longer in favor, is it possible to employ a solution similar to that used by the framework team in the previous scenario? Let's consider the idea of a "company customer."

What if the company customer were to field integration stories from the many applications groups? This would then be a similar solution to the one employed by the framework team. As the central focus of integration requests, the company customer would indeed have the best and broadest view from which to help with synchronization of cross cutting development efforts. For the many companies now facing enterprise application integration issues, this "company customer" might have an excellent vantage point.

But who would be in the company customer team? Even more important, how will the company prevent this new team from becoming yet another architecture group, destined to fail? Maybe the solution lies in learning from the past.

Many architecture groups have been driven by a technical mantra which fell on deaf ears, ears that were more interested in hearing solutions that make sense to the business. Driven by a focus to define a corporate technology stack, or something similar, architecture teams of the past may have lost sight of that which matters most—building solutions meaningful to the company. The company customer would assess and prioritize development efforts based on business needs and not technologies.

Company Customer Composition

Similar to the customer team created in the first encounter, the company customer will need a diverse collection of members. To succeed, I think it would be best to rotate members from all customer teams within an organization through the company customer.

Of course a great deal of this discussion is based on an assumption that there are customer teams and not the single customer as proposed in early XP writings. It seems clear that we need to further our definition of the customer as a team and not an individual. As the XP community clarifies the composition of the customer team, it might become easier to understand which member(s) might be good candidates for the company customer. It might also become clearer if and when a company customer team is needed.

Conclusion

I am interested to see if the idea of a company customer raises any interest within the agile community. Two years ago, XP helped me to save a project from being shut down. It also helped a group of frustrated developers start laughing and enjoying their time at work. As more developers and managers find the XP difference to be a breath of fresh air, I think XP will need to continue to grow and embrace the change it has initiated.

Of course it is a given that any company would be happy to be facing too many successful projects. As a strong advocate of XP, I want to see XP, and other agile methodologies embraced by the software development community at large. But although XP works well for a single project, we need discussion and definition for corporate XP. Projects that share dependencies on each other or projects within a company (large enough that having one large XP project simply does not make sense) will need some common focus and steering to prevent the integration issues of the past, or that which I have called extreme chaos.

Maybe it makes sense to create customers for a customer, or maybe XP might help us to create a company customer that can act as a benign corporate guide. Or maybe there are many other emerging solutions that will help synchronize XP projects. My hope is that this chapter will spawn more conversation in this area within the XP and agile communities at large.

CHAPTER TWENTY

Stealth Methodology Adoption

Kevin Aguanno

Many people have struggled with the challenge of how to introduce agile methods into their organization. As with any change in processes, there are those who will strongly resist the introduction of agile methods,[1] and they could scuttle your efforts. You need to consider how to introduce your changes to these individuals so that they do not feel threatened by the changes, and even actively support your efforts.

Thomas Kuhn, the 20th century philosopher, studied the nature of these changes in the context of scientific developments. In Kuhn's famous book, *The Structure of Scientific Revolutions*,[2] he shows us that the conflict between those who are supporting traditional methods and those who are proposing new methods is normal. In his book, he shows us how traditional beliefs form a core *paradigm* from which scientists can view the world. The supporters of new methods are proposing a new paradigm – essentially changing the way that scientists view the world – and encounter (naturally[3]) tremendous resistance to this fundamental change. In fact, Kuhn notes that "normal science often suppresses fundamental novelties because they are necessarily subversive of its basic commitments."[4] So, in order for proponents to promote their new methods, they need to counter the suppression of the traditionalists, forming a *scientific revolution*. Revolutionaries are naturally marginalized by traditionalists as part of their resistance to the change.

In the context of the emergence of agile development methods, one notes that the failure of traditional methods to cope with projects that have unstable requirements or high rates of change is the type of evidence that Kuhn points out is a prelude to a scientific revolution. Kuhn notes that this discrepancy between fact and traditional theory is the cauldron in which new theories are brewed: the failure of existing rules is the prelude to a search for new ones.[5]

When faced with these conflicts between theory and reality, Kuhn notes that the natural tendency of traditionalists is to apply the traditional methods more rigidly and to try and make minor adjustments to the traditional methods to incorporate the anomalies.[6] For software development models, these anomalies emerged almost from the start of their history: In 1970, Royce defined the "traditional" Waterfall development model,[7] where the project passes through a number of sequential phases from Design through Build through Test to Deploy. Almost immediately, people noticed that this model worked well in theory, but that in actual practice, a large body of projects existed where requirements were changing throughout the project – something the Waterfall model does not accommodate.

The first solution was to incorporate the concept of iterative development. Basili and Turner came up with this concept in 1975,[8] and labeled it Iterative Enhancement. In this model, a core framework is built, and then the project progresses through a number of iterative cycles in which additional functionality is added on to the framework, allowing the product to grow over time. This method was seen as an immediate improvement over the original Waterfall model, and it led to many subsequent variants.

In 1988, Boehm looked at the Iterative Enhancement model and noted that it prioritized the work for each of its iterations based upon functionality – i.e. build the most important remaining functions next. He saw that this could lead to some problems when faced with complex solutions with high levels of uncertainty. When a project contains a lot of technological uncertainty (and therefore risk) Boehm noted that the iterative model could lead to failure if the "easy" work happened to get done first while the work with the most uncertainty got left until later. If this happened, the complex bits of work finished last could require fundamental design changes that would require very high amounts of rework. In effect, the end result in these situations is not much different from Royce's Waterfall method. Boehm proposed a different solution: Spiral Development.[9] In Boehm's new method, the work for each iteration is prioritized based upon the uncertainty (or level of risk) associated with the work, such that the highest-risk items are developed first. Using this method, dramatic design shifts happen very early in the project, minimizing their impact on project budgets and timelines, and reducing the total amount of rework.

The evolution of new methods to address high-complexity and high-uncertainty project continued with the widespread popularity of Rapid Application Development (RAD)[10] in the early 1990s. The 1990s was a fertile decade for new solutions to this problem, giving birth to Agile Development and its associated methods: The Crystal Methods,[11] Lean Development,[12] Dynamic Systems Development Method (DSDM),[13] Scrum,[14,15] Extreme Programming,[16] Feature-Driven Development,[17] and others.

With the emergence of a large number of methods to address a common problem, the leaders of these methods gathered together[18] to discuss their common problems, namely how to overcome the natural resistance to new methods and get them adopted into organizations. The result was a realization that all of these methods shared a few common underlying principles and beliefs.[19] With a common framework of reference, the proponents of these methods then began the process of converting the traditionalists over to the new methods. Using Kuhn's terms, they were *revolutionaries* trying to push forward a *paradigm shift*, one where agile methods would be accepted and respected alongside their more traditional counterparts.

During this definitive period for agile methods, debate ensued as to the correct method for promoting agile methods, and how best to adopt them within an organization. This quiet debate over the concept of "selling agile" has been widely discussed, generating many conflicting opinions. In informal discussions among agile proponents, and through more public fora including the *Selling Agile* discussion group on Yahoo.com,[20] experts agree on a few approaches to adopting agile methods into a project or into an organization. These approaches are discussed below; however, foremost among these approaches is the need to avoid "selling" agile at all.

If you try to actively "sell" agile, you are, in effect, trying to convince others to change their traditional beliefs and start thinking in a new way. By the very nature of the approach, you are confronting traditional practices and trying to point out their weaknesses in relation to the new method. For those with long-held and strong beliefs in the traditional methods, you will be seen as confrontational and 'extreme' (pun intended). You may become marginalized by others, reducing any chances you have of effecting any change.

Instead of trying to "sell" others on agile approaches, a directly persuasive approach, consider using more stealthy means to convince others to adopt these techniques. Act as a role model for others, adopting the methods for your own work (where you can) and lead by example. Others will see your different approach and your improved effectiveness. By becoming more successful yourself, others will naturally want to mimic your contributing behaviors and techniques. When leading by example, you can encourage others to adopt your methods without using confrontational, persuasive techniques; rather, you are using more stealthy approaches that "fly under the radar," and persuade others without directly offending their traditional views and without attracting too much attention from the "methodology police" (a process audit or corporate standards department).

Focus on the Benefits

When discussing your approaches with others, try to remain pragmatic, focusing on the business benefits behind the new techniques. While agile methods may not fit every project, they do provide valuable benefits when applied against specific business problems. Consider each of these benefits when evaluating whether a particular agile technique might be useful on your own project.

There are three main types of benefits from agile techniques: reducing risk, improving control, and improving communications. Each of these benefits has a number of aspects that are described in detail in Chapter 1, the introduction to this book.

By focusing on the benefits, you can often reduce implementation resistance by showing the significant benefits that can be achieved through using these methods. This approach ("selling the sizzle," in marketing parlance) brings the parties out of their daily concerns for a moment and allows them to share a vision of a better situation – for some people, providing such a vision is the key to winning them over to your approach.

Introduce Agile Methods to your Project

To obtain the maximum benefits from any new process you adopt within your organization, change all of the related processes at once. With this approach, every new process that drives incremental value will be starting to generate that value all at once. Why prolong the pain? Why not just get it all over with at once?

For small changes, the above approach may work; however, for more comprehensive changes, you must consider the impact on the people affected by the changes. Imagine that one day you come in to work and your entire world is turned upside down. You may have sat in on some training sessions on the new processes, but they seemed academic – without real hands-on work with the new processes, it all seemed rather abstract and hard for you to envision. You will be overwhelmed and not effective at performing your job under the new processes until you have had time to adjust to the change, learning new ways of doing your job and getting to know who you will now be interacting with under the new paradigm.

Introducing agile methods faces the same challenges. In theory, a wholesale adoption of a new process is good; in practice, it rarely succeeds. (One exception to this rule is when a new organization (or team) is being formed, with all new processes. In this case, no one will be effective until the new processes are assimilated; in these situations, there would be no negative impact from adopting agile techniques *en masse*.) For most situations, you will have to figure out how to introduce the agile methods bit by bit, allowing those affected to adjust to the changes as you go along, else you risk crippling the group's performance.

To take this measured approach, follow the tips provided below. These tips have been gathered from a broad range of sources on change management and agile method adoption.

Understand Stakeholders and their Relative Power

Before you begin to phase in agile techniques, you should first identify the project stakeholders and understand their individual concerns. Do not get trapped in the common belief that only the concerns of the formal project sponsor matter – seek out those who really do have a stake in the success (or failure) of the project, and understand their concerns. I often call this "sniffing out the hidden agendas."

One technique that helps uncover the few individuals whose opinions should carry more weight is called stakeholder organizational mapping. Using this technique, you follow a six step process identified by Barreca: [21]

1   Build an organization chart showing the formal interrelationships between the project stakeholders.

2   Identify the formal roles of the stakeholders on the project (e.g. user, evaluator, decision maker, or approver).

3   Evaluate the receptiveness of each stakeholder to change in general (leaders, followers, and resisters).

4   Assess your level of influence over these individuals

5   Evaluate what type of support you believe each individual will give towards your proposed changes (hostile, non-supporter, neutral, supporter, or sponsor)

6   Identify the informal influence pathways. The influence
     pathways will often not follow hierarchical lines, but shows
     who really wields influence within the group.

An example of this technique in use is shown in Figure 20-1.
Here, we see a sample stakeholder organizational map showing
three areas of interest:

- **Political Structure.** This shows you the subset of
  stakeholders who are really interested (positively or
  negatively) in the outcome of the project, and who have
  some influence over its operating conditions.

- **Inner Circle.** This is a smaller group of people within the
  political structure who can (and will) actively wield their
  power to help or hinder the project.

- **Power Sponsor.** This individual is the one who is paying
  the bill on the project, or whose reputation is at stake as
  the "owner" of the project. The Power Sponsor has the
  ability to make unilateral decisions affecting the outcome
  of the project, or who will use his or her power and
  influence to get others to come on board with his or her
  decision. Do not confuse the Power Sponsor with the
  regular project sponsor, the one delegated to sign off on
  project documents and make decisions on everyday project
  issues. The Power Sponsor may be the sponsor, the
  sponsor's boss, or someone else in the organization who is
  pulling the strings behind the scenes to make the project
  happen.

By using the stakeholder organization map, you can focus your
communication efforts ("selling") on those in power who may
resist your proposed changes. Do not waste too much time
with those who will support what you will propose – they will

be in your corner anyways; rather, target your efforts at specific individuals who may be converted into supporters (or at least neutralized).

When addressing those who are non-supporters (or those who are hostile) consider using the old "triple-decker approach" favored by so many management consultants: when speaking with the target person in an effort to persuade them to accept your approach, make sure you speak with the person above him or her on the stakeholder organization map and also with those who are below him or her – that way, they will hear the idea from you, from his or her "boss," and from employees in his or her department. When hearing about the wisdom of adopting some agile methods from so many directions at once,

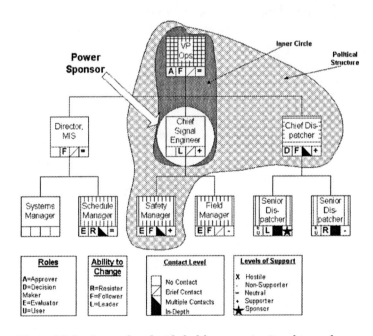

Figure 20-1: A completed stakeholder organizational map shows the power dynamics for this project. This example is reproduced from an article by Jeanne Barreca.[21]

most people will find it difficult to go against the thinking of so many. At heart, most people want to fit in with the larger group, and this technique takes advantage of that.

Understand the Business Case

To gain the support of business stakeholders, neither focus on the technology, nor the buzzwords in the approach; instead, focus on their specific business problems and how what you are proposing will address those problems. In other words, you need to speak in business terms.

Just learning the current business buzzwords will not make you an effective persuader to your stakeholders any more than learning the right technology buzzwords makes you an effective programmer. You need to understand the *specific* problems being addressed by the business case that justified the project investment. At some point, someone should have put together (even if only in their heads) an estimate of the cost of the project along with an estimate of the expected benefits to be received if the project is successful. This person would have compared the two to see if the project made economic sense before approving the start of the project.

Sometimes the project is to generate profits, at other times, it is to minimize losses. Some projects are not meant to make money, but rather to gain (or preserve) market share. And still others may be initiated just to comply with changing government legislation. Government itself (and non-profit organizations) may initiate projects to increase levels of service, without requiring that a project make or save money. Whatever the reason, the person initiating the project should have a clear idea of why the project was started in the first place. Find that person, and find out what his or her expectations are for the project outcome.[22]

Once you have understood what is behind the project business case, you can now talk to the stakeholders using the paradigm of the business case itself. Identify ways in which agile methods can support the business case by lowering risk, improving quality, gaining early market share, etc. (See the section on the benefits of agile methods discussed in Chapter 1 for more ideas on how agile can support the business case.)

The key here is to speak to the stakeholders on their own terms, helping them solve their business problems. If agile methods will help solve those problems, then explain to the stakeholders how using agile methods will benefit them, using specific non-technical examples.

Use White Label Methods

I once had lunch with a CFO named Terry who was very upset at his IT group. I asked him what the matter was, and he told me that he had just approved the initiation of a huge project. In fact, the project was the biggest project the organization had ever undertaken. Terry explained that the business needed to respond to a competitor who offered a wide range of online services to their customers that Terry's organization did not yet offer. They were losing market share due to the convenience and the lower prices that the competitor could now offer as a result of the cost savings introduced by the new online ordering system.

The company was under very tight financial con-straints, and Terry had to find a way of doing the work cost effectively. The CEO preferred hiring an outside consultancy to come in and build the application, but Terry was convinced that the company had the skills to do the work in house. Also, Terry believed that in its tightly-constrained financial position, the company needed to find ways of keeping costs low, and doing the work in house would be the cheapest solution. While the CEO was skeptical, Terry promised him that the costs would be lower and that the in-house group would be able to do the level of work required. After all, Terry had seen them build some pretty remarkable software over the years – this could not be all that difficult now, could it?

I asked Terry why he was upset at his IT group – what had they done to anger him? Terry replied that the IT group had come to him with a budget that was in line with his expectations and promised that they could meet the schedule. I interrupted him and asked "Well, then, what's the problem?" Terry replied that what really angered him was that the team was going to take the most important project he has ever initiated, one on the success of which Terry has hung his reputation, and were going to deliver it using something called "Extreme Programming." He became agitated, and shouted "Extreme? Extreme! How could they do something so risky when my job is on the line?"

Over the course of lunch, I succeeded in calming Terry down. After considering his outburst, I realized that his concern was not in the method that was being proposed, but rather his objection to the *name* of the method. I tried a different approach.

"Terry, forget about this 'Extreme' business and let's talk some sense here. I know you have good people in your IT department. Maybe they can do it another way and still bring it in on time and on budget," I suggested.

"Do you really think so? I am worried now that we have a bunch of cowboys down there who are going to just hack something together without any controls or quality," Terry said.

"Well, then, how about this? We get them to focus most of their efforts on quality. Make that the primary goal of the project, while of course staying on time, and trying to live within the budget. Would that address your concern?"

"Yes, it would. What are you proposing?"

"First, let's forget about following the normal company processes – they would just slow things down and not add much value. Do you agree?"

"Of course." Terry was very interested now.

"What we can do, is have the teams develop the application in pieces. We will start with building one part, then have them test and demonstrate that piece to us. In that way, you will know *for sure* that they are making progress – no one will be able to pull the wool over your eyes."

"I like the sound of this."

"It gets better. When the IT group delivers each piece, you can sit down and review the work in progress, have a chance to play with it, and give them your feedback early, rather than waiting for the end of the project, when they would normally show you what they have built. This allows you to redirect the team should they start to go off course from what you intended. You will have complete control. Does this sound good to you so far?"

"Yes, this is exactly what we need."

"We need to break the product into small enough pieces so that they can deliver something to you every two weeks. That way, you are never at risk for more than a couple of weeks' work if they do get off course. At the beginning of each cycle, you will look at what originally-identified features are still left to do, plus whatever new requirements you have come up with, and any defects or feedback that you came up with from your reviews, and reprioritize for them, telling them what specific pieces you would like them to work on in the next two-week round. Of course, they will help you prioritize by telling you what pieces make technical sense to do together, or which features are dependent on other ones being done first, but you get to make the final decisions. So far, so good?"

"Yes, I love it. But what about quality? You said they would be focused on quality."

"Yes, they will be. By allowing you to reprioritize their efforts every two weeks, you are more likely to get what you need at the end of the project, even if your requirements have changed during the project, and I am sure they will on this one."

Terry interrupted: "I expect that things will change a lot – we really don't know for sure yet what we are doing in this area – it is all new to us. I suspect our vision for this will change somewhat during the development, as we start to see it take shape."

"Then what I am suggesting is perfect for your situation. You can redirect the team as you go to make sure they stay in line with your vision. Now, every two weeks, the team will develop a piece of that vision, and deliver it to you fully tested. They will gather your acceptance criteria up front, and use those criteria as inputs into their design and development process. In fact, they may even use your acceptance criteria as their own test criteria to make sure that what they deliver is guaranteed to meet your acceptance criteria before it leaves your hands. Every time they deliver a new piece, they will completely test the whole thing so that, by the time the project is done, the first bits have been tested several times over, almost guaranteeing better quality than if the team had just been through the testing cycle once at the end of a traditional project."

"I like what you are proposing. Tell me more. Does this really work?"

"Of course it works – I use this approach myself all the time. In fact, there is even another technique that you could decide to use that would make the quality even better: we call it Pair Programming."

346

"What's that?" Terry asked.

"Pair Programming is a technique that will dramatically improve your quality and reduce the risk of schedule slips late in the project. Here's how it works. First, you place two programmers at each keyboard – in effect, sharing a desk and a computer. Only one programs at any given time, with the other one looking over his or her shoulder instantly performing code and design reviews as the code is written. You normally do your code reviews at the end of a project, but here you are doing them throughout. This way, any defects are highlighted immediately, and the programmer has a chance to fix things while he or she is still writing the code, rather than waiting until much later when a tester may find a defect that takes many hours of investigation to uncover and fix. Also, design issues can be pointed out right away – issues that could cost you dearly later if you have to change your design near the end of the project to fix a defect. This saves you a lot of time, and may save you money, even with the doubled cost of development. However, don't count on this as a way of saving costs – if you are lucky, you'll come out about even – instead, consider this a way of reducing schedule and quality risks."

"This sounds like what I wanted – something that keeps this project on schedule and almost guarantees good quality."

"Well, there are no guarantees," I chuckled, "but you certainly will notice the difference between this approach and your traditional, sequentially-phased software development methods."

"I like this. Why don't my IT guys know this stuff? If they could do this stuff, then they would not have to scare me with all this talk about 'Extreme Programming.'"

I smiled to myself as I paid the bill, making a note to myself that I should immediately talk to the head of the IT group and tell him that he can go ahead and use XP, as long as he stops calling it by its real name.

Practice Stealth Methodology Adoption

Instead of trying to adopt an entire methodology at once, and making the adoption public, try a different approach, one I call Stealth Methodology Adoption. Pick the agile techniques that make the most sense on your own project. Then consider the ones that will work within the culture of your team and your organization. Finally, look at the availability of tools (such as automated testing tools) and expertise. Use these factors to prepare a shortlist of agile techniques that will work for you.

Your shortlist will help you stay focused on realistic goals for your agile evolution. Do not expect to get the full benefit from these techniques on day one – phase them in, adopt them gradually, to allow teams time to experiment and learn. You should spend some time understanding the business case (as discussed above) and using that understanding to prioritize which techniques from your shortlist should be adopted first, second, and so on. This prioritization effort is very important, for by strategic ordering of these techniques, you can dramatically affect the achievement of the business results planned in the business case.

Of all the agile techniques that can end up on your shortlist, here are five that I find are the easier ones to adopt that still drive tremendous business value.

Iterative Development. The engine that makes most of the other agile techniques possible, iterative development is the first agile technique that you should consider. If you are in an environment of restrictive processes that enforce Waterfall-type sequential development, then you can still stealthily adopt iterative development onto your project. Instead of standing up on a chair and waving a red flag and shouting out that you are breaking the organizational rules, find ways of subverting the existing process to your own ends. If the official method is Waterfall, then by all means use it; however, you can structure your project so that it becomes a series of short waterfalls, each of a fixed duration. By breaking down development into a number of subprojects, each with its own design-develop-test waterfall, you are complying with the organizational rules, but still allowing you to do what is, in fact, iterative development.

Feature-Driven Development. Instead of building out a *project* work breakdown structure (WBS) consisting of tasks and then estimating and scheduling each task, consider an alternative approach. This first approach follows the standard industry practices promoted by the Project Management Institute (PMI); yet, it leaves project team members feeling micromanaged. Even worse, continually changing requirements will lead to chaos as the work breakdown structure is frequently updated, re-estimated, and then rescheduled in a project planning tool such as Microsoft Project.™

Instead, build a *product* breakdown structure (a WBS that focuses on deconstructing the deliverable into externally-observable features).[23] You can then estimate the work required to build the features and then assign the prioritized features to different iterations. In Project, you can create time-boxed iterations in the plan. In each iteration, just list the features that you are planning for that iteration, scheduling each feature to take up the entire timeboxed period.

As a PM, you should spend your time tracking the delivery of useful features, and not worry as much about the behind-the-scenes pieces that the team is developing. Let the team do their own job – do not try to micromanage them. Using feature-based planning will give you more meaningful tracking metrics and will allow you to converse meaningfully with the customer on progress and issues.

Test-Driven Development. Once you have designed your approach based upon features, you can then begin to start your technical design based upon customer acceptance test criteria. You need to spend time with your customers up front to understand their acceptance criteria for the project in detail. Then, once you have this information, you can use it to plan out your own design, ensuring that you build only what the customers care about – what they will be testing. These same tests can be used as the final tests by the developers to make sure that the application delivers what the customers are expecting.

By using Test-Driven Development, you are not only very efficient in your design (only building what customers will be testing, and no more) but also you are almost guaranteeing customer approval of the end product. After all, you have already gathered their acceptance criteria and pre-tested the solution to make sure it meets all of those criteria before handing it off to the customers. Finally, there is yet one more benefit to this agile technique – the resulting quality of the application (as measured by compliance with customer expectations/test specifications) will be much higher.

Customer Involvement in Prioritization and Planning. Why try to fight change? Change is inevitable in this fast-paced business world, and we need to find ways to adapt to it in order for us to deliver useful software. What better way to guarantee that you are delivering useful software than by allowing the customer to provide feedback throughout the project on how much value you are delivering compared to his or her current business needs. In effect, we are talking about allowing the customer to get involved in helping guide the project towards delivering business value.[22]

Not only will you improve your chances of delivering value, but also you will improve the visibility of progress (easing customers who are nervous from bad past experiences), reduce the chance of misunderstandings leading the project team away from the customer's true intent, and get the customer's immediate involvement in decisions where tradeoffs need to be made.

Continuous Testing. While Test-Driven Development increases the chances of customer acceptance of your project deliverables, it does not guarantee that defects will be found early enough to be fixed before they start impacting the project schedule. One of the biggest problems with the Waterfall method is that it does not predict/control/deal with design defects found late in the test cycle at the end of the project. These force the project to cycle back and reopen the design phase before cycling through all the phases again, leading to significant schedule delays.

Iterative development, on the other hand, allows testing to happen during each iteration. If you combine these two concepts (iterative and test-driven development) you come up with the concept of *continuous testing*. Using this technique, you work with a set of acceptance criteria (test specifications) that you will measure the product against as it evolves throughout the project iterations. You continually run all test cases (using automated tools, if possible) against every build of the product, and track its evolving quality during (and across) iterations. Through continuous testing, you will have a much greater likelihood of meeting the customer's stated quality criteria and expectations (as expressed in their acceptance tests), both improving the quality of the product and improving the chances of final customer acceptance.[24]

Negotiate Agile Contracts

To allow you to employ agile methods more freely on your projects, consider negotiating agile contracts that support the methods. While projects may operate under many different kinds of contracts, the most common are Fixed Price contracts that place all of the budget risk on the vendor, and Time and Materials contracts that place all of the budget risk on the sponsor. Figure 20-2 shows the relative placement of several contract types along this spectrum. Agile contracts can be negotiated at any point along this spectrum, but have different characteristics depending up on who is accepting most of the budget risk.

With agile methods, Time and Materials contracts are the easiest to work under. The main reason behind this is the active involvement of the project sponsor in prioritization, feedback, and raising changing requirements. Under Time and Materials contracts, the sponsor takes all of the budget risk, which is appropriate if the sponsor will be participating at this level in activities that may impact the budget.

Of course, not every project will be able to operate under Time and Materials contracts. In many cases, you will

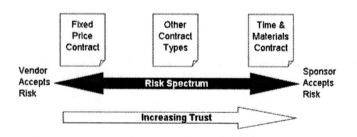

Figure 20-2: Contract types appear along a risk-transfer spectrum, with all the risk on the vendor at one end, and all of the risk on the sponsor on the other end.

have to create Fixed Price contracts for your project. In Chapter 12, we reviewed different ideas for creating Agile Fixed Price contracts that would still allow the project the flexibility of dealing with sponsor-generated changes, while protecting the vendor from the risk of budget overruns.

No matter which approach you take, contracts that allow for agile methods and that transfer risk accordingly are a good start when trying to introduce agile methods into an organization. You may want to start down this route as one of your early activities in your evolution towards a fully-agile development environment.

Don't Start with Pair Programming

Despite my (true) story above about convincing a CFO to adopt Extreme Programming on his project, the hardest XP practice to introduce into an organization is Pair Programming. Of all 12 XP practices, it is by far the hardest to convince sponsors to pay for, and even the hardest to convince developers to adopt.

Sponsors find Pair Programming's claims of reduced costs very hard to accept, especially when you have no track record doing agile work for the customer. Without trust, customers will see it as just doubling costs and wasting effort. When you are working with a sponsor whom you suspect will be less than supportive of such an idea, do not attempt to adopt this practice until you have some agile successes under your belt and have started to gain their trust.

Developers may also resist the adoption of Pair Programming. I have heard developers complaining that it feels awkward to have someone peering over their shoulder as they work, and that it makes them self-conscious and less productive. Some developers complain that being "babysat" by another developer makes them feel as if no one trusts in their abilities, reducing team morale. There is also the possibility of more socializing and less work. Gerold Keefer, in Chapter 18, points out some of the research that indicates Pair Programming may not always be effective. In light of these criticisms, you should take time to consider the suitability of the practice to your individual team, and perhaps discuss the approach with them, gathering their individual feedback, before making any decisions about adopting the approach.

If you think you want to try introducing Pair Programming to a sponsor or team who may be receptive, do not double up completely on developers. Instead, start with a second part time developer, and call the work "early code inspections" rather than Pair Programming. It will be easier to convince your sponsor and the team on the merits of focusing on improved quality (reduced errors) and perhaps shortened testing/fix time at the end of the project.

Get Started Today!

Agile methods allow us to adapt to the changing world around us. Traditional methods simply do not adapt efficiently to these changes, and lead to increased costs and timelines. Agile methods have their role to play in modern product development.

They are not for every organization, nor for every project. You need to have a supportive culture, experienced team members, and an appropriate project. (For example, you would not want to try agile methods for planning the nationwide rollout of cash register upgrades for a large retailer. In this case, little change might be expected, and more traditional methods might be better.)

When starting down the agile road, pick and choose the agile methods that might help you maximize the business value that your project delivers. Do not get caught up on adopting a whole method. Instead, find the pieces that make the most sense to you – that you are sure will return value to your organization – and start with those practices first. Over time, your project (or your organization) will adopt more and more techniques, becoming more agile and responsive to change in the mean time.

Pick your battles wisely: find the ones you know that you will be able to win, and start there. Use stealth (if you need to) when introducing agile methods to reduce visibility of the changes and to reduce the resulting objections. Once you have some successes under your belt, you can let your secrets out of the bag, and be seen as a role model for others to follow.

Don't wait – get started today!

PART FIVE

Resources

Chapter Notes

Chapter One

[1] Beck, Kent. *Extreme Programming Explained: Embracing Change.* Boston: Addison Wesley, 1999.

[2] Schwaber, Ken and Beedle, Mike. *Agile Software Development with Scrum.* Upper Saddle River, NJ: Prentice Hall, 2002.

[3] Palmer, Steven. "Feature-Driven Development." Borland Developer Network Web site. <http://bdn.borland.com/article/borcon/files/2136/paper/2136.html>.

[4] Poppendieck, Mary and Poppendieck, Tom. *Lean Software Development: An Agile Toolkit for Software Development Managers.* Boston: Addison Wesley, 2003.

[5] Cockburn, Alistair. "Crystal Light Methods." Available at <http://alistair.cockburn.us/crystal/articles/clm/crystallightmethods.htm>.

[6] Highsmith, Jim. "History: The Agile Manifesto." Agile Alliance Web site, 2001. < http://www.agilemanifesto.org/history.html>.

[7] Aguanno, Kevin. "Ever-Changing Requirements: Use Agile Methods to Reduce Project Risk." *Proc. Informatics 2004.* Canadian Information Processing Society (CIPS). May 2004.

[8] Aguanno, Kevin. "Manage Change Better With Scrum." *Inside Project Management*. 2.8 (2002) 1-6.

[9] The Lean Construction Institute Web site is available at <http://www.leanconstruction.org/>.

[10] The Standish Group. The CHAOS Report. 1994. <http://www.standishgroup.com/sample_research/chaos_1994_1.php>.

[11] Royce, W.W. "Managing the Development of Large Software Systems: Concepts and Techniquees." *Proc. WESCON*. (1970) 1-9.

[12] Aguanno, Kevin. "The Waterfall Development Method." *Inside Project Management*. 2.8 (2002).

[13] Boehm, Barry. *Software Engineering Economics*. Upper Saddle River, NJ: Prentice Hall, 1981.

[14] See Chapter 5 for more details on the benefits of high-bandwidth communications vehicles.

[15] Highsmith, Jim. *Agile Project Management*. Boston: Addison Wesley, 2004.

[16] The C3 Team. "Chrysler Goes to 'Extremes.'" *Distributed Computing*. Oct. 1998, 24-28.

Chapter Two

[1] Beck, Kent; Cockburn, Alistair; Jeffries, Ron; and Highsmith, Jim. Agile Manifesto. <http://www.agilemanifesto.org> 2001.

[2] Highsmith, Jim. *Agile Software Development Ecosystems*. Boston: Addison-Wesley, 2002.

[3] Highsmith, Jim; Orr, K.; Cockburn, Alistair. "Extreme Programming." *E-Business Application Delivery*. 4-17, Feb. 2000.

[4] Basili, V. and Turner, A.J. "Iterative Enhancement: A Practical Technique for Software Development." *IEEE Transactions on Software Engineering.* 1.4 (1975) 390-96.

[5] Cockburn, A. and Highsmith, J. "Agile Software Development: The Business of Innovation." *IEEE Computer.* Sept. 2001, 120-22.

[6] Royce, W.W. "Managing the Development of Large Software Systems: Concepts and Techniques." *Proc. WESCON.* (1970) 1-9.

[7] Beck, Kent. "Embrace Change with Extreme Programming." *IEEE Computer.* Oct. 1999, 70-77.

[8] Boehm, Barry. "Get Ready for Agile Methods, With Care." *IEEE Computer.* Jan. 2002, 64-69.

[9] Boehm, Barry. "A Spiral Model of Software Development and Enhancement." *IEEE Computer.* 21.5 (1988) 61-72.

[10] We use the terms CMM and SW-CMM interchangeably to denote the Software CMM from the Software Engineering Institute.

[11] Paulk,Mark C. "Key Practices of the Capability Maturity Model, Version 1.1." *Technical Report CMU/SEI-93-TR-25,* 1993.

[12] Paulk, Mark C. "Extreme Programming from a CMM Perspective." IEEE Software. 18.6 (2001) 19-26.

[13] Schwaber, Ken. "Controlled Chaos: Living on the Edge." Agile Alliance Web Site. <http://www.agilealliance.org/articles/articles/ap.pdf>, 2002.

[14] Turk, Dan; France, Robert; and Rumpe, Bernhard. "Limitations of Agile Software Processes." *Proc. 3rd International Conference on eXtreme Programming and Agile Processes in Software Engineering - XP2002,* 2002.

[15] Poppendieck, Mary. Lean Programming. Agile Alliance Web Site. <http://www.agilealliance.org/articles/articles/LeanProgramming.htm> 2001.

[16] The C3 Team. "Chrysler Goes to Extremes." *Distributed Computing.* Oct. 1998, 24-28.

[17] Glass, R. "Agile Versus Traditional: Make Love, Not War." *Cutter IT Journal.* Dec. 2001, 12-18.

[18] CMM will be replaced by CMMI; see "How Will Sunsetting of the Software CMM Be Conducted" at <http://www.sei.cmu.edu/cmmi/adoption/sunset.html>.

[19] The Personal Software Process (PSP) is closely related to the CMM. Humphrey, W.S. *A Discipline for Software Engineering.* Reading, MA: Addison Wesley Longman, 1995.

[20] Email conversation with Sandra Shrum, SEI.

[21] Turner, Richard and Jain, Apurva. "Agile meets CMMI: Culture Clash or Common Cause?" *Proc. eXtreme Programming and Agile Methods - XP/Agile Universe 2002.* (2002) 153-165.

[22] Highsmith, Jim. "What is Agile Software Development?" *Crosstalk.* Oct. 2002, 4-9.

[23] DeMarco, Tom and Boehm, Barry. "The Agile Methods Fray." *IEEE Computer.* June 2002, 90-92.

[24] Paulk, Mark C. "Agile Methodologies and Process Discipline." *Crosstalk.* Oct. 2002, 15-18.

[25] Glazer, H. "Dispelling the Process Myth: Having a Process Does Not Mean Sacrificing Agility or Creativity." *Crosstalk.* Nov. 2001.

[26] Paulisch, Frances and Völker, Axel. "Agility: Build on a Mature Foundation." *Proc. Software Engineering Process Group Conference - SEPG 2002,* 2002.

[27] As XP is the most documented method, it often is used as a representative sample of Agile Methods.

[28] XP supports the following Level 2 practices according to Paulk (2001): *requirements management, software project planning, software project tracking and oversight, software quality assurance,* and *software configuration management,* but not *software subcontract management.*

[29] XP supports the following Level 3 practices according to Paulk (2001): *organization process focus, organization process definition, software product engineering, inter-group coordination,* and *peer reviews.* XP does not support the Level 3 practices *training program* and *integrated software management.*

[30] Agile Methods rely on undocumented (tacit) knowledge and avoid documentation.

[31] Rakitin, S.R. "Manifesto Elicits Cynicism." *IEEE Computer.* 34.12 (2001) 4.

[32] Bowers, P. "Highpoints from the Agile Software Development Forum." *Crosstalk.* Oct. 2002, 26-27.

[33] Jeffries, Ron. "Extreme Programming and the Capability Maturity Model." XP Programming Web Site. <http://www.xprogramming.com/xpmag/xp_and_cmm.htm>.

Chapter Three

[1] Highsmith, Jim. Posted on the *Agile Vs Self Adapting Wiki.* <http://alistair.cockburn.us/crystal/wiki/AgileVsSelfAdapting>.

[2] Schwaber, Ken. *Agile Software Development with Scrum.* Upper Saddle River: Prentice Hall, 2002. pp 24-25.

[3] Highsmith, Jim. *Agile Project Management: Creating Innovative Products.* Boston: Addison-Wesley, 2004.

[4] Chin, Gary. *Agile Project Management: How to Succeed in the Face of Changing Project Requirements.* New York: AMACOM, 2004.

Chapter Four

[1] See <http://www.sei.cmu.edu/cbs/spiral2000/february2000/ Royce/> for an overview of RUP as an example of a "Spiral process."

[2] Boehm, Barry. *Software Engineering Economics.* Upper Saddle River, NJ: Prentice Hall, 1981.

[3] Beck, Kent. *Extreme Programming Explained.* Boston: Addison-Wesley, 2000.

Chapter Five

[1] Beck, Kent. *Extreme Programming Explained: Embrace Change.* Boston: Addison-Wesley, 1999.

[2] Coad, P., E. Lefebvre, and J. De Luca. *Java Modeling In Color With UML: Enterprise Components and Process.* Upper Saddle River: Prentice Hall, 1999.

[3] Cockburn, Alistair. *Agile Software Development.* Boston: Addison-Wesley, 2001.

[4] Highsmith, Jim. *Agile Software Development Ecosystems.* Boston: Addison-Wesley, 2002.

[5] Schwaber, K., and M. Beedle. *Agile Software Development with Scrum.* Upper Saddle River: Prentice Hall, 2001.

[6] Highsmith, Jim, and Alistair Cockburn. "Agile Software Development: The Business of Innovation." *IEEE Software* 34.9 (2001): 120-122.

[7] Cockburn, Alistair, and Jim Highsmith. "Agile Software Development: The People Factor." *IEEE Software* 34:11 (2001): 131-133.

[8] Boehm, Barry, and D. Port. "Balancing Discipline and Flexibility with the Spiral Model and MBASE." *CrossTalk* Dec. 2001: 23-30. <http://www.stsc.hill.af.mil/crosstalk/2001/12/boehm.pdf>.

[9] Software Engineering Institute. *Capability Maturity Model® Integration^SM V1.1 (CMMI^SM)*. Pittsburgh: SEI, 2002. <http://www.sei.cmu.edu/cmm>.

[10] Humphrey, Watts. *A Discipline for Software Engineering*. Boston: Addison-Wesley, 1997.

[11] Paulk, Mark C. "Agile Methodologies and Process Discipline." *CrossTalk* Oct. 2002: 15-18.

[12] Highsmith, Jim. "What Is Agile Software Development?" *CrossTalk* Oct. 2002: 4-9.

[13] Cockburn, Alistair. "Agile Software Development Joins the Would-Be Crowd." *Cutter IT Journal* Jan. 2002: 6-12.

[14] Sullivan, K., P. Chalasani, S. Jha, and V. Sazawal. "Software Design as an Investment Activity: A Real Options Perspective." *Real Options and Business Strategy: Applications to Decision Making*. Ed. L. Trigeorgis. London: Risk Books. Dec. 1999.

[15] Mathiassen, L. "Reflective Systems Development." *Scandinavian Journal of Information Systems*. Vol. 10, No. 1, 2. Gothenburg, Sweden: The IRIS Association, 1998: 67-117.

[16] Hohmann, L. *Journey of the Software Professional*. Upper Saddle River: Prentice-Hall, 1997.

[17] Jones, Capers. *Software Assessments, Benchmarks, and Best Practices*. Boston: Addison-Wesley, 2000.

[18] Cockburn, Alistair. "Selecting a Project's Methodology." *IEEE Software* 17.4 (2000): 64-71.

[19] McCarthy, J., and A. Monk. "Channels, Conversation, Cooperation and Relevance: All You Wanted to Know About Communication But Were Afraid to Ask." *Collaborative Computing* 1.1 (Mar. 1994): 35-61.

[20] Allen, T.J. *Managing the Flow of Technology*. Cambridge, MIT Press, 1977.

[21] Olson, G. M., and J. S. Olson. "Distance Matters." *Human-Computer Interaction* 15 (2001): 139-179.

[22] Goldratt, E. *The Goal*. Great Barrington: North River Press, 1992.

[23] Goldratt, E. *Theory of Constraints*. Great Barrington: North River Press, 1990.

[24] DeMarco, T., and T. Lister. *Peopleware: Productive Projects and Teams*. 2nd Ed. New York: Dorset House, 1999.

[25] Herring, R., and M. Rees. "Internet-Based Collaborative Software Development Using Microsoft Tools." *Proc. 5th World Multiconference on Systemics, Cybernetics and Informatics*. Orlando, Florida. July 2001: 22-25. <http://erwin.dstc.edu.au/Herring/Software EngineeringOverInternetSCI2001.pdf>.

[26] Brown, N. "Disciplines Delivering Success." *Proc. Software Technology Conference, 1997*. <http://stc-online.org/cd-rom/1997/track1.pdf>.

Chapter Six

[1] Wheatley, Margaret. *Leadership and the New Science: Discovering Order in a Chaotic World*. San Francisco: Berrett-Koehler Publishers, 1999.

[2] Cockburn, Alistair. *Agile Software Development*. Boston: Addison Wesley Longman, 2001.

[3] The original wiki web site is at <http://c2.com/cgi-bin/wiki>.

Chapter Seven

[1] Smith, John. *A Comparison of RUP and XP.* Rational Software White Paper, 2001.

[2] Beck, Kent. *Extreme Programming.* Boston: Addison-Wesley, 2000.

[3] Cockburn, Alistair. *Agile Software Development. Boston:* Addison-Wesley, 2002.

[4] Tomayko, James E. "A Comparison of Pair Programming to Inspections for Software Defect Reduction." *Computer Science Education.* 2002.

[5] Tomayko, James E. "Using Extreme Programming to Develop Software Requirements." *Soft-Ware 2002.* Berlin: Springer-Verlag, 2002. 315-31.

[6] Davis, Alan. *Software Requirements.* Englewood Cliffs, N.J.: Prentice-Hall, 1990.

[7] Tomayko, James E. "An Historian's View of Software Engineering." *Proc. of the IEEE Conference on Software Engineering Education and Training.* Los Alamitos, California: IEEE Computer Society Press, 2000.

[8] Leffingwell, D. and Widrig, D. *Managing Software Requirements: A Unified Approach.* Boston: Addison-Wesley, 2000.

[9] Boehm, Barry. "Requirements that Handle IKIWISI, COTS, and Rapid Change." *Computer.* Los Alamitos, California: IEEE Press. July 2000. 99-102.

[10] Thayer, Richard and Dorfman, Merlin, eds. *Software Requirements Engineering.* Los Alamitos, California: IEEE Computer Society Press, 1997.

Chapter Eight

[1] Ambler, S.W. *Agile Modeling: Best Practices for the Unified Process and Extreme Programming.* New York: John Wiley & Sons, 2002.

[2] Standish Group. *ChAOS: A Recipe for Success, 1998.* Published Report. 1998.

[3] Thomas, M. "IT Projects Sink or Swim." *British Computer Society Review*, 2001.

[4] Beck, K. *Extreme Programming Explained – Embrace Change.* Reading, MA: Addison Wesley Longman, 2000.

[5] Frankel, D.S. *Model Driven Architecture: Applying MDA to Enterprise Computing.* Indianapolis: Wiley Publishing, 2003.

[6] Amber, S.W. *The Object Primer 3rd Edition: Agile Model Driven Development with UML 2.* New York: Cambridge University Press, 2004.

[7] Available on the Web at <http://www.borland.com>.

[8] Available on the Web at <http://www.compuware.com>.

[9] Available on the Web at <http://www.cai.com>.

Chapter Nine

[1] Beck, K. *Extreme Programming Explained – Embrace Change.* Reading, MA: Addison Wesley Longman, 2000.

[2] Ambler, S.W. *Agile Modeling: Best Practices for the Unified Process and Extreme Programming.* New York: John Wiley & Sons, 2002.

[3] Cockburn, A. *Agile Software Development.* Reading, MA: Addison Wesley Longman, 2002.

[4] Ambler, S.W. *The Object Primer 3rd Edition: Agile Model Driven Development with UML 2.* New York: Cambridge University Press, 2004.

Chapter Ten

[1] RUP for Extreme Programming plug-ins are available for free from IBM at <http://www-106.ibm.com/developerworks/rational/library/4156.html>.

[2] CRC cards were first Introduced at OOPSLA in 1989 by Kent Beck and Ward Cunningham as an approach for teaching object-oriented design. A good introduction to CRC Cards and how to prepare them is found in Rubin, David M. *Introduction to CRC Cards.* January 1998. <http://www.softstar-inc.com/Download/Intro%20to%20CRC.pdf>.

[3] Palmer, Stephen. "Feature-Driven Development and Extreme Programming." *The Coad Letter.* 70 (2002). <http://bdn.borland.com/article/0,1410,29684,00.html>.

[4] See the Agile Manifesto at <http://www.agilemanifesto.org>.

[5] Poppendieck, Mary and Poppendieck, Tom. *Lean Software Development: An Agile Toolkit.* Boston: Addison Wesley, 2003. The section on agile contracts is available on the Web at <http://www.poppendieck.com/pdfs/Contracts_Excerpt_from_Lean_Software_Devleopment.pdf>.

Chapter Eleven

[1] <http://www.agilealliance.org>.

[2] Armour, F., Miller, G. *Advanced Use Case Modelling*, Boston: Addison Wesley, 2000.

[3] Bach, J., "Heuristic Risk-Based Testing." *Software Testing and Quality Engineering Magazine.* 11,1999.

[4] Basili, V., Caldiera, G., and Rombach, H. "Experience Factory." *Encyclopaedia of Software Engineering.* Vol. 1. John Wiley & Sons, 1994.

[5] Beck, K. *Extreme Programming Explained: Embrace Change.* Boston: Addison Wesley, 2000.

[6] Birk, A. "A Knowledge Management Infrastructure for Systematic Improvements in Software Engineering." *PhD Theses in Experimental Software Engineering.* Vol. 3. Fraunhofer IRB Verlag, 2001.

[7] Cockburn, A. *Writing Effective Use Cases.* Boston: Addison Wesley, 2001.

[8] Cockburn, A. *Agile Software Development.* Boston: Addison Wesley, 2002.

[9] Constantine, L., Lockwood, L. *Software For Use.* Boston: Addison Wesley, 1999.

[10] Dorofee, A. J., Walker, J., et al. *Continuous Risk Management Guidebook.* Pittsburgh, PA: Software Engineering Institute, 1996.

[11] Kohler, K. and Paech, B. "Task-driven Requirements in object-oriented Development." *Perspectives on Requirements Engineering.* Eds. J. Leite and J. Doorn. Kluwer Academic Publishers, 2003.

[12] Kontio, J. "The Riskit Method for Software Risk Management, version 1.00, CS-TR-3782." *Computer Science Technical Reports.* College Park, MD: University of Maryland, 1997.

[13] Kovitz, B.L. *Practical Software Requirements. A Manual of Content and Style.* Greenwich: Manning Publications Co., 1998.

[14] McPhee, Ch., and Eberlein, A. "Requirements Engineering for Time-to-Market Projects." *Proc. 9th Conference and Workshop on the Engineering of Computer-based Systems.* ECBS, Sweden, 2002.

[15] Maiden, N., and Rugg, G. "ACRE: Selecting Methods For Requirements Acquisition." *Software Engineering Journal.* May, 1996.

[16] Mead, N. R. "Why Is It so Difficult to Introduce Requirements Engineering Research Results into Mainstream Requirements Engineering Practice?" *Proc. Fourth International Conference on Requirements Engineering.* Illinois, June 2000.

[17] Morris, P., Masera, M., and Wilikens, M. "Requirements Engineering and Industrial Uptake." *Requirements Engineering.* 3, 1998.

[18] Potter, B., and Sinclair, J. *Formal Specification and Z.* London: Prentice Hall, 1996.

[19] van Schouwen A.J., Parnas, D. L., and Madey J. "Documentation of Requirements for Computer Systems." *Proc. IEEE International Symposium On Requirements Engineering,* San Diego, California, 1993.

[20] van Lamsweerde, A. "Requirements Engineering in the Year 00: A Research Perspective." *Proc. 22nd International Conference on Software Engineering,* Ireland, June 2000.

[21] Vegas, S., "Characterization Schema for Selecting Software Testing Techniques." Thesis. Madrid: Universidad Prolitecnica de , February 2002.

[22] Wiegers, K.E. "Read My Lips: No New Models!" *IEEE Software.* September/October 1998.

[23] With context we mean important factors influencing the software project.

[24] Note that for now we do not propose to denote probabilities by number.

Chapter Twelve

[1] Highsmith, Jim. *Agile Software Development Ecosystems.* Reading, MA: Addison Wesley, 2002.

[2] Beck, Kent. *Extreme Programming Explained.* Reading, MA: Addison Wesley, 1999.

[3] Johnson, Jim, et al. "Collaborating on Project Success." *Software Magazine.* Feb./Mar. 2001. <http://www.softwaremag.com/archive/2001feb/CollaborativeMgt.html>.

[4] Williams, Laurie, et al. "An Initial Exploration of the Relationship Between Pair Programming and Brooks' Law." *Proc. Agile Development Conference 2004.*

[5] Bosworth, Michael T. *Solution Selling.* New York: McGraw-Hill, 1995.

[6] Peeters, Vera and Van Cauwenberghe, Pascal. "The XP Game Explained." *Extreme Programming Perspectives.* Eds. Marchesi, Succi, Wells, and Williams. New York: Pearson, 2003.

[7] Schwaber, Ken and Beedle, Mike. *Agile Software Development With Scrum.* Upper Saddle River, NJ: Prentice Hall, 2002.

[8] Leach, Lawrence P. *Critical Chain Project Management.* Norwood, MA: Artech House Publishers, 2000.

[9] Poppendieck, Mary. *Lean Software Development: An Agile Toolkit.* Reading, MA: Addison Wesley, 2003.

[10] Cockburn, Alistair. *Agile Software Development.* Reading, MA: Addison Wesley, 2002.

[11] Kerth, Norm. *Project Retrospectives: A Handbook for Team Reviews.* New York: Dorset House, 2001.

[12] Weinberg, Gerald. *Quality Software Management: Systems Thinking.* New York: Dorset House, 1997.

[13] Senge, Peter. *The Fifth Discipline.* New York: Random House, 1990.

Chapter Thirteen

[1] Constantine, Larry L. "Unified Hegemony," *Software Development, 8,* (11), November. Reprinted in L. Constantine, ed. *Beyond Chaos: The Expert Edge in Managing Software Development.* Boston: Addison-Wesley, 2001.

[2] Fowler, Martin. "Put Your Process on a Diet," *Software Development, v. 8,* 12, December.

[3] Beck, Kent. *Extreme Programming Explained,* Reading, MA: Addison-Wesley, 2000.

[4] Jeffries, Ron et al. *Extreme Programming Installed.* Boston: Addison-Wesley, 2001.

[5] Constantine, Larry L. "The benefits of visibility," *Computer Language Magazine,* September 1992. Reprinted in *The Peopleware Papers,* Upper Saddle River, NJ: Prentice Hall, 2001.

[6] Ambler, Scott. *Agile Modeling: Effective Practices for Extreme Programming and the Unified Process.* New York: Wiley, 2002.

[7] Highsmith, Jim. *Adaptive Software Development: A Collaborative Approach to Managing Complex Systems.* New York: Dorset House, 2000.

[8] Baker, F.T. "Chief programmer team management of production programming," *IBM Systems Journal, 11* (1), 1972.

[9] Cockburn, Alistair. *Writing Effective Use Cases.* Boston: Addison-Wesley, 2001.

[10] Cockburn, Alistair. *Agile Software Development.* Boston: Addison-Wesley, 2002.

[11] Constantine, Larry L. and Lockwood, L. *Software for Use: A Practical Guide to the Models and Methods of Usage-Centered Design,* Reading, MA: Addison-Wesley, 1999.

[12] Constantine, Larry L. and Lockwood, L. "Usage-Centered Engineering for Web Applications," *IEEE Software, 19* (2): 42-50, March/April 2002.

[13] Fowler, Martin. *Refactoring: Improving the Design of Existing Code.* Reading, MA: Addison-Wesley, 1999.

[14] Jeffries, Ron. "Card magic for Managers," *Software Development, 8,* (12), December 2000. Reprinted in L. Constantine, ed. *Beyond Chaos: The Expert Edge in Managing Software Development.* Boston: Addison-Wesley, 2001.

[15] Constantine, Larry L. "Cutting Corners: Shortcuts in Model-Driven Web Development," *Software Development, 8,* (2), February 2000. Reprinted in L. Constantine, ed. *Beyond Chaos: The Expert Edge in Managing Software Development.* Boston: Addison-Wesley, 2001.

Chapter Fourteen

[1] Ambler, S.W. *Agile Modeling: Best Practices for the Unified Process and Extreme Programming.* New York: John Wiley & Sons, 2002.

[2] Jeffries, R. *Essential XP: Documentation.* <http://www. xprogramming.com/xpmag/expDocumentationInXp.htm> 2001.

[3] Although I have cheated a bit here and applied the practices *Model to Communicate* and *Model to Understand* to the creation of documentation I want to emphatically point out where AM is concerned the concepts of "model" and "document" are orthogonal. I apologize if this is a bit frustrating, but unfortunately the world is a fuzzy place. Embrace fuzziness!

[4] Agile Alliance. *Manifesto for Agile Software Development.* <http://www.agilealliance.org/> 2001.

[5] Ambler, S. W. *Agile Database Techniques: Effective Strategies for the Agile Software Developer.* New York: Wiley, 2003.

[6] McGovern, J.; Ambler, S.W.; Stevens, M.E.; Linn, J.; Sharan, V.; and Jo, E.K. *The Practical Guide to Enterprise Architecture.* Upper Saddle River, NJ: Pearson Education Group, 2004.

[7] Beck, K. *Extreme Programming Explained – Embrace Change.* Reading, MA: Addison Wesley Longman, 2000.

[8] Highsmith, J.A. *Adaptive Software Development: A Collaborative Approach to Managing Complex Systems.* New York: Dorset House Publishing, 2000.

[9] Hunt, A. and Thomas, D. *The Pragmatic Programmer: From Journeyman to Master.* Reading, MA: Addison Wesley Longman, 2000.

[10] Cockburn, A. *Agile Software Development.* Reading, MA: Addison Wesley Longman, 2002.

Chapter Fifteen

There are no notes for Chapter 15.

Chapter Sixteen

[1] Personal email exchange with the author.

[2] Poole, Charles and Huisman, Jan Willem. "Using Extreme Programming in a Maintenance Environment." *IEEE Software.* 18.6 (2001) 42-50.

[3] Schuh, Peter. "Recovery, Redemption, and Extreme Programming." *IEEE Software.* 18.6 (2001) 38-41.

[4] DeMarco, Tom. *The Deadline: A Novel About Project Management.* New York: Dorset House Publishing, 1997.

Chapter Seventeen

[1] Miller, G.A. "The Magical Number Seven, Plus or Minus Two: Some Limits on Our Capacity for Processing Information." *Psychology Review.* 63 (1956) 81-97. Available on the Web at <http://www.well.com/user/smalin/miller.html>.

[2] Schwaber, K. and Beedle, M. *Agile Software Development with Scrum.* Upper Saddle River, NJ: Prentice Hall, 2002. p. 36.

[3] Chin, Gary. *Agile Project Management: How to Succeed in the Face of Changing Project Requirements.* New York: AMACOM, 2004. p. 88.

[4] Schwaber, K. and Beedle, M. *Agile Software Development with Scrum.* Upper Saddle River, NJ: Prentice Hall, 2002. p. 36-7.

[5] Ibid. 37.

[6] Thomsett, Rob. *Radical Project Management.* Upper Saddle River, NJ: Prentice Hall, 2002. p.45.

[7] Cockburn, Alistair. *The Crystal Methods: How to Make a Methodology Fit.* 2004. <http://alistair.cockburn.us/crystal/talks/cm/1>.

[8] Cockburn, Alistair. *Crystal Clear: A Human-Powered Methodology for Small Teams.* Boston: Addison Wesley, 2004.

[9] Cockburn, Alistair. *Surviving Object-Oriented Projects.* Boston: Addison Wesley, 1998. p. 77-93.

[10] Cohen, D.; Lindvall, M.; and Costa, P. *Agile Software Development: A DACS State-of-the-Art Report.* Rome, NY: DACS, 2003. p. 23.

[11] Cockburn, Alistair. Cited in Cohen, D.; Lindvall, M.; and Costa, P. *Agile Software Development: A DACS State-of-the-Art Report.* Rome, NY: DACS, 2003. p. 24.

[12] Aguanno, Kevin. "Manage Change Better with Scrum." *Inside Project Management.* 2.8 (2002) 1-6.

[13] Agile Alliance. "Principles Behind the *Agile Manifesto.*" Agile Manifesto Web Site. <http://www.agilemanifesto.org/principles.html>.

[14] Aguanno, Kevin. "Ever-Changing Requirements? Use Agile Methods to Reduce Project Risk." *Proc. Informatics 2004.* Toronto, May 2004.

[15] Nolan, Sean. "Calculating Costs of a Software Error-Prevention System." *Baseline Magazine.* March 2004.

[16] Gage, Debbie and McCormick, John. "Why Software Quality Matters." *Baseline Magazine.* March 2004.

Chapter Eighteen

[1] Beck, K. et. al. "Chrysler goes to 'Extremes.'" *Distributed Computing.* Issue 10, 1998.

[2] Beck, K. "Embracing Change with Extreme Programming." *IEEE Computer.* Issue 10, 1999.

3 Beck, K. *Extreme Programming Explained.* Boston: Addison-Wesley, 2000.

4 Beck, K. *Planning Extreme Programming.* Boston: Addison-Wesley, 2001.

5 Beizer, B. *Software Testing Techniques.* Thomson Computer Press, 1990.

6 Brooks, F. *The Mythical Man-Month.* Boston: Addison Wesley, 1995.

7 Cockburn, A. "Selecting a Project's Methodology." *IEEE Software.* Issue 4, 2000.

8 Crispin, L. "Extreme Rules of the Road." *STQE Magazine.* Vol. 4, 2000.

9 DeMarco, T. and Lister, T. *Peopleware.* New York: Dorset House, 1997.

10 Dittert, K. "XP und 'Pair Programming.'" *OBJEKTspektrum.* Issue 4, 2001.

11 Eckstein, J. "Resistance to change: Issues with early and often delivery?" *Proc. OOPSLA 2001*, 2001.

12 Grenning, J. "Launching Extreme Programming at a Process-Intensive Company." *IEEE.* Issue 6, 2001.

13 Griffin, A. "Managing Problem People in XP Implementation." *Proc. XP Universe 2001*, 2001.

14 Gutknecht, J. et al. "The school of Niklaus Wirth: the art of simplicity." *dpunkt Verlag.* 2000.

15 Haungs, J. "Pair Programming on the C3 project." *IEEE Computer.* Issue 2, 2001.

16 Hendrickson, C. "Will Extreme Programming kill your customer?" *Proc. OOPSLA 2001*, 2001.

17 Jeffries, R. "Extreme Testing." *STQE Distributed Computing.* Issue 2, 1999.

[18] Jeffries, R., et al. *Extreme Programming Installed.* Boston: Addison Wesley, 2000.

[19] Keefer, G. "The CMMI in 45 Minutes." Technical Paper, 2001.

[20] Keefer, G. "A CMMI Compatible Risk Management Process." *PSQT.* 2002.

[21] Martin, R.C. "Interview with Robert C. Martin." *ObjectView.* Issue 4.

[22] Myers, G.J. *The Art of Software Testing.* New York: John Wiley & Sons, 1979.

[23] Nawrocki, J. and Wojciechowski, A. "Experimental Evaluation of Pair Programming." *Proc. ESCOM*, 2001.

[24] Nosek, J.T. "The Case for Collaborative Programming." *Communications of the ACM.* Vol. 4, 1998.

[25] Oppenheim, Alan V. "A Personal View of Education." *IEEE Signal Processing.* Vol. 4, 1992.

[26] Pearse, T., Freeman, T. and Oman, P. "Using Metrics to Manage the End Game of a Software Project." *Proc. Sixth International Software Metrics Symposium*, 1999.

[27] Robertson, J. and Robertson, S. *Mastering the Requirements Process.* Boston: Addison-Wesley, 1999.

[28] Schuh, P. "Recovery, Redemption and Extreme Programming." *IEEE Software.* Issue 6, 2001.

[29] Tschirky, F., Brabec, B. and Kern, M. "Avalanche Rescue Systems in Switzerland: Experience and Limitations." *Diss.* Eidg. Institut für Schnee- und Lawinenforschung, 2000.

[30] Williams, L. et al. "Strengthening the Case for Pair Programming." *IEEE Software.* Issue 4, 2000.

[31] Williams, L. and Kessler, R.R. "Experimenting with Industry's 'Pair-Programming' Model in the Computer Science Classroom." *Journal on Software Engineering Education*. Issue 12, 2000.

[32] Williams, L. and Cockburn, A. "The Costs and Benefits of Pair Programming." *Proc. XP2000 Conference*, 2000.

[33] Williams, L. and Upchurch, R.L. "In Support of Student Pair-Programming." *Proc. SIGCSE Conference 2001*, 2001.

[34] Griffin, Scott D. Keynote talk at *SEPG 2000*.

[35] As quoted by Linda Rising in Chapter 16.

[36] See the work of Laurie Williams at the University of Utah. Email: lwilliam@cs.utah.edu.

[37] Tzu, Sun. *The Art of War*.

[38] Drucker, Peter. "The Next Society: Survey of the Near Future." *The Economist*. Nov. 3, 2001.

[39] Beck, Kent. "Extreme Programming: A Humanistic Discipline of Software Development." *Proc. FASE 1998*. 1-6

[40] Beck. Kent. *Test Driven Development: By Example.* Boston: Addison Wesley, 2002.

[41] Muller, Matthias M. and Hagner, Oliver. "Experiment about Test-First Programming." *Proc. Conference on Empirical Assessment in Software Engineering (EASE).* Keele, UK: 2002.

[42] Williams, L. and Maximilien, M. *Assessing Test-Driven Development at IBM.* 2003.

[43] Cockburn, A. "Reexamining the Cost of Change Curve." XProgramming.com Website. 2000.

[44] Elssamadisy, A. and Schalliol, G. "Recognizing and Responding to 'Bad Smells' in Extreme Programming." *Proc. ICSE.* 2002.

[45] Viljamaa, J. "Refactoring I: Basics and Movivation." *Proc. Seminar on Programming Paradigms.* University of Helsinki, October 2000.

[46] Muller, Matthias M. "Are Reviews an Alternative to Pair Programming?" *Proc. Conference on Empirical Assessment in Software Engineering (EASE).* Keele, UK, 2003.

[47] Padberg, F. and Muller, M. "Extreme Programming from an Engineering Economics Viewpoint." EDSER Workshop. 2002.

[48] Williams, L. and Erdogmus, H. "On the Economic Feasibility of Pair Programming." EDSER Workshop. 2002.

[49] Beck, K. and Vlissides, J. "XP." *C++ Report.* June 1999.

[50] Wells, D. "VCAPS Project." Wiki report. 2003.

[51] Keefer, G. "Mutual Programming: A Practice to Improve Software Development Productivity." AVOCA Technical Paper, 2002.

[52] Keefer, G. "Task Stack Planning." AVOCA Technical Paper, 2003.

Chapter Nineteen

[1] Taber, Cara and Fowler, Martin. "Planning and Running and XP Iteration." Available online at <http://www.martinfowler.com/articles/planningXpIteration.html>. Originally published as "An Iteration in the Life of an XP Project." *Cutter IT Journal.* 13.11 (Nov. 2000).

Chapter Twenty

[1] For an example, see Gerold Keefer's work in Chapter 18 of this book.

[2] Kuhn, Thomas S. *The Structure of Scientific Revolutions.* 3rd Ed. Chicago: University of Chicago Press, 1996.

[3] Ibid, page 12.

[4] Ibid, page 5.

[5] Ibid, pages 68-9.

[6] Ibid, page 81.

[7] Royce, W.W. "Managing the Development of Large Software Systems: Concepts and Techniques." *Proc. WESCON.* (1970) 1-9.

[8] Basili, V. and Turner, A.J. "Iterative Enhancement: A Practical Technique for Software Development." *IEEE Transactions on Software Engineering.* 1.4 (1975) 390-6.

[9] Boehm, B. "A Spiral Model of Software Development and Enhancement." *IEEE Computer.* 21.5 (1988) 61-72.

[10] RAD was developed by James Martin circa 1991.

[11] Cockburn, A. *Crystal Clear: A Human-Powered Methodology for Small Teams.* Boston: Addison Wesley, 2004.

[12] Poppendieck, Mary and Poppendieck, Tom. *Lean Software Development: An Agile Toolkit for Software Development Managers.* Boston: Addison Wesley, 2003.

[13] DSDM Consortium. *DSDM Web site.* <http://www.dsdm.com/>.

[14] Schwaber, K. and Beedle, M. *Agile Software Development with Scrum.* Upper Saddle River, NJ: Prentice Hall, 2002.

[15] Aguanno, K. "Manage Change Better Using Scrum." *Inside Project Management.* 2.8 (2002) 1-6.

[16] Beck, Kent. *Extreme Programming Explained: Embrace Change*. Boston: Addison Wesley, 1999.

[17] Coad, P., Lefevre, E., and DeLuca, E. *Java Modeling in Color with UML: Enterprise Components and Process*. Prentice Hall, 1999.

[18] Highsmith, Jim. "History: The Agile Alliance." The Agile Manifesto Web site. <http://www.agilemanifesto.org/history.html>. 2001.

[19] Beck, K. et al. "The Agile Manifesto." The Agile Manifesto Web site. <http://www.agilemanifesto.org/>. 2001.

[20] The Selling Agile discussion group (formed in April 2004) is available from Yahoo! Groups at <http://finance.groups.yahoo.com/group/SellingAgile/>.

[21] Barreca, Jeanne R. "Understanding Your Customer's Power Structure." *Inside Project Management*. 3.10 (2003) 1-4.

[22] Aguanno, K. "'Business Value' as a Factor in Software Design Projects." *Project Magazine*. 3.7 (2002). <http://www.projectmagazine.com/v3i7/valuev3i7.html>.

[23] Aguanno, K. "Work More Efficiently Using a Focused Work Breakdown Structure." *Inside Project Management*. 3.1 (2003) 1-3.

[24] Aguanno, K. "So You Think You're Done? What to Do After the Launch." *Proc. ProjectWorld 2001, Toronto*. March 2001.

Managing Agile Projects

Contributor Profiles

M any of the chapters in this book are reprints of earlier works. The authors of those works have contributed them to this book to help spread knowledge of how to manage agile projects better. Most of the materials have been reworked and updated from their previously-published versions, to help ensure that this book has the latest materials available on the topic.

Authors contributing to this book were not paid for their contributions—this book is one more example of their giveback to the professional community. Those at the forefront of the agile methods movement need to be recognized and commended for their groundbreaking efforts. The following pages contain brief background information on each of the contributors as well as Web site URLs and email addresses. Visit the URLs to find out more about the individual contributors, their other related activities, and to find out about the products and services that they offer.

Editor: Kevin Aguanno

Kevin Aguanno is a driven, results-oriented solution designer and project manager with over seventeen years of experience working with a wide range of industries.

Mr. Aguanno specializes in managing complex application development and systems integration projects. He has been brought in as a trouble shooter to turn around many troubled projects, and is known in the industry for this expertise. He has spoken at conferences and has published articles on managing agile projects.

He is a member of both PMI and the Association for Project Management in the U.K., holding the PMP and MAPM designations respectively. Winner of several international awards, Mr. Aguanno is a proven manager and public speaker active in research and writing on the topic of project management.

Kevin has written several books, including *Beyond the PMP: Advanced Project Management Certification Options*, and *101 Ways to Reward Your Team Members for $20 (or Less!)* His articles appear regularly in various professional journals.

Author's Web site: **www.mmpubs.com/aguanno**

Author's Email: **aguanno@ca.ibm.com**

Scott Ambler

Scott Ambler is a Senior Consultant with Ronin International, Inc. since its inception in 1999. He actively works with Ronin clients on large-scale software development projects and on software process improvement (SPI) efforts around the world.

Scott is Canadian and still lives in Canada although he spends a large portion of his time consulting in the United States and Europe. He has worked in the IT industry since the mid-1980s and with object technology since the early 1990s. He has written several books and white papers on object-oriented software development, software process, Agile Modeling (AM), Agile Database Techniques, the Enterprise Unified Process (EUP), and other topics.

Scott is a Senior Contributing Editor with *Software Development* magazine and a member of the *Flashline* Software Development Productivity Council.

He is the Thought Leader of the Agile Modeling methodology, and is the author of *Agile Modeling,* and *The Elements of UML 2.0 Style.*

Author's Web sites: **www.agiledata.org**
www.agilemodeling.com
www.ambysoft.com

Author's Email: **swa@ambysoft.com**

Sanjiv Augustine

S anjiv Augustine is Director of Technology at CC Pace, a full service technology services firm offering consulting, staffing, IT outsourcing and software solutions to the financial services industry. Sanjiv is a leading agile management consultant in Washington, DC, founder of the Yahoo! Agile Project Management (APM) group, and a frequent presenter at industry conferences. He has deployed eXtreme Programming (XP) at large financial institutions, and has managed several XP projects varying in size from five to over one hundred people. Sanjiv's interest in Complex Adaptive Systems led him to develop a new APM framework that will be published in a Prentice-Hall book scheduled for late 2004 release.

Headquartered in Fairfax, Virginia, CC Pace is recognized globally as a leading innovator in Agile Project Management and ranks in the *Washington Business* Journal's top 20 largest software developers. Since 1980, CC Pace has delivered business and technology-based solutions to more than 60 financial services institutions. CC Pace tools and methodologies are the foundation upon which operational efficiency, profitability, and speed-to-market become an everyday reality for our clients.

Author's Web site: **www.ccpace.com**

Author's Email: **sanjiv.augustine@ccpace.com**

Alistair Cockburn

Alistair Cockburn, is an internationally recognized expert in object technology, methodology, and project management, one of the authors of the Agile Software Development Manifesto, and creator of the the Agile Development Conference. He is the author of *Surviving OO Projects, Agile Software Development, Writing Effective Use Cases*, and *Crystal Clear: A Human-Powered Methodology for Small Teams*. Much of his written material can be found at his website.

Author's Web site: **Alistair.Cockburn.us**

Author's Email: **alistair.cockburn@acm.org**

David Cohen

David Cohen is a software engineer for Computer Associates International, Inc. He is currently heavily involved in the design and development of a distributed, highly-scalable workflow system. He uses his expertise in Business Process Modeling to model, design, and implement comprehensive workflow solutions across the company.

David was formerly a Junior Scientist at Fraunhofer Center for Experimental Software Engineering Maryland. He specialized in the software development lifecycle, including hands-on Agile development experience, and user interface usability modeling. David also worked on the development of collaborative, Internet-based tools to facilitate knowledge transfer between individuals and organizations and build experience bases supporting the Experience Factory Model.

David has published a number of white papers on agile development, usability testing, and user interface design.

Author's Email: **David.Cohen@ca.com**

Larry Constantine

Larry Constantine, IDSA, is an award-winning designer, consultant, and trainer who helps clients throughout the globe improve their products and processes. An innovative visual and interaction designer and winner of the 2001 Performance-Centered Design Competition, he specializes in complex and challenging design problems where user performance is critical.

In a career spanning four decades he has contributed many of the core concepts and techniques of modern software engineering theory and practice. With Lucy Lockwood, he developed essential use cases and the widely used usage-centered design process based on essential models. His publications include more than 150 papers and 18 books, among them *Software for Use*, written with Lucy Lockwood and winner of the Jolt Award for best book of 1999, and the software engineering classic, *Structured Design*, written with Ed Yourdon.

Author's Web site: **lconstantine@foruse.com**

Author's Email: **www.foruse.com**

Patricia Costa

Patricia Costa has been involved in the design and development of software applications as well as in research on various software engineering areas since 1996. Currently she is a scientist at the Fraunhofer Center for Experimental Software Engineering, Maryland. Her work includes experimental and applied research on processes and methods for improving software architectures and software products in general, agile methods, knowledge management, security, and software measurement and experimentation.

She has a B.Sc. and a M.Sc. degree in Computer Science from the Federal University of Minas Gerais, Brazil (earned in 1996 and 1999, respectively) and a M.Sc. degree in Telecommunications Management from University of Maryland, University College (2002).

Author's Web site:　**fc-md.umd.edu/people/pcosta**

Author's Email:　**pcosta@fc-md.umd.edu**

David Hussman

D avid Hussman has been
building software for
more than 10 years. In
that time, he has developed in the
following fields: medical, digital
audio, digital biometrics, retail,
and education. For the past four
years, David has coached large and
small teams in the U.S., Canada,
and Russia.

As well as speaking and
presenting at agile conferences in
the U.S. and Europe, David has contributed to several books,
published at numerous agile conferences, contributed to the
Cutter Consortium, and recently completed a series of
interviews for Capella University courses.

Author's Web site: **www.supergofaster.com**

Author's Email: **david.hussman@sgfco.com**

Ronald E. Jeffries

Ron Jeffries has been developing software since 1961, when he accidentally got a summer job at Strategic Air Command HQ, and they accidentally gave him a FORTRAN manual. He and his teams have built operating systems, language compilers, relational and set-theoretic database systems, manufacturing control, and applications software, producing about a half-billion dollars in revenue, and he wonders why he didn't get any of it.

For the past few years he has been learning, applying, and teaching Extreme Programming, teamed with Kent Beck, Ken Auer, Ward Cunningham, and Martin Fowler.

Author's Web site: **www.XProgramming.com**

Author's Email: **ronjeffries@acm.org**

Gerold Keefer

Gerold Keefer was educated at FHTE (Fachhochschule für Technik Esslingen), Department of Telecommunications. Since 1993 he has been working as a consultant in the field of software development, quality management and process improvement in a range of major companies. He has been repeatedly a speaker at the PSQT, SQM and CONQUEST conferences both in Europe and the U.S..

"Extreme Programming Considered Harmful" was the first (and up to now) best received analysis on the limitations of Extreme Programming, personally recognized by thought leaders including Ivar Jacobson, Tom Gilb, Grady Booch and Karl Wiegers.

His current interest is on common sense CMMI implementations with a focus on zero-overhead, quantitative processes. Gerold Keefer is the CEO and founder of AVOCA LLC a quality management consultancy, founded in 1999.

Author's Web site: **www.avoca-vsm.com**

Author's Email: **gkeefer@avoca-vsm.com**

Kirstin Kohler

K irstin Kohler has been a project manager, researcher, and consultant with Fraunhofer IESE since 1999. She actively works with customers on industrial projects, and provides consultancy and training services. She regularly participates in conferences and writes articles covering current research topics in software engineering for publication in journals, proceedings, and book chapters. Her special research focus is on requirements engineering, usability engineering, and on the gap between these two disciplines. Before joining Fraunhofer IESE, she worked at Hewlett Packard for several years in user interface development, quality assurance, and software process improvement of user-centered design processes. She holds the equivalent of Master of Science degrees in Software Engineering and Biological Science.

Fraunhofer IESE performs research and development in the areas of innovative software development approaches, quality and process engineering, requirements and usability engineering, software architectures, continuing improvement and Learning Organizations as well as IT-based learning. In order to prepare software developers and users for current and future IT requirements, new technologies, methods, processes, and tools are being developed, which provide a sound engineering-style basis for industrial software development.

Author's Email: **kohler@iese.fhg.de**

Mike Lindvall

Mikael Lindvall is a scientist at Fraunhofer Center for Experimental Software Engineering Maryland. Dr. Lindvall specializes on best practices and methodologies as well as experience and knowledge management in software engineering. He is also interested in software architecture evaluation and evolution. He is currently working on ways of building experience bases for best practices to attract users to both contribute and use experience bases as well as on methods to quickly understand a software architecture and identify architectural violations. Dr. Lindvall received his PhD in computer science from Linköpings University, Sweden in 1997. Lindvall's PhD work focused on evolution of object-oriented systems and was based on a commercial development project at Ericsson Radio in Sweden.

Author's Web site: fc-md.umd.edu/people/mlindvall

Author's Email: mlindvall@fc-md.umd.edu

Barbara Paech

B arbara Paech holds the Software Engineering Chair at the University of Heidelberg. Until October 2003, she was a department head at the Fraunhofer Institute of Experimental Software Engineering. Her teaching and research focuses on methods and processes to ensure quality of software with adequate effort. For many years, she has been particularly active in the area of requirements and rational engineering. She has headed several industrial, national and international research and transfer projects. She is spokeswoman of the special interest group "Requirements Engineering" in the German computer science society.

She holds a PhD in Computer Science from the Ludwig-Maximilans-Universität München (1990) and a Habilitation in Computer Science from the Technical Universität München (1998).

Author's Web site: **www-swe.informatik.uni-heidelberg.de/**

Author's Email: **paech@informatik.uni-heidelberg.de**

Linda Rising

L inda Rising has a Ph.D. from Arizona State University in the area of object-based design metrics. Her background includes university teaching experience as well as work in industry in the areas of telecommunications, avionics, and strategic weapons systems. She has been working with object technologies since 1983.

She is the editor of *A Patterns Handbook, A Pattern Almanac 2000*, and *Design Patterns in Communications Software*, and has a number of publications including articles in *IEEE Software* and *STQE*. These and other articles are available on her web site. She is a regular contributor to the DDC-I On-line Newsletter: ddci.com/news_latest_news_archive.shtml. She is the co-author with Mary Lynn Manns of a new book—*Fearless Change: Patterns for Introducing New Ideas*.

Linda has presented tutorials and workshops at JAOO, OOPSLA, and other conferences.

Linda Rising is an independent consultant who can help your organization get going with Scrum or retrospectives or patterns. Her favorite implementation of these important practices is to combine agility with retrospectives with patterns writing to capture organizational best practices.

Author's Web site: **www.lindarising.org**

Author's Email: **risingl@acm.org**

Jim Tomayko

James E. Tomayko is a Teaching Professor in the School of Computer Science at Carnegie Mellon University, and a Visiting Scientist at the Software Engineering Institute (SEI).

Dr. Tomayko founded and participates in the Software Development Studio for the MSE program, which provides students with a laboratory for direct application of concepts learned in coursework. Previously, he was leader of the Academic Education Project at the SEI, and Director of the MSE. He has worked in industry through employee, contract, or consulting relationships with NCR, NASA, Boeing Defense and Space Group, Fontanus, Carnegie Works, Xerox, the Westinghouse Energy Center, Keithley Instruments, PPG, and Mycro-Tek.

Dr. Tomayko is the co-author of *Human Aspects of Software Engineering* available at www.charlesriver.com/titles/ humanaspsoftwareeng.html.

Author's Email: jet@cs.cmu.edu

Pascal Van Cauwenberghe

Pascal Van Cauwenberghe is a consultant who helps his customers to improve their software process while delivering results, and vice versa. Active in IT since 1990, he was involved in engineering, banking, communications and distributed applications.

He's been using agile, XP, Systems Thinking, Theory of Constraints and Lean methods for the past few years and regularly speaks about them at conferences and industry events.

He's actively involved in Agile, XP and Systems Thinking groups in the Benelux and is one of the organizers of the Benelux XP Day conference. He's the co-author of the "XP Game", a playful simulation used worldwide to introduce extreme programming techniques.

Author's Web sites: **http://www.nayima.be**
http://www.xp.be
http://www.xpday.be

Author's Email: **pvc@nayima.be**

Susan Woodcock

S usan Woodcock is the Vice President of Strategic Services at CC Pace, a full service technology services firm offering consulting, staffing, IT outsourcing and software solutions to the financial services industry. Susan has over a decade of experience in project management, strategic business planning, and business process redesign specializing in the mortgage and capital markets industries. In her role, Susan is heading research and development at CC Pace where they are cultivating methodology and software innovations such as the application of agile development and management techniques to packaged system implementations, incorporation of usability practices into traditional technology consulting services, and software product innovation techniques.

Headquartered in Fairfax, Virginia, CC Pace is recognized globally as a leading innovator in Agile Project Management and ranks in the *Washington Business* Journal's top 20 largest software developers. CC Pace tools and methodologies are the foundation upon which operational efficiency, profitability, and speed-to-market become an everyday reality for our clients.

Author's Web sites: **www.ccpace.com**

Author's Email: **susan.woodcock@ccpace.com**

Bibliography

Agile Alliance. *Manifesto for Agile Software Development.* <http://www.agilealliance.org/> 2001.

Aguanno, K. "'Business Value' as a Factor in Software Design Projects." *Project Magazine.* 3.7 (2002). <http://www.projectmagazine.com/v3i7/valuev3i7.html>.

- - -. "Manage Change Better Using Scrum." *Inside Project Management.* 2.8 (2002) 1-6.

- - -. "So You Think You're Done? What to Do After the Launch." *Proc. ProjectWorld 2001, Toronto.* March 2001.

- - -. "Work More Efficiently Using a Focused Work Breakdown Structure." *Inside Project Management.* 3.1 (2003) 1-3.

- - -. "Ever-Changing Requirements: Use Agile Methods to Reduce Project Risk." *Proc. Informatics 2004.* Canadian Information Processing Society (CIPS). May 2004.

- - -. "The Waterfall Development Method." *Inside Project Management.* 2.8 (2002).

Allen, T.J. *Managing the Flow of Technology.* Cambridge: MIT Press, 1977.

Amber, S.W. *The Object Primer 3rd Edition: Agile Model Driven Development with UML 2.* New York: Cambridge University Press, 2004.

- - -. *Agile Database Techniques: Effective Strategies for the Agile Software Developer.* New York: Wiley, 2003.

- - -. *Agile Modeling: Best Practices for the Unified Process and Extreme Programming.* New York: John Wiley & Sons, 2002.

Armour, F., Miller, G. *Advanced Use Case Modelling.* Boston: Addison Wesley, 2000.

Bach, J., "Heuristic Risk-Based Testing." *Software Testing and Quality Engineering Magazine.* 11 (1999).

Baker, F.T. "Chief programmer team management of production programming." *IBM Systems Journal.* 11.1 (1972).

Barreca, Jeanne R. "Understanding Your Customer's Power Structure." *Inside Project Management.* 3.10 (2003) 1-4.

Basili, V. and Turner, A.J. "Iterative Enhancement: A Practical Technique for Software Development." *IEEE Transactions on Software Engineering.* 1.4 (1975) 390-96.

Basili, V., Caldiera, G., and Rombach, H. "Experience Factory." *Encyclopaedia of Software Engineering.* Vol. 1. John Wiley & Sons, 1994.

Beck, K. "Embracing Change with Extreme Programming." *IEEE Computer.* 10 (1999) 70-77.

- - -. "Extreme Programming: A Humanistic Discipline of Software Development." *Proc. FASE 1998.* 1-6

- - -. *Extreme Programming Explained: Embrace Change.* Boston: Addison Wesley, 1999.

- - -. *Planning Extreme Programming.* Boston: Addison-Wesley, 2001.

- - -. *Test Driven Development: By Example.* Boston: Addison Wesley, 2002.

Beck, K. et. al. "Chrysler goes to 'Extremes.'" *Distributed Computing*. 10 (1998) 24-28.

Beck, Kent; Cockburn, Alistair; Jeffries, Ron; and Highsmith, Jim. *Agile Manifesto*. <http://www.agilemanifesto.org> 2001.

Beck, K. and Vlissides, J. "XP." *C++ Report*. June 1999.

Beizer, B. *Software Testing Techniques*. Thomson Computer Press, 1990.

Birk, A. "A Knowledge Management Infrastructure for Systematic Improvements in Software Engineering." *PhD Theses in Experimental Software Engineering*. Vol. 3. Fraunhofer IRB Verlag, 2001.

Boehm, Barry. "A Spiral Model of Software Development and Enhancement." *IEEE Computer*. 21.5 (1988) 61-72.

- - -. "Get Ready for Agile Methods, With Care." *IEEE Computer*. Jan. 2002, 64-69.

- - -. "Requirements that Handle IKIWISI, COTS, and Rapid Change." *Computer*. Los Alamitos, California: IEEE Press, July 2000. 99-102.

- - -. *Software Engineering Economics*. Upper Saddle River, NJ: Prentice Hall, 1981.

Boehm, Barry and D. Port. "Balancing Discipline and Flexibility with the Spiral Model and MBASE." *CrossTalk*. Dec. 2001, 23-30. <http://www.stsc.hill.af.mil/crosstalk/2001/12/boehm.pdf>.

Bosworth, Michael T. *Solution Selling*. New York: McGraw-Hill, 1995.

Bowers, P. "Highpoints from the Agile Software Development Forum." *Crosstalk*. Oct. 2002, 26-27.

Brooks, F. *The Mythical Man-Month*. Boston: Addison Wesley, 1995.

Brown, N. "Disciplines Delivering Success." *Proc. Software Technology Conference, 1997.* <http://stc-online.org/cd-rom/1997/track1.pdf>.

Chin, G. *Agile Project Management: How to Succeed in the Face of Changing Project Requirements.* New York: AMACOM, 2004.

Coad, P., Lefebvre, E. and De Luca, J. *Java Modeling In Color With UML: Enterprise Components and Process.* Upper Saddle River: Prentice Hall, 1999.

Cockburn, A. *Agile Software Development.* Reading, MA: Addison Wesley Longman, 2002.

- - -. "Agile Software Development Joins the Would-Be Crowd." *Cutter IT Journal.* Jan. 2002, 6-12.

- - -. *Crystal Clear: A Human-Powered Methodology for Small Teams.* Boston: Addison Wesley, 2004.

- - -. "Crystal Light Methods." Available at <http://alistair.cockburn.us/crystal/articles/clm/crystallightmethods.htm>.

- - -. "Reexamining the Cost of Change Curve." XProgramming.com Website. 2000.

- - -. "Selecting a Project's Methodology." *IEEE Software.* 17.4 (2000) 64-71.

- - -. *Writing Effective Use Cases.* Boston: Addison Wesley, 2001.

Cockburn, A. and Highsmith, J. "Agile Software Development: The Business of Innovation." *IEEE Computer.* Sept. 2001, 120-22.

- - -. "Agile Software Development: The People Factor." *IEEE Software.* 34.11 (2001) 131-133.

Constantine, Larry L. (Ed.) *Beyond Chaos: The Expert Edge in Managing Software Development.* Boston: Addison-Wesley, 2001.

- - -. "Cutting Corners: Shortcuts in Model-Driven Web Development." *Software Development.* 8.2 (2000).

- - -. "The benefits of visibility," *Computer Language Magazine.* September 1992.

- - -. "Unified Hegemony." *Software Development.* 8.11(2001).

Constantine, Larry L. and Lockwood, L. *Software for Use: A Practical Guide to the Models and Methods of Usage-Centered Design.* Reading, MA: Addison-Wesley, 1999.

- - -. "Usage-Centered Engineering for Web Applications." *IEEE Software.* 19.2 (2002) 42-50.

Crispin, L. "Extreme Rules of the Road." *STQE Magazine.* 4 (2000).

Davis, Alan. *Software Requirements.* Englewood Cliffs, N.J.: Prentice-Hall, 1990.

DeMarco, Tom. *The Deadline: A Novel About Project Management.* New York: Dorset House Publishing, 1997.

DeMarco, Tom and Boehm, Barry. "The Agile Methods Fray." *IEEE Computer.* June 2002, 90-92.

DeMarco, T. and T. Lister. *Peopleware: Productive Projects and Teams.* 2nd Ed. New York: Dorset House, 1999.

Dittert, K. "XP und 'Pair Programming.'" *OBJEKTspektrum.* 4 (2001).

Dorofee, A. J., Walker, J., et al. *Continuous Risk Management Guidebook.* Pittsburgh, PA: Software Engineering Institute, 1996.

Drucker, Peter. "The Next Society: Survey of the Near Future." *The Economist.* Nov. 3, 2001.

DSDM Consortium. DSDM Web site. <http://www.dsdm. com/>.

Eckstein, J. "Resistance to change: Issues with early and often delivery?" *Proc. OOPSLA 2001.* 2001.

Elssamadisy, A. and Schalliol, G. "Recognizing and Responding to 'Bad Smells' in Extreme Programming." *Proc. ICSE.* 2002.

Fowler, Martin. "Put Your Process on a Diet." *Software Development.* 8.12.

- - -. *Refactoring: Improving the Design of Existing Code.* Reading, MA: Addison-Wesley, 1999.

Frankel, D.S. *Model Driven Architecture: Applying MDA to Enterprise Computing.* Indianapolis: Wiley Publishing, 2003.

Glass, R. "Agile Versus Traditional: Make Love, Not War." *Cutter IT Journal.* Dec. 2001, 12-18.

Glazer, H. "Dispelling the Process Myth: Having a Process Does Not Mean Sacrificing Agility or Creativity." *Crosstalk.* Nov. 2001.

Goldratt, E. *The Goal.* Great Barrington: North River Press, 1992.

- - -. *Theory of Constraints.* Great Barrington: North River Press, 1990.

Grenning, J. "Launching Extreme Programming at a Process-Intensive Company." *IEEE.* 6 (2001).

Griffin, A. "Managing Problem People in XP Implementation." *Proc. XP Universe 2001.* 2001.

Gutknecht, J. et al. "The school of Niklaus Wirth: the art of simplicity." *dpunkt Verlag.* 2000.

Haungs, J. "Pair Programming on the C3 project." *IEEE Computer.* 2 (2001).

Hendrickson, C. "Will Extreme Programming kill your customer?" *Proc. OOPSLA 2001.* 2001.

Herring, R. and M. Rees. "Internet-Based Collaborative Software Development Using Microsoft Tools." *Proc. 5th World Multiconference on Systemics, Cybernetics and Informatics.* Orlando, Florida. July 2001, 22-25. <http://erwin.dstc.edu.au/Herring/Software EngineeringOverInternetSCI2001.pdf>.

Highsmith, J.A. *Adaptive Software Development: A Collaborative Approach to Managing Complex Systems.* New York: Dorset House Publishing, 2000.

- - -. *Agile Project Management.* Boston: Addison Wesley, 2004.

- - -. *Agile Software Development Ecosystems.* Reading, MA: Addison Wesley, 2002.

- - -. "History: The Agile Manifesto." Agile Alliance Web site. 2001. < http://www.agilemanifesto.org/history.html>.

- - -. "What is Agile Software Development?" *Crosstalk.* Oct. 2002, 4-9.

Highsmith, Jim and Alistair Cockburn. "Agile Software Development: The Business of Innovation." *IEEE Software.* 34.9 (2001) 120-122.

Highsmith, Jim; Orr, K.; Cockburn, Alistair. "Extreme Programming." *E-Business Application Delivery.* 4.17 (2000).

Hohmann, L. *Journey of the Software Professional.* Upper Saddle River: Prentice-Hall, 1997.

Humphrey, Watts. *A Discipline for Software Engineering.* Boston: Addison-Wesley, 1997.

Hunt, A. and D. Thomas. *The Pragmatic Programmer: From Journeyman to Master.* Reading, MA: Addison Wesley Longman, 2000.

Jeffries, Ron. "Card magic for Managers." *Software Development.* 8.12 (2000).

- - -. *Essential XP: Documentation.* <http://www.xprogramming.com/xpmag/expDocumentationInXp.htm> 2001.

- - -. "Extreme Programming and the Capability Maturity Model." XP Programming Web Site. <http://www.xprogramming.com/xpmag/xp_and_cmm.htm>.

- - -. "Extreme Testing." *STQE Distributed Computing.* 2 (1999).

Jeffries, Ron et al. *Extreme Programming Installed.* Boston: Addison-Wesley, 2001.

Johnson, Jim, et al. "Collaborating on Project Success." *Software Magazine.* Feb./Mar. 2001. <http://www.softwaremag.com/archive/2001feb/CollaborativeMgt.html>.

Jones, Capers. *Software Assessments, Benchmarks, and Best Practices.* Boston: Addison-Wesley, 2000.

Keefer, G. "A CMMI Compatible Risk Management Process." *PSQT.* 2002.

- - -. "Mutual Programming: A Practice to Improve Software Development Productivity." AVOCA Technical Paper. 2002.

- - -. "Task Stack Planning." AVOCA Technical Paper. 2003.

- - -. "The CMMI in 45 Minutes." Technical Paper. 2001.

Kerth, Norm. *Project Retrospectives: A Handbook for Team Reviews.* New York: Dorset House, 2001.

Kohler, K. and B. Paech. "Task-driven Requirements in object-oriented Development." *Perspectives on Requirements Engineering.* Eds. J. Leite and J. Doorn. Kluwer Academic Publishers, 2003.

Kontio, J. "The Riskit Method for Software Risk Management, version 1.00, CS-TR-3782." *Computer Science Technical Reports.* College Park, MD: University of Maryland, 1997.

Kovitz, B.L. *Practical Software Requirements: A Manual of Content and Style.* Greenwich: Manning Publications Co., 1998.

Kuhn, Thomas S. *The Structure of Scientific Revolutions.* 3rd Ed. Chicago: University of Chicago Press, 1996.

Leach, Lawrence P. *Critical Chain Project Management.* Norwood, MA: Artech House Publishers, 2000.

Leffingwell, D. and D. Widrig. *Managing Software Requirements: A Unified Approach.* Boston: Addison-Wesley, 2000.

Maiden, N. and G. Rugg. "ACRE: Selecting Methods For Requirements Acquisition." *Software Engineering Journal.* May, 1996.

Martin, R.C. "Interview with Robert C. Martin." *ObjectView.* Issue 4.

Mathiassen, L. "Reflective Systems Development." *Scandinavian Journal of Information Systems.* Vol. 10.1 and 10.2 (1998) 67-117.

McCarthy, J. and A. Monk. "Channels, Conversation, Cooperation and Relevance: All You Wanted to Know About Communication But Were Afraid to Ask." *Collaborative Computing.* 1.1 (1994) 35-61.

McGovern, J.; Ambler, S.W.; Stevens, M.E.; Linn, J.; Sharan, V.; and Jo, E.K. *The Practical Guide to Enterprise Architecture.* Upper Saddle River, NJ: Pearson Education Group, 2004.

McPhee, Ch. and A. Eberlein. "Requirements Engineering for Time-to-Market Projects." *Proc. 9th Conference and Workshop on the Engineering of Computer-based Systems.* ECBS, Sweden, 2002.

Mead, N. R. "Why Is It so Difficult to Introduce Requirements Engineering Research Results into Mainstream Requirements Engineering Practice?" *Proc. Fourth International Conference on Requirements Engineering.* Illinois, June 2000.

Morris, P., Masera, M., and Wilikens, M. "Requirements Engineering and Industrial Uptake." *Requirements Engineering.* 3 (1998).

Muller, Matthias M. "Are Reviews an Alternative to Pair Programming?" *Proc. Conference on Empirical Assessment in Software Engineering (EASE).* Keele, UK, 2003.

Muller, Matthias M. and Oliver Hagner. "Experiment about Test-First Programming." *Proc. Conference on Empirical Assessment in Software Engineering (EASE).* Keele, UK: 2002.

Myers, G.J. *The Art of Software Testing.* New York: John Wiley & Sons, 1979.

Nawrocki, J. and A. Wojciechowski. "Experimental Evaluation of Pair Programming." *Proc. ESCOM.* 2001.

Nosek, J.T. "The Case for Collaborative Programming." *Communications of the ACM.* 4 (1998).

Olson, G. M. and J. S. Olson. "Distance Matters." *Human-Computer Interaction.* 15 (2001) 139-179.

Oppenheim, Alan V. "A Personal View of Education." *IEEE Signal Processing.* 4 (1992).

Padberg, F. and M. Muller. "Extreme Programming from an Engineering Economics Viewpoint." EDSER Workshop. 2002.

Palmer, Steven. "Feature-Driven Development." Borland Developer Network Web site. <http://bdn.borland.com/article/borcon/files/2136/paper/2136.html>.

Paulisch, Frances and Axel Völker. "Agility: Build on a Mature Foundation." *Proc. Software Engineering Process Group Conference - SEPG 2002.* 2002.

Paulk, Mark C. "Agile Methodologies and Process Discipline." *Crosstalk.* Oct. 2002, 15-18.

- - -. "Extreme Programming from a CMM Perspective." *IEEE Software.* 18.6 (2001) 19-26.

- - -. "Key Practices of the Capability Maturity Model, Version 1.1." *Technical Report CMU/SEI-93-TR-25.* 1993.

Pearse, T., Freeman, T. and Oman, P. "Using Metrics to Manage the End Game of a Software Project." *Proc. Sixth International Software Metrics Symposium.* 1999.

Peeters, Vera and Pascal Van Cauwenberghe. "The XP Game Explained." *Extreme Programming Perspectives.* Eds. Marchesi, Succi, Wells, and Williams. New York: Pearson, 2003.

Poole, Charles and Jan Willem Huisman. "Using Extreme Programming in a Maintenance Environment." *IEEE Software.* 18.6 (2001) 42-50.

Poppendieck, Mary. *Lean Programming.* Agile Alliance Web Site. <http://www.agilealliance.org/articles/articles/LeanProgramming.htm> 2001.

Poppendieck, Mary and Tom Poppendieck. *Lean Software Development: An Agile Toolkit for Software Development Managers.* Boston: Addison Wesley, 2003.

Potter, B., and J. Sinclair. *Formal Specification and Z.* London: Prentice Hall, 1996.

Rakitin, S.R. "Manifesto Elicits Cynicism." *IEEE Computer.* 34.12 (2001) 4.

Robertson, J. and S. Robertson. *Mastering the Requirements Process.* Boston: Addison-Wesley, 1999.

Royce, W.W. "Managing the Development of Large Software Systems: Concepts and Techniques." *Proc. WESCON.* (1970) 1-9.

Schuh, Peter. "Recovery, Redemption, and Extreme Programming." *IEEE Software.* 18.6 (2001) 38-41.

Scwaber, Ken. *Agile Project Management with Scrum.* Redmond, Washington: Microsoft Press, 2004.

- - -. "Controlled Chaos: Living on the Edge." Agile Alliance Web Site. <http://www.agilealliance.org/articles/articles/ap.pdf>, 2002.

Schwaber, K. and M. Beedle. *Agile Software Development with Scrum.* Upper Saddle River, NJ: Prentice Hall, 2002.

Senge, Peter. *The Fifth Discipline*. New York: Random House, 1990.

Smith, John. *A Comparison of RUP and XP.* Rational Software White Paper. 2001.

Software Engineering Institute. *Capability Maturity Model® IntegrationSM V1.1 (CMMISM).* Pittsburgh: SEI, 2002. <http://www.sei.cmu.edu/cmm>.

Sullivan, K., P. Chalasani, S. Jha, and V. Sazawal. "Software Design as an Investment Activity: A Real Options Perspective." *Real Options and Business Strategy: Applications to Decision Making.* Ed. L. Trigeorgis. London: Risk Books. Dec. 1999.

Taber, Cara and Fowler, Martin. "An Iteration in the Life of an XP Project." *Cutter IT Journal.* 13.11 (2000).

- - -. "Planning and Running and XP Iteration." Available online at <http://www.martinfowler.com/articles/planningXpIteration.html>.

Thayer, Richard and Dorfman, Merlin, eds. *Software Requirements Engineering.* Los Alamitos, California: IEEE Computer Society Press, 1997.

The Standish Group. *ChAOS: A Recipe for Success.* Published Report. 1998.

- - -. *The CHAOS Report.* 1994. <http://www.standishgroup.com/sample_research/chaos_1994_1.php>.

Thomas, M. "IT Projects Sink or Swim." *British Computer Society Review.* 2001.

Thomsett, Rob. *Radical Project Management.* Upper Saddle River, NJ: Prentice Hall, 2002.

Tomayko, James E. "A Comparison of Pair Programming to Inspections for Software Defect Reduction." *Computer Science Education.* 2002.

- - -. "An Historian's View of Software Engineering." *Proc. of the IEEE Conference on Software Engineering Education and Training*. Los Alamitos, California: IEEE Computer Society Press, 2000.

- - -. "Using Extreme Programming to Develop Software Requirements." *Soft-Ware 2002*. (2002)   315-31.

Tschirky, F., Brabec, B. and Kern, M. "Avalanche Rescue Systems in Switzerland: Experience and Limitations." *Diss. Eidg. Institut für Schnee- und Lawinenforschung*. 2000.

Turk, Dan; France, Robert; and Rumpe, Bernhard. "Limitations of Agile Software Processes." *Proc. 3rd International Conference on eXtreme Programming and Agile Processes in Software Engineering - XP2002*. 2002.

Turner, Richard and Apurva Jain. "Agile meets CMMI: Culture Clash or Common Cause?" *Proc. eXtreme Programming and Agile Methods - XP/Agile Universe 2002*. (2002) 153-165.

van Lamsweerde, A. "Requirements Engineering in the Year 00: A Research Perspective." *Proc. 22nd International Conference on Software Engineering*. Ireland, June 2000.

van Schouwen A.J., Parnas, D. L., and Madey J. "Documentation of Requirements for Computer Systems." *Proc. IEEE International Symposium On Requirements Engineering*. San Diego, California, 1993.

Vegas, S., "Characterization Schema for Selecting Software Testing Techniques." Thesis. Madrid: Universidad Prolitecnica de, February 2002.

Viljamaa, J. "Refactoring I: Basics and Movivation." *Proc. Seminar on Programming Paradigms*. University of Helsinki, October 2000.

Weinberg, Gerald. *Quality Software Management: Systems Thinking*. New York: Dorset House, 1997.

Wells, D. "VCAPS Project." Wiki report. 2003.

Wheatley, Margaret. *Leadership and the New Science: Discovering Order in a Chaotic World*. San Francisco: Berrett-Koehler Publishers, 1999.

Wiegers, K.E. "Read My Lips: No New Models!" *IEEE Software*. September/October 1998.

Williams, L. and A. Cockburn. "The Costs and Benefits of Pair Programming." *Proc. XP2000 Conference*. 2000.

Williams, L. and H. Erdogmus. "On the Economic Feasibility of Pair Programming." EDSER Workshop. 2002.

Williams, L. and M. Maximilien. *Assessing Test-Driven Development at IBM*. 2003.

Williams, L. and R. L. Upchurch. "In Support of Student Pair-Programming." *Proc. SIGCSE Conference 2001*. 2001.

Williams, L. and R. R. Kessler. "Experimenting with Industry's 'Pair-Programming' Model in the Computer Science Classroom." *Journal on Software Engineering Education*. 12 (2000).

Williams, Laurie, et al. "An Initial Exploration of the Relationship Between Pair Programming and Brooks' Law." *Proc. Agile Development Conference 2004*. 2004.

- - -. "Strengthening the Case for Pair Programming." *IEEE Software*. 4 (2000).

417

How would you like to deliver projects more quickly and with greater customer satisfaction in an environment of frequent scope changes?

Based on a live recording of a presentation Mr. Aguanno has delivered many times to project managers and software developers in Canada, the U.S., Europe, Asia, and Australia. One of his most popular presentations.

This presentation outlines the underlying principles of Agile Development and details of how it differs from traditional development projects. Then, using an agile project management method called Scrum, it illustrates how agile management methods used in software development may be extended to projects from other application areas outside of information technology. Participants will come away from the presentation with a high-level understanding of the Agile Development philosophy and how it differs from traditional development approaches, enough of an understanding of Scrum to be able to determine if and how it could be implemented on a project, and a list of resources for further information on Agile Development and Scrum.

Audio Cassette	$12.00	ISBN 1-895186-08-0
CD-ROM (mp3)	$12.00	ISBN 1-895186-13-7

Published in 2003 by Multi-Media Publications Inc.

Order online at www.mmpubs.com/aguanno/publications.html

419

Printed in the United States
38643LVS00002B/64